THE LAST
BATTLE

THE LAST BATTLE

WHEN U.S. AND GERMAN SOLDIERS
JOINED FORCES IN THE WANING HOURS
OF WORLD WAR II IN EUROPE

STEPHEN HARDING

DA CAPO PRESS
A Member of the Perseus Books Group

Designed by Pauline Brown
Maps by Steve Walkowiak

Typeset in Palatino LT Std by the Perseus Books Group

Library of Congress Cataloging-in-Publication Data

Harding, Stephen, 1952–
  The last battle: when U.S. and German soldiers joined forces in the waning hours of
World War II in Europe / Stephen Harding.
     pages cm
  Includes bibliographical references and index.
  ISBN 978-0-306-82208-7 (hardcover : alk. paper)—ISBN 978-0-306-82209-4
(e-book) 1. World War, 1939–1945—Campaigns—Austria—Tyrol. 2. World War,
1939–1945—Prisoners and prisons, German. 3. Prisoners of war—Austria—Itter—
History—20th century. 4. Prisoners of war—France—History—20th century.
5. Daladier, Edouard, 1884–1970—Captivity, 1940–1945. 6. Reynaud, Paul, 1878–
1966—Captivity, 1940–1945. I. Title.
  D765.45.T9H37 2013
  940.54'213642—dc23

                                                                    2012044706

First Da Capo Press edition 2013

Published by Da Capo Press
A Member of the Perseus Books Group
www.dacapopress.com

Da Capo Press books are available at special discounts for bulk purchases in the U.S.
by corporations, institutions, and other organizations. For more information, please
contact the Special Markets Department at the Perseus Books Group, 2300 Chestnut
Street, Suite 200, Philadelphia, PA 19103, or call (800) 810-4145, ext. 5000, or e-mail
special.markets@perseusbooks.com.

10 9 8 7 6 5 4 3 2

*As always,
for Mari, with love*

CONTENTS

Photos following page 118

vii

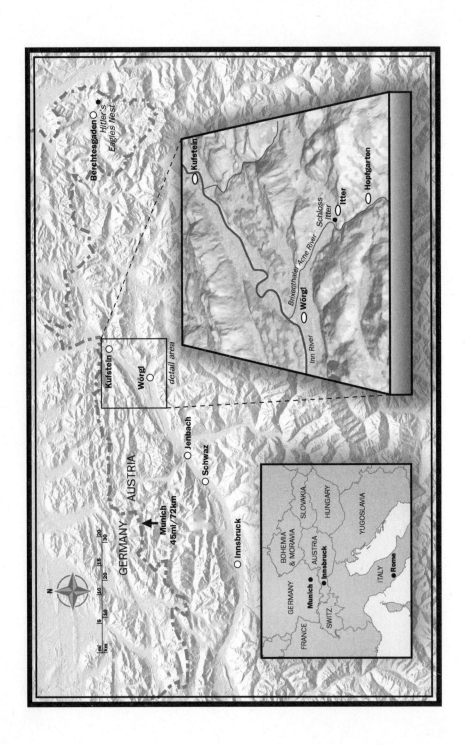

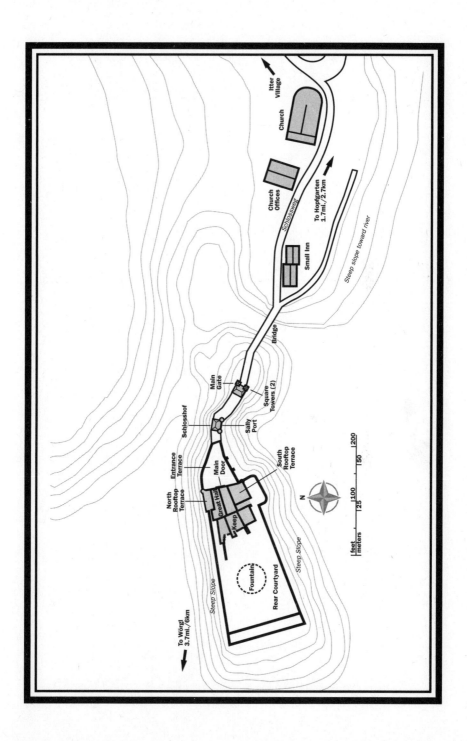

To Itter Village

Church

Church Offices

Schlossweg

Small Inn

To Hopfgarten
1.7mi./2.7km

Steep slope toward river

Bridge

Main Gate

Square Towers (2)

Schlosshof

Sally Port

Entrance Terrace

North Rooftop Terrace

Main Door

Great Hall

Keep

South Rooftop Terrace

N

Steep Slope

Steep Slope

Fountain

Rear Courtyard

To Wörgl
3.7mi./6km

feet   25   50   100   200
meters

PRELUDE

ON THE MORNING OF MAY 4, 1945, Captain John C. "Jack" Lee Jr. sat cross-legged atop the turret of his M4 Sherman tank, comparing the narrow streets before him with the terrain features marked on the map that lay partially open across his lap. Lee, a stocky twenty-seven-year-old from Norwich, New York, had spent the last five months leading Company B of the 23rd Tank Battalion—and, at times, much of the entire U.S. 12th Armored Division—on a headlong advance across France, into Germany, and now, in what would turn out to be the last days of World War II in Europe, into the Austrian Tyrol.

Lee's tank was parked at the intersection of two streets in the town of Kufstein, Austria, three miles southwest of the German border on the south bank of the swift-flowing Inn River. All three of the 23rd's tank companies had crossed the frontier the day before, leading the 12th Armored Division's Combat Command R on its drive southward from the suburbs of Munich. Lee's company had spearheaded the drive into Kufstein and had fought its way through a well-defended German roadblock before quickly clearing the town of its few defenders. Now, with the situation stabilized and lead elements of the 36th Infantry Division moving in to assume responsibility for the area, Lee and his men could catch a few minutes' rest.

JUST A FEW MILES TO THE SOUTHWEST another tired officer was also scanning a map, trying to determine what the coming hours would hold for him and his men. Josef "Sepp" Gangl, a decorated Bavarian-born major in the

German Wehrmacht, knew that the American juggernaut was rolling his way and that its arrival would likely be heralded by thunderous artillery barrages, the roar of tank fire, and the rattle of automatic weapons.

Gangl was not unduly troubled by the possibility of his own death; he'd come to grips with his own mortality fighting the Russians on the Eastern Front and the Allies in Normandy. He was concerned about the men he led, however, for not all were soldiers, and many weren't even German. A few days earlier, knowing the war was lost and loath to spend any more lives defending a system he'd long before stopped believing in, Gangl had declared his own personal armistice and joined forces with the Austrian anti-Nazi resistance. His only goal now was to keep the advancing Americans—and, for that matter, any German units still loyal to the führer and the Reich—from butchering the men who'd chosen to follow him.

———

ATOP A ROCKY PROMONTORY overlooking the flatlands over which the Americans would soon advance, a gaggle of argumentative Frenchmen were also pondering what fate had in store for them. Peering over the battlements of a castle that had stood atop its mountain for centuries, and that had been their prison until that very morning, the men knew their newfound freedom was no protection against the wrath of die-hard SS units still roaming the thick forest around them. They needed deliverance, and they needed it soon. If help did not come before the sun set, they would almost certainly die within the walls of their Tyrolean fortress.

———

THE WARMTH OF THE SPRING SUN and Jack Lee's exhaustion made it difficult for him to focus on the map. He was profoundly tired and hoped, more fervently than he let on to his men, that Kufstein would be Company B's last battle. Like virtually every other soldier in the European theater of operations, Lee knew that the war could end at any moment—Adolf Hitler had killed himself five days earlier, and organized German opposition was crumbling—and, while the young officer would in some ways hate to see the conflict come to a close, he didn't want any of his men to be the last American killed in Europe.

As Lee pondered what the war's end would mean to him and his fellow tankers, events were unfolding literally just down the road that would shatter his men's dreams of peace. Though he didn't yet know it, Lee was about to be thrust into an unlikely battle involving the alpine castle whose icon was obscured by a fold in his map, a group of combative French VIPs, an uneasy alliance with the enemy, a fight to the death against overwhelming odds, and the last—and arguably the strangest—ground combat action of World War II in Europe.

CHAPTER 1

A MOUNTAIN STRONGHOLD

THE CASTLE THAT WAS SOON to figure so largely in Jack Lee's life lay fourteen road miles to the southwest of where the young officer sat perched atop his tank. Schloss Itter, as it's called in German, sits on a hill that commands the entrance to Austria's Brixental valley. The structure bestrides a ravine, with a short bridge linking the castle to the flank of the mountain. The village of Itter spreads out to the east from the castle, some 2,300 feet above sea level and nestled beneath Hohe Salve, the 6,000-foot mountain in the middle alpine region historically known as Tyrol.

Though it would be of little concern to Lee and his men in the coming hours, Castle Itter already had a long, rich, and often violent history. The surrounding area had been inhabited at least since the middle Bronze Age (1800 to 1300 BCE), and the fact that the valleys of the Inn and Brixental Rivers provide a fairly flat and direct route between Central Europe and the Italian peninsula ensured that Tyrol saw more than its share of conflict. Conquered by Rome in 15 BCE, the region was successively invaded by the Ostrogoths, various German tribes, and Charlemagne's Franks. In the ninth century CE Tyrol came under the sway of the Bavarians, who built two sturdy stone keeps and a surrounding wall atop the hill that would later be home to Schloss Itter, and in 902 a Count Radolt passed ownership of the fortified site to the Roman Catholic diocese of Regensburg.[1]

Seeking to better protect his expanding Tyrolean possessions—and, of course, better enforce the collection of diocesan taxes—Regensburg's Bishop Totu[2] ordered that the keeps and wall be replaced by a more substantial fortress. Construction of the full-fledged castle was a leisurely and often-interrupted process, however, and took more than a century to complete. In 1239 Rapoto III of Ortenburg, Bavaria's count palatine,[3] seized the fortress as a result of his vicious feud with the then current bishop of Regensburg, Siegfried. The latter captured Rapoto in 1240, and, in order to win his freedom, the defeated nobleman was forced to cede many of his properties in Bavaria and Tyrol to the Regensburg bishopric. Among the properties passed to Siegfried were the castle at Itter and the village that had grown just outside its walls; the names of both fortress and village first appear in the historical record in 1241.[4]

Though ostensibly men of both God and peace, the bishops of Regensburg were also princes of the Holy Roman Empire. As temporal rulers the bishops were often heavy-handed and needlessly severe, and Schloss Itter saw frequent service as a base from which the bishops launched punitive expeditions against their sorely oppressed subjects. Though Tyrol came under Hapsburg rule in 1363, Schloss Itter and the nearby village remained within the ecclesiastical control of the Regensburg bishops until 1380, when Bishop Konrad VI von Haimberg sold them to the archbishop of Salzburg—Pilgrim II of Puchein—for 26,000 Hungarian guilders.

Looted and partially destroyed during the 1515–1526 Tyrolean peasant uprising,[5] Schloss Itter was rebuilt beginning in 1532. For the last few years of the sixteenth century, the fortress was home to an ecclesiastical court charged with suppressing witchcraft in the region, and local legend holds that in 1590 the last witch to be burned in the Tyrol met her end on a pyre in the schloss's main courtyard.[6] It is also at about this time—and most probably at the order of those whose job it was to root out witches—that the famous phrase from Dante's fourteenth-century epic poem *Divine Comedy* was first inscribed, in German, on the wall above the doors leading to Schloss Itter's vaulted entranceway: "Abandon hope, all ye who enter here."

The castle changed hands several times over the following two and a half centuries, and by 1782 was part of the personal lands of Joseph II, who had become Holy Roman emperor two years earlier following the death of his mother, Hapsburg empress Maria Theresa. So fond was Joseph of his

Tyrolean fortress that when Pope Pius VI journeyed to Austria shortly after Joseph's ascension to the throne, the monarch insisted that the pope consecrate the altar in Schloss Itter's small but exquisite chapel. The pope did so—mainly in an attempt to heal a rift between Joseph and the church—and also left behind at the castle an ornate Gothic crucifix and other ecclesiastical treasures.

Despite his fondness for Schloss Itter, Joseph II—like most of the castle's previous owners—chose to live elsewhere. In late December 1805 he was replaced by another, though admittedly far grander, absentee landlord, Napoléon Bonaparte. The diminutive French emperor gained title to the schloss as a result of the Treaty of Pressburg, which followed his victories over Austria at Ulm and Austerlitz, in mid-October and early December 1805, respectively. Bonaparte did not long retain title, however, for in 1809 he presented Schloss Itter to his loyal ally King Maximilian I of Bavaria.[7] The latter did little to ensure the upkeep of his new fortress, and, when in 1812 the councilors of Itter village offered Maximilian the relatively paltry sum of 15 Austro-Hungarian guldens for the entire edifice, the king accepted with alacrity. The villagers in fact had no intention of rehabilitating Schloss Itter; they intended it merely to be a source of construction materials. Over the following decades stones from the castle's walls and wooden beams from its interior were used to build the village *gasthaus* and various other structures.

The castle remained in disrepair even after Tyrol returned to Austrian rule following the 1814–1815 Congress of Vienna. But in 1878 the obviously canny village government sold the schloss—by that time little more than a scenic ruin—for an impressive 3,000 guldens to a Munich-based entrepreneur named Paul Spiess, who planned to turn it into a large and presumably very exclusive inn. The would-be hotelier launched a comprehensive renovation, ultimately giving Schloss Itter a central, multistory housing wing with fifty guest rooms, backed by a taller keep-like structure and flanked by smaller wings containing kitchens, servants' quarters, and storage areas. Spiess also repaired the encircling walls, rebuilt the crumbling gatehouse, landscaped the ravine, and repaved the narrow, 150-yard-long road between the castle and the village. Despite Spiess's investment, the hotel ultimately failed, and in 1884 the disappointed businessman sold the property to one of Europe's most acclaimed—and beautiful—musicians, the famed German piano virtuoso and composer Sophie Menter.

Born in Munich in 1846, Menter was something of a prodigy. The child of talented musicians—her father was a cellist and her mother a singer—she played her first public concert while still in her teens. At the age of twenty-three she became a student of Franz Liszt, who often referred to her as his "piano daughter" and ultimately declared her to be the world's finest living female pianist. In 1872 she married the Bohemian cellist David Popper, with whom she toured for several years. Menter's purchase[8] of Castle Itter was the culmination of a long-held desire for a stately home that would serve as both a private refuge from the rigors of her professional life and a salon for other musicians, and she refurbished several of the ground-floor rooms for use as practice areas and small performance spaces.

Over the eighteen years that Menter owned Castle Itter, she hosted such notable musical guests as Richard Wagner and Pyotr Ilyich Tchaikovsky, and her friend and mentor Liszt was a frequent and very welcome visitor. Indeed, so welcome was he that his several visits always commenced with ceremonial cannon salutes, and his passage up the approach road took him beneath flower-bedecked triumphal arches. While Liszt enjoyed these grand gestures, he used his time as Menter's guest to work. During a visit in November 1885, for example, he arose each morning at four, worked steadily for three hours, took a brief pause to attend Mass in the castle's chapel, and then went back to work until midafternoon.[9] In letters to Menter he was deeply appreciative of the time he'd spent at her "fairy-like" castle, referring to his time there as "magic memories."[10]

Sophie Menter continued to live at Castle Itter following the end of her marriage to Popper in 1886, and she often used the schloss for public events such as her October 1891 benefit performance to support the new choral society forming in the market town of Wörgl, four miles to the northwest of the schloss. She also continued to provide a creative atmosphere for famous visitors. During one two-week visit in September 1892, Tchaikovsky most probably scored Menter's "Ungarische Zigeunerweisen," a seventeen-minute work for piano and orchestra based on Hungarian Gypsy melodies that Menter and Tchaikovsky premiered in St. Petersburg, Russia, in February 1893.

Sadly, the costs of keeping up the aging structure forced Menter to sell Schloss Itter in 1902.[11] The buyer was one Eugen Mayr of Berlin, a wealthy physician and entrepreneur who equipped parts of the structure with electric lighting and had modern plumbing installed in the kitchens and primary living areas. Mayr used the castle as a suitably majestic venue for his August 1904 wedding to Maria Kunert, and he then spent several years and a small fortune giving the structure a neo-Gothic facelift. The addition of crenellated battlements and extensive interior woodwork—as well as the installation of several huge paintings depicting various stirring scenes from German mythology—left the castle with the fairytale look so popular during the first years of the twentieth century, which allowed Herr Mayr and his bride to achieve some success operating Itter as a boutique hotel.

The Schloss-Hotel Itter, as it was known, gained both prestige and increasing numbers of well-heeled guests following the end of World War I. The growing popularity of downhill skiing ensured that formerly sleepy villages throughout the Tyrol became popular holiday destinations, and the hamlet of Itter—which enterprising locals quickly dubbed "the Pearl of Tyrol"—was no exception. The castle was far and away the toniest place to lodge while enjoying the area's winter sports and gradually became almost as popular during the off-season. In 1925 the First Austrian Republic's deputy governor of Tyrol, Dr. Franz Grüner, bought Schloss Itter, primarily as a venue in which to display his impressive—and vast—collection of artwork and sculpture. Ironically, in 1932 Édouard Daladier, who during World War II would be one of Itter's VIP prisoners, stayed at the castle while visiting Wörgl to explore the growing city's experimental issuance of local currency as a way to stimulate economic recovery from the worldwide depression.[12]

That depression ultimately helped bring about Adolf Hitler's rise to power, of course, which in turn led in March 1938 to the Anschluss—Nazi Germany's annexation of Austria. And that sad event ultimately led directly to Schloss Itter's transformation from fairytale castle and hotel into something decidedly more sinister.

————

FOLLOWING THE ANSCHLUSS, Nazi Germany set about erasing all vestiges of independent Austria—a process that began with the former nation being renamed the German province of Ostmark.[13] The country was divided into seven administrative districts, the Reichsgaue, with Itter and the rest of Tyrol governed by a Nazi functionary based in Vorarlberg, some ninety miles to the southwest.

Life at Schloss Itter remained essentially unchanged for the first few months of the German occupation; the Nazis were too busy absorbing Austria into the "Greater Reich." One aspect of that absorption—the extension into the former Austria of the Nazi secret police and concentration-camp systems—was to have a direct effect on the castle and those who would later be held there, though it took place outside Itter's walls.

While the majority of Austrians welcomed the 105,000 troops of Lieutenant General[14] Fedor von Bock's 8th Army when they rolled across the border at five thirty in the morning on March 12, 1938, other residents of the newly created Ostmark were less inclined to become citizens of the "Greater Reich." Anti-Nazi resistance cells began forming throughout Austria soon after the Anschluss, and Tyrol—with its staunch Roman Catholicism, compact geography, and traditional sense of regional identity—quickly became a center of ongoing opposition to German rule and its increasingly onerous regulations. Like other nascent resistance groups throughout Austria, those in Tyrol were initially fragmented by suspicion, and rightly so. The Gestapo[15] was vigorous in its efforts to quash any opposition to Nazi rule and was often aided by pro-German Austrians who were only too willing to inform on neighbors they suspected of being less than wholehearted in their support of the new order.

Despite the Gestapo's best efforts, resistance cells survived, not only in larger cities such as Vienna, Salzburg, and Innsbruck, but also in towns and villages throughout the country. And while the score of resistance members in Wörgl initially had to bide their time and conserve their limited resources, as did most of their compatriots, they were able, over the months and years of German occupation, to slowly and carefully build the organization that would ultimately play a key role in the Schloss Itter story. And ironically, like the Austrian resistance as a whole, the cell in Wörgl was to be helped in its anti-Nazi efforts by no less an organization than the German army.

Within days of the Anschluss the entire Austrian army, the Bundesheer, was transferred en masse into the Wehrmacht—Nazi Germany's unified armed forces—an action that for a variety of reasons was welcomed by the majority of Bundesheer troops.[16] Moreover, the annexation of Austria created an even larger pool of manpower for Germany; between 1938 and 1945 some 1.3 million Austrian men were drafted into German military service. Austrian soldiers fought in every branch of the German armed forces and on every battlefront, and more than 240,000 of them died in combat or from sickness or accidents.[17]

While many Austrians served the Third Reich willingly and even fervently,[18] others endured their military duty only because any attempt to avoid conscription or to desert once in the ranks would have resulted in the harshest of punishments. Though the Germans attempted to keep certain Austrians they considered to be unreliable—leftists, nationalists, and others[19]—out of the military, many young men who secretly abhorred the Nazis ended up as "German" soldiers. And in the process of enduring their Wehrmacht time, many anti-Nazi Austrians learned—and extensively practiced in combat—the military skills that in the final months of the war would prove to be so valuable to the Austrian resistance and to the inhabitants of Schloss Itter.

SOME SOURCES INDICATE that Castle Itter's transformation from picturesque schloss-hotel and art venue into formidable prison was ultimately carried out at the direct order of Reichsführer der SS Heinrich Himmler himself. Himmler landed at an airfield outside Vienna just hours after German troops crossed the Austrian frontier on March 12, to personally lead the pacification of Austria—a process that would, in Himmler's view, require the arrest of anyone who might pose even the slightest threat to the new order. The diminutive former chicken farmer therefore took immediate personal control of all existing police forces and of the Austrian SS, which since 1934 had worked covertly to undermine Austrian independence and lay the groundwork for the Anschluss.[20]

Even as the majority of Austrians welcomed incoming German units with cheers and flowers, widespread arrests were already underway of those whose politics, religion, or ethnicity was deemed unacceptable. Himmler needed places to put the masses of new prisoners until they could be moved to established prisons and concentrations camps in Germany,[21] and it is entirely possible that Castle Itter's robust construction and relatively remote location attracted the attention of the notoriously secretive reichsführer. His attention must have wandered, however, for it wasn't until early 1940 that the German government leased the castle from Dr. Franz Grüner for unspecified official use.

The exact nature of that use remains unclear for the first two years following the signing of the lease agreement, though some sources indicate that the castle may have been used as an initial detention and interrogation site for high-value prisoners marked for deportation to Germany. We do know for certain that in early 1942 the castle was designated as the Ostmark headquarters for the German Alliance for Combating the Dangers of Tobacco.[22]

Despite its strangely ominous name, this Nazi-established and tax-funded organization was indeed dedicated to fighting tobacco use in "greater" Germany. While it might seem exceedingly odd that Adolf Hitler and his minions would be morally opposed to anything, the führer was widely known to abhor smoking. He believed the habit eroded public morals and undermined the health and effectiveness of military personnel. His attitude was by no means outside the mainstream; despite, or perhaps because of, its citizens' widespread tobacco use, Germany had since the mid-nineteenth century been a leader in researching the medical dangers of smoking. Under Nazi control, the Alliance for Combating the Dangers of Tobacco undertook its mission primarily by issuing pamphlets and press releases outlining the health risks associated with smoking, and the regional headquarters established at Schloss Itter was responsible for disseminating those products throughout the former Austria.

As important as the antismoking crusade might have been to Hitler, however, Himmler never lost his initial interest in using Schloss Itter for more nefarious purposes. On November 23, 1942, he got Hitler to sign an order directing SS-Lieutenant General Oswald Pohl, who as director of the SS Main Economic Administration Department (SS-Wirtschafts-Verwaltungshaupamt) was in charge of administering the concentration-camp system,[23] to begin the process of acquiring the castle outright for "special SS use." Himmler intended to convert Schloss Itter into a detention facility for *ehrenhäftlinge*, "honor prisoners" whom the Germans considered famous enough, powerful enough, or potentially valuable enough to be kept alive and in relatively decent conditions.

On February 7, 1943, members of Pohl's staff officially requisitioned the castle and all its outbuildings on Himmler's direct orders, abruptly terminating the lease arrangement that had provided Grüner with a respectable income for the previous three years. Officially referred to as an evacuation camp (*Evakuierungslager*), the castle was put under the operational control of the regional concentration-camp command at Dachau,[24] some ninety miles to the northwest. As one of that sprawling camp's 197 satellite facilities in southern Germany and northern Austria, Schloss Itter was to draw its funding, guard force, and support services directly from its soon-to-be-infamous parent facility.

The castle's transformation from an antismoking administrative center into a high-security facility for honor prisoners began immediately following its requisitioning. Plans for the conversion were apparently overseen by no less a personage than architect Albert Speer, Hitler's minister of armaments and war production,[25] with the actual construction supervised by SS-Second Lieutenant Petz.[26] A member of Dachau's facilities branch, he arrived at Itter on February 8 with twenty-seven prisoners—twelve from Dachau and fifteen from Flossenbürg[27]—all of whom had before their arrests been carpenters, plumbers, and the like.[28] Petz also took along some ten members of Dachau's SS-Totenkopfverbände (SS-TV) unit[29] to act as a security detail during the conversion work; they would be replaced by permanent guards once the castle's transformation was completed.

The first order of business for Petz and his slave laborers was to pack up most of Schloss Itter's remaining quality furnishings and artworks, a task that was carried out under the watchful eye of the owner. We don't know how Grüner felt about the outright expropriation of his castle and the cessation of the lucrative lease that had been in force for the previous three years, but we do know that for the official handover of the structure to Petz, Grüner wore a Nazi Party membership pin in his lapel. Once the furnishings and art had been crated, Petz ordered his prisoner-workers to begin dismantling the altar, consecrated by Pope Pius VI, in the schloss's small chapel. He also ordered the removal of the Gothic crucifix and all other Christian symbols; this may have been out of an excess of Nazi zeal on his part, or it may have been to deny the castle's future prisoners any chance of spiritual succor. Once the chapel had been stripped, its accoutrements were crated and joined the furnishings and artworks on trucks bound for a Salzburg warehouse owned by Grüner.

With the decks cleared, Petz was ready to put his prisoners to work on the castle's conversion. As was common in the concentration-camp system, the SS officer usually did not interact with the workers directly; he passed on his orders through a prisoner-functionary known as a kapo, a title with essentially the same meaning as the American prison term "trusty."

Though prisoners themselves, kapos often received better treatment than those they oversaw, and many were notoriously brutal to their fellow inmates in an attempt to curry even greater favor with their SS overlords. Fortunately for the prisoners on the Schloss Itter work party, their appointed kapo, a German political prisoner named Franz Fiedler,[30] was by all accounts a decent man who did all he could to shield his charges from the worst of Petz's frequent rages.

One source of those outbursts was the fact that Petz was under intense pressure from his superiors at Dachau to finish the work at Schloss Itter as quickly as possible. The SS officer knew that any delay could well mean his immediate reassignment to some location vastly more dangerous than the Austrian Tyrol, so his anxiety level was in all probability intense from the start. He thus wasted no time in putting his prisoners to work on the castle's transformation, and he directed them to start at basement level and work their way up.

Schloss Itter's cellars were extensive and, as might be expected, both cold and damp. This was not necessarily a disadvantage, however, because none of the existing five large rooms in the basement area were intended for use as living spaces. The two driest were converted into bulk food-storage areas—one for fruit and the other for potatoes and other vegetables—while the other three became, respectively, carpentry, plumbing, and electrical workshops. The stone staircase leading up to the ground floor was repaired and fitted with a handrail, and the already stout door leading into the cellar was reinforced and fitted with intricate double locks.

The ten rooms converted on the ground floor were largely given over to living and working areas for the SS-TV troops who would ultimately form the castle's permanent guard force. Using lumber trucked in from SS supply depots in Bavaria, the inmate-artisans constructed a dormitory meant to house up to thirty-five troops: a facility boasting individual lockers for each soldier, an arms room with a stout door secured with multiple locks, latrines with toilets and showers, and a kitchen with sinks, stoves, and pantry. Sophie Menter's delightful music room was divided in half; one side was turned into a day room for the enlisted troops and the other into an orderly room that would be the domain of the guard detachment's senior noncommissioned officer.

The prisoner-workers then set about converting the first floor's[31] existing nine rooms. Two were fitted out as offices for the future commander of the permanent SS-TV detachment and his executive officer; a third was made into a small, private lounge for the two officers; a fourth was a latrine; and the remaining five became the first of an eventual nineteen cells for the VIP prisoners soon to be incarcerated at Schloss Itter.

Because the prisoner accommodations were intended to house person-ages of great value to the Reich, they were decidedly more comfortable than the cells most of the Nazis' captives were forced to inhabit. The schloss's VIP cells—1 through 5 on the first floor, 6 through 9 on the second, and 10 through 19 on the third—were based on the existing guest rooms, and each was intended to house no more than two prisoners. Exterior bars were fitted over the windows in any room that had them, and the door of each room was fitted with two stout exterior locks. In anticipation of the possible need to completely isolate certain prisoners, about half of the room-cells had rudimentary sinks and toilets.

Conditions were far better in the fourth-floor suite to be occupied by the man picked to command the SS troops assigned to the castle. That officer—and his spouse, should he be accompanied—would enjoy an exquisitely furnished living room, bedroom, private kitchen, and dining room. In ad-dition to the usual amenities, the commander's suite also boasted a tele-phone system that would enable him to speak directly with the regional command authorities in Dachau and, in case he needed immediate military assistance, with the commandant of the Wehrmacht's Mountain Warfare Noncommissioned Officer School in nearby Wörgl.[32]

Once finished with the conversion of the castle's main building, the prisoner-workers moved on to the structure known as the schlosshof, a freestanding second gatehouse some fifty feet behind the smaller first struc-ture and separated from it by a triangular enclosed courtyard used as a parking area. Built of the same stone used for the castle, the schlosshof was pierced in the center by an arched entryway whose steps led up to a walled terrace and the main building. In addition to the entryway, the schlosshof housed a garage, a stable, and a storage area for gardening and landscaping equipment and supplies. The slave laborers—who slept in the building's cramped upper floor at the end of each long, hard workday—added a small medical clinic, consisting of a waiting room, an examination room, an office for an enlisted medic, and a rudimentary dental office.

The final task Petz assigned to his prisoner-workers was to install those systems that would make the castle escape-proof. Because Schloss

Itter already had massive walls, steep-sided ravines on its west, north, and east sides, and what was essentially a dry moat on its south side, it required only the addition of strategically placed tangles of concertina wire and a large, intricate lock on the front gate. To further discourage any freedom-minded prisoner, Petz had some of his SS-TV men install floodlights around the inside perimeter of the main wall. The troops also constructed three small, wooden-sided positions for MG-42 machine guns overlooking the castle's front and rear courtyards.

Schloss Itter's conversion into a VIP detention facility was essentially completed on April 25, 1943, though final modifications to the castle's electrical system had not been finished by the date Petz's original orders directed him to return to Dachau with his prisoner-workers and their guards. Not wanting to delay his departure—and, we can assume, anxious not to thereby incur the wrath of his superiors—Petz took his prisoner-workers and most of their guards back to Dachau but ordered the inmate who'd been overseeing the electrical work to stay behind and finish the job, with two SS-TV men as overseers.[33]

While the names of the two guards are lost to history, we do know the identity of the prisoner-electrician—a man destined to play an important role in later events at Schloss Itter. He was thirty-six-year-old Zvonimir "Zvonko" Čučković[34] (pronounced Kook-o-vich), a Roman Catholic and native of Sisak, Croatia, who before the April 1941 German invasion of Yugoslavia had been an electrical technician living in Belgrade with his wife, Ema, and son, also named Zvonimir.[35] Following his nation's capitulation, Čučković joined the anti-German resistance but was arrested by the Gestapo in December 1941. After spending time in prisons in Belgrade, Graz, Vienna, and Salzburg, he was transferred to Dachau on September 26, 1942.

Though initially destined for liquidation, Čučković was saved from death when during his arrival interrogation he stressed—in accented but fluent German—that his background as an electrical technician might allow him to be of some service to his captors. They agreed, and he was allotted to Petz's camp-maintenance crew. From November 1942 to February 1943 Čučković was assigned to an external work detail at Traunstein, a Dachau subcamp some fifty miles southeast of Munich, but he was returned to Dachau specifically to join Petz's expedition to Schloss Itter. There, he and an Austrian prisoner named Karl Horeis were responsible for upgrading the castle's entire electrical system, as well as for various other tasks. Petz's decision to allow the Croat to remain behind when the rest of the slave laborers were returned to Dachau was a testament to Čučković's skill; ultimately, it would also save his life.

With Schloss Itter ready to receive prisoners, it only remained for the administrators at Dachau to staff the new facility. Fourteen members[36] of that camp's SS-TV unit, as well as one member of the organization's female auxiliary[37] (and six Alsatian guard dogs), were tapped to form the castle's guard force, officially referred to as SS-Special Commando[38] Itter. The men were for the most part older, less capable troops with no combat experience. Most had served as guards at the larger camps and were happy to be posted to the relatively comfortable schloss. We might also assume that the more forward-looking of the guards assigned to the castle—those who had begun to realize that an Allied victory would probably mean execution for anyone connected with the operation of the death camps—welcomed the opportunity to spend whatever was left of the war guarding VIP prisoners in an alpine redoubt far removed from the horrors of the Final Solution.

If the guards believed they would be able to pass the rest of the war in an oasis of relative calm, however, they were sorely mistaken, for the two officers assigned as their superiors were definitely not of the laissez-faire school of military leadership. The junior of the two and the man tapped to serve as the second in command of Special Commando Itter, SS-Second Lieutenant Stefan Otto, was a member of the Sicherheitsdienst (SD), the security and intelligence arm of the SS. While his primary duty would be to glean useful information from any VIP prisoner ultimately remanded to Schloss Itter, every member of the castle's guard force knew he would also be closely watching them for any sign of laxness, either military or ideological. Any soldier unlucky enough to get on Otto's bad side could well end up reassigned to a frontline combat unit or even a penal battalion.

And worse, for reasons now unknown, the SS planners at Dachau chose to give command of Schloss Itter—a facility intended to house several of the highest-ranking and potentially most valuable prisoners in the Third Reich—to a brutish, unsophisticated, and politically inept officer widely known within the SS as a man almost as cruel to his own troops as he was to those unfortunate enough to become his prisoners.

———

To PUT IT SIMPLY, SS-Captain Sebastian "Wastl" Wimmer was a nasty piece of work. A native Bavarian, he was born in 1902 in Dingolfing—a small town some fifty miles northeast of Munich. In 1923 Wimmer joined the latter city's police department as a patrolman and eventually rose to the rank of sergeant in spite of, or perhaps because of, a reputation for securing quick confessions by beating suspects nearly to death during interrogation. Barely literate, unkempt, and given to violent drunken rages, he was the ideal recruit for the nascent SS. He joined the organization in March 1935,[39] having resigned from the Munich police the previous month.

We don't know Wimmer's motivation for enlisting in the SS. While it might certainly have been the act of a politically committed man seeking to win martial glory in an elite organization that espoused ideals that mirrored his own, it is more likely that, given what we know of his personality, Wimmer saw the organization as his ticket out of a dead-end job and a way to gain official sanction to continue brutalizing those who in all probability had always made him feel inferior—intellectuals, the wealthy, and, of course, Jews and the others whom the Nazis scornfully referred to as "subhumans."

Whatever his motivations, Wimmer was soon to see—and become part of—the dark side of Adolf Hitler's New Germany. After initial training at Dachau, the newly minted SS-TV officer[40] was assigned to the camp's permanent battalion-sized guard staff, known as SS-Wachsturmbann Oberbayern.[41] Though Dachau in 1935 was just two years old and still relatively small—its enlargement and the addition of crematoria would not begin until 1937—it nonetheless housed several thousand inmates, largely Jews and political prisoners. And while systematic prisoner executions had not yet begun, Wimmer and the other guards were essentially free to humiliate, brutalize, and, if they could provide a reasonable justification, kill inmates with impunity.

Wimmer was apparently good at his job, for by September 1937 he had risen to the rank of first lieutenant. That same month the director of the concentration-camp system, SS-Major General Theodor Eicke, ordered the single-battalion SS-Wachsturmbann Oberbayern enlarged to five battalions and redesignated as SS-Totenkopfstandarte 1 Oberbayern. Like the two other regiment-sized units[42] Eicke formed from concentration camp guard forces in 1937, Oberbayern was intended from the start to be a military organization. It would not engage in direct combat with armed enemy forces, however; all three of the initial Totenkopfstandarten were to be used to conduct what Eicke euphemistically referred to as "police and security duties" behind the battlefront. Given that Eicke was the originator of the "inflexible harshness" doctrine applied to concentration-camp prisoners, it comes as no surprise that the wartime duties of the Totenkopfstandarten would actually consist of rounding up, harshly interrogating, and usually executing enemy political and military leaders, Jews, and other "undesirables."

Both Totenkopfstandarte Oberbayern and Wimmer first got to practice their new roles during the 1938 German annexation of the Sudeteland. Two Oberbayern battalions preceded regular Wehrmacht units into the disputed region—the northern and western border areas of Czechoslovakia inhabited largely by ethnic Germans—to identify and round up anyone deemed a threat to the annexation effort. While many of these unfortunates ended up in Dachau and other concentration camps in Germany, some didn't survive their initial seizure by Wimmer and his comrades.

The reprehensible skills Wimmer demonstrated in the Sudetenland were put to extensive use during Germany's September 1939 invasion of Poland. Tasked to operate in the province of Kielce, Upper Silesia, behind the lines of Major General Walter von Reichenau's 10th Army, Wimmer and the other troops of Totenkopfstandarte Oberbayern[43] tortured and killed large numbers of Jews, anti-Nazi Catholic clergy, mental patients, Polish nationalist activists, and Polish soldiers attempting to escape capture. Mass murders were committed at such villages as Ciepielow, Nisko, and Rawa Mazowiecka;[44] indeed, so heinous were the atrocities committed by the Totenkopfstandarten troops under the guise of "police and security" operations that several senior Wehrmacht officers complained directly to Himmler. Their pleas were ignored, however, and Wimmer and his accomplices continued their murderous rampage until all three of the original Totenkopfstandarten were withdrawn from Poland in late 1939.[45] The units' withdrawal did not, of course, mean that German atrocities in Poland came to an end. New Totenkopfstandarten moved in to continue the horrific work and were joined by SS einsatzgruppen (special task forces)—units intended solely to carry out systematized mass executions in very short periods of time.[46]

Following their withdrawal from Poland, the three original Totenkopfstandarten were used to form the 3rd SS Panzer Division,[47] commanded by

Theodor Eicke. Equipped largely with captured Czech weapons, the division took part in the German invasions of France and the Low Countries, with Wimmer apparently serving in one of the division's panzer-grenadier (motorized infantry) regiments. Not surprisingly, given its provenance and fanaticism, the 3rd SS Panzer Division committed a variety of war crimes, including the May 1940 murder of ninety-seven captured members of the British army's 2nd Battalion, the Royal Norfolk Regiment, in the French village of Le Paradis.

The SS division's propensity for committing war crimes only increased following its April 1941 transfer to the Eastern Front, where it saw action with Army Group North in the advance on Leningrad. Russia was harder on the division than France had been: despite initial tactical successes in the spring and summer of 1941, by winter Eicke and his troops were being heavily battered by the Red Army. By the spring of 1942 the 3rd SS Panzer Division was encircled by superior Soviet forces near the town of Demyansk, south of Leningrad, and had lost almost 80 percent of its combat strength.

Wimmer, however, was not among the casualties. In January 1942 he was transferred to the 2nd SS Panzer Division, "Das Reich," which was itself engaged in fierce combat with the Red Army as part of Field Marshal Fedor von Bock's Army Group Center. The reason for the transfer is unclear, as is the exact nature of Wimmer's duties, but it seems likely that he reverted to the sort of "police and security" tasks he'd earlier undertaken in Poland. This assumption is bolstered by the fact that in September 1942 he was transferred yet again, but this time out of the combat zone to the relative safety of a staff job at a then little-known concentration camp just outside the city of Lublin, in central Poland. Officially referred to as a "prisoner of war camp of the Waffen-SS in Lublin," it became infamous simply as Majdanek.

Though established in October 1941 primarily as a slave-labor camp—prisoners were put to work in nearby factories producing weapons and vehicles for the German war effort—Majdanek also quickly became a de facto extermination center where Russian POWs, Polish Jews, and political prisoners were shot, hanged, and gassed. Sebastian Wimmer was personally responsible for Majdanek's day-to-day operations. In that capacity he undertook such mundane tasks as ordering supplies and equipment, overseeing personnel and staffing operations, and managing the warehouses that held the clothing and personal items confiscated from prisoners.

However, Wimmer also played an active role in the camp's more horrific activities. In addition to deciding which prisoners would be worked
to death in the nearby factories and which would be killed outright, he also
ruthlessly quashed any sign of resistance from those he and his guards so
cruelly oppressed. Any inmate who showed even the slightest hesitation
to follow an order or perform a task was made an example of, usually in
the most public and painful way. As a true disciple of Theodore Eicke's
"inflexible harshness" doctrine, Wimmer made sure that every prisoner in
Majdanek—whether Polish or Russian, POW or Jew, man, woman, or
child—suffered as much as possible.

Wimmer spent some five months at Majdanek, and his performance there
so impressed his superiors that in mid-February 1943 he was transferred back
to where his SS career had begun: Dachau. Though his position title was the
same as the one he'd had at Majdanek—chief of the preventive detention
camp—Wimmer's personal power was even greater than it had been in
Poland, because Dachau was literally the center of the concentration-camp
universe for SS-TV men. And while he ostensibly answered to camp commandant SS-Lieutenant Colonel Martin Weiss, Wimmer was the man in
charge of most of Dachau's day-to-day operations and, arguably, one of
the camp service's most powerful younger officers.

And this may be one possible answer to the question about how a man
like Wimmer—a textbook sociopath with a penchant for violence and a reputation for brutality toward both prisoners and his own soldiers—obtained
such a plum and politically sensitive job as commandant of Schloss Itter.
Crude Wimmer might have been, but he most obviously was not stupid.
Despite its importance within the camp system, Dachau was a decidedly
unpleasant place to work. Why put up with masses of unwashed prisoners
and the pervasive stench of burning human flesh when by pulling some
strings and calling in a few personal favors he could get himself a cushy
posting at a castle-hotel turned VIP prison? Why, his wife, Thérèse, who'd
spent most of the war years living with her parents in southern Germany,
could even join him, and they could both spend the remainder of the war
in safety and relative luxury. And if part of the price he had to pay for such
good fortune was to be civil to a bunch of VIP prisoners, why not? After
all, he could still brutalize his own men whenever he chose.

There is, of course, one other possibility. It might well have been that
the planners at Dachau tapped Wimmer for the Schloss Itter command not

in spite of his proven record of brutality but because of it. While the VIPs soon to be incarcerated in the hotel-turned-prison would have to be relatively well cared for as long as there was a chance they could be exchanged for important Germans held by the Allies, they might also need to be eliminated should the tide of war turn against Germany. The man in charge at Schloss Itter would therefore have to be ready, willing, and able to kill the VIP prisoners at a moment's notice, without compunction and without remorse. And "Wastl" Wimmer had certainly proven that he could be that man.

———

HOWEVER WIMMER'S ASSIGNMENT as commandant of Schloss Itter came about, we know (from Zvonimir Čučković's meticulous notes) that he arrived at the castle on the morning of Wednesday, April 28, 1943. His deputy, Stefan Otto of the SD, and the members of the permanent guard force had reached the castle two days earlier and were drawn up at attention in the small courtyard just inside the front gate. Wimmer and his wife had been driven down from Dachau in an open-top Opel staff car, which pulled up in front of the assembled guard troops, followed by a small truck whose cargo bay was packed with suitcases, boxes, and small pieces of furniture. The staff car's enlisted SS driver leapt out and dashed around to open the car's right-side door; Wimmer stepped down, his eyes scanning the soldiers before him.

Discreetly watching the scene through a closed window on the second floor of the schlosshof, Čučković could not hear what Wimmer then said to the gathered SS men. But from the officer's gestures and the grim looks on the faces of the troops, the Croat assumed the brief address concerned the need for discipline and the certainty of punishment should Wimmer in any way find that discipline to be lacking. Having finished speaking, the SS-TV officer undertook a brief inspection of the men, Otto trailing at his side, and then barked an order that sent the soldiers rushing to the rear of the truck to begin unloading what were apparently the Wimmers' luggage and personal effects. After waiting a moment to ensure his goods were being handled with the proper respect, the new commandant of Schloss Itter strode purposefully toward the castle's main entrance, his wife hurrying to keep up.

Wimmer's urgency stemmed from the fact that he had just days to en-sure that Schloss Itter was ready to receive its first prisoners. While he had not yet been told exactly who those notables would be, he knew that their value to the Reich—as either hostages or pawns in complex diplomatic ma-neuverings of which he had no knowledge and in which he most probably had absolutely no interest—would require that they be kept alive and well. He also undoubtedly understood that he would be held personally respon-sible for any harm that came to any of his VIP captives, a situation we might assume caused a fairly high level of anxiety in a man who had thus far spent his SS career humiliating, brutalizing, and murdering the prisoners put in his charge.

In the days immediately following Wimmer's arrival at Schloss Itter, Čučković noted that the new commandant kept his troops hopping with surprise inspections and practice alerts. During the latter the SS guards responded to mock prisoner escapes—announced by the blaring of a klaxon fixed to the roof of the castle's gatehouse—primarily by manning the MG-42 machine guns overlooking the courtyards. Čučković noted dryly that the guards didn't seem to realize that an escaped prisoner would be on the outside of the walls, headed for the cover of the nearby forests, rather than hanging about inside the castle waiting to be shot.

Čučković watched the Germans' preparations carefully, recording his observations in a small notebook that he had managed to steal from the SS guardroom and kept hidden behind a loose board in the schlosshof. He had to be extremely careful, of course, since he was still the only prisoner in a castle full of SS troops, but he hoped that his notes would someday prove useful in some way to the Allied cause.

And then, on the morning of Sunday, May 2, 1943, two Mercedes staff cars flying SS pennants from their fenders rolled through Schloss Itter's main gate and into the small triangular courtyard just behind it. From his vantage point in the schlosshof Čučković watched Wimmer rush out to meet the vehicles; the Croat was trying to get a better look at the first car's uniformed occupants when he saw three men alight from the second ve-hicle. Though the men were all dressed in drab and threadbare civilian suits, they seemed somehow familiar to Čučković. With a shock of recog-nition, he realized that the first VIP prisoners had arrived, and Schloss Itter was now officially open for business.

CHAPTER 2

FIRST ARRIVALS

ZVONKO ČUČKOVIĆ'S SHOCK on seeing the three men step from the Mercedes staff car in Schloss Itter's lower front courtyard that May day was understandable. Though the Croat had been incarcerated in one German prison or another for sixteen months, he easily recognized the newly arrived prisoners—Édouard Daladier, General Maurice Gamelin, and Léon Jouhaux—because their faces had regularly appeared on the front pages of newspapers across Europe even before the 1939 outbreak of war.

The fact that he was now seeing three of the most influential men in prewar France in the hands of the SS was somehow even more disturbing than his own initial arrest had been.[1] And while Čučković did not know the details of how the men had come to be prisoners, he was certain that their journey from the various halls of power in Paris to the decidedly colder and less hospitable halls of Schloss Itter had not been an easy one.

———

AT SIXTY-ONE, THE STOCKY, barrel-chested, and pugnacious Édouard Daladier was the youngest of the newly arrived prisoner trio. Arguably one of France's most important and prominent politicians in the years between the end of the First World War and the outbreak of the Second, he'd been born in 1884, the son of a baker. Intelligent and ambitious, he'd first worked as a history teacher and then made the leap into politics in 1912, when at the age of twenty-eight he won his first elected office: mayor of his home-town of Carpentras, near Avignon, in the Vaucluse department of France's Mediterranean southeast. His political rise was interrupted by World War I, during which he saw four years of brutal trench warfare, first as an enlisted soldier and then as a decorated officer.[2]

Following the armistice Daladier had returned to politics, serving in a series of increasingly important positions in the left-leaning Radical Social-ist Party. He'd been named the organization's leader in 1927 and served in several interwar governments as a minister responsible for, among other things, the foreign affairs and defense portfolios. In the latter position he pressed for the reform and modernization of the French army, an effort he continued when he was first named premier in January 1933; his gov-ernment lasted just nine months, however, and was swept from power when it proved incapable of forming a coherent policy to deal with the con-tinuing effects of the Great Depression. Daladier's second stint as premier, which began on January 30, 1934, lasted less than two weeks because his overly firm response on February 6 to widespread antiparliamentarist ri-ots in Paris organized and led by right-wing groups resulted in sixteen deaths and thousands of injuries.[3]

While Daladier's response to the riots led to the fall of his government, the fascist threat inherent in the street fighting prompted him to take his Radical Socialist Party into a leftist coalition with the French Communist Party and its longtime rivals, the Socialists. Known as the Popular Front, the alliance won power in the 1936 elections and the leader of the Socialists, Léon Blum, became premier.[4] He named Daladier his minister of national defense and war, a position the latter held until Blum resigned in June 1937. Daladier again served as minister of national defense and war when Blum briefly returned to the premiership in March and April 1938. The quick col-lapse of the second Blum ministry led French president Albert Lebrun to turn to Daladier, whose third and final term as France's premier began on April 10, 1938.

It was, of course, a period fraught with political intrigue and the real possibility of war. German forces had marched into Austria less than a month earlier, and Adolf Hitler was making increasingly strident demands regarding the Czech Sudetenland. Though Daladier was personally opposed to negotiating with Hitler—believing that to do so would only whet the Nazi leader's appetite for further expansion—his vivid memories of the butchery he'd witnessed in the trenches during World War I and his belief that France was not ready for war led him to join British prime minister Neville Chamberlain in signing the September 1938 Munich Agreement that gave the Sudetenland to Germany. Though the French people lauded Daladier as a peacemaker on his return from Munich, he—unlike the gullible Chamberlain—had no illusions that the dismemberment of Czechoslovakia had prevented war. His intent, he later said,[5] was to use the "reprieve" provided by Munich to strengthen both France's defenses and its national resolve.

Though Daladier set about improving his nation's military power—especially in terms of combat aircraft—the process was far from complete when Germany's September 1, 1939, invasion of Poland sparked the general European war the French premier had long believed to be inevitable. While several members of his government—including his Conservative Party justice minister, Paul Reynaud—urged him to take swift and decisive action following France's declaration of war, Daladier sought to minimize French losses and continue the military buildup he felt was absolutely necessary if France was to have any chance of successfully engaging the German juggernaut. Unfortunately for Daladier, his caution was widely seen as weakness, and support for his policies soon began to erode both within his government and among his increasingly bellicose people, and, on March 21, 1940, he resigned as premier and was immediately replaced by Reynaud.

Despite stepping down from the premiership, Daladier remained in government as Reynaud's minister of national defense and war. This was an act of political pragmatism on the latter's part, for the two men were poles apart ideologically and were in the first stages of a personal enmity that would eventually grow to epic proportions.[6] Their personal differences notwithstanding, Reynaud realized that Daladier was well versed in the intricacies of defense procurement and military reform and kept him in the cabinet. It was a rocky relationship at best, for in addition to their clear distaste for one another, Daladier was a supporter of General Maurice Gamelin, the elderly chief of the French army's General Staff, whom Reynaud believed to be too old and inept to properly defend France against a German assault. Daladier had appointed Gamelin to his lofty position and took personally any criticism of the army chief.

Even after Gamelin's bungling failed to halt the German invasion of France that began on May 10, 1940—ineptitude that led Reynaud to replace him just eight days later with the even older and arguably more hidebound General Maxime Weygand—Daladier continued to defend Gamelin as a brilliant military leader brought low by the incompetence and cowardice of others. This attitude helped ensure that the antagonism already existing between Daladier and Reynaud flared into outright hatred. Reynaud made it increasingly difficult for Daladier to carry out the duties of his ministry, and that situation, coupled with the certainty that the appallingly swift collapse of the French army would soon lead to a German occupation, prompted Daladier to join several other prominent politicians who believed they could carry on the struggle from Morocco, a French colony.

The group—which in addition to Daladier included former interior minister Georges Mandel, former secretary of state for finance Pierre Mendès-France, and former minister of marine Caesar Campinchi[7]—sailed for Casablanca on June 21 aboard the steamer *Massilia*, arriving four days later to a decidedly chilly reception. France had capitulated the day after the ship left Le Verdon-sur-Mer,[8] and General Charles-Auguste Noguès, the commander in chief of French forces in North Africa and governor-general of Morocco, was waiting to see which way the political wind was blowing in Paris. Though he personally believed that France was capable of carrying on the fight against Germany from North Africa, he did not want to seem overly welcoming to the politicians aboard *Massilia*—this despite having been appointed to the Moroccan governorship by Daladier. Noguès therefore ordered Daladier and several others detained on the ship under guard.

That detention lasted until June 27, when Daladier was able to travel to Noguès's headquarters in Rabat. Though the two men agreed that French forces in North Africa had both the will and the wherewithal to continue the fight against Germany, Noguès refused to act without clear instructions from the rump government in Bordeaux. As Daladier later recalled, the general "was seeking government authorization to break with official policy and fight on, even if the government had to disavow its involvement in the process."[9] Noguès's first few cables had gone unanswered, but on June 28 the general received a very definite reply: he was to abstain from any military action. Further, he was to detain Daladier and the other politicians in Morocco until after the scheduled July 10 vote in the National Assembly that was expected to ratify the Franco-German armistice and grant "full and extraordinary powers" to Marshal[10] Philippe Pétain to form a new government to administer that part of France not yet occupied by German forces.

Having determined that cooperation with the new order was the better part of valor, Noguès immediately ordered that Daladier and the others not be allowed to board ship for the return passage to Bordeaux until after the crucial July 10 vote. When that balloting was over—and with Pétain confirmed as the new master of unoccupied France and his capital established at Vichy, a resort town about seventy miles northwest of Lyon—Noguès permitted Daladier to take ship for Bordeaux. He was not arrested upon his August 10 arrival, but he was immediately informed that the Vichy government intended to prosecute him—along with Blum, Gamelin, Mandel, Reynaud, former air force minister Guy La Chambre, and former army comptroller general Robert Jacomet—for their "responsibility" for France's defeat by Germany. It was, of course, a political witch hunt intended to find scapegoats rather than the truth, but Daladier approached the trial as an opportunity to put Pétain and his collaborationist regime under the spotlight.

The trial was to be held in the town of Riom, some twenty miles southwest of Vichy, and the prospective defendants were told to stay in the vicinity. Daladier lodged with various friends in and around Vichy until September 6, when he was taken into custody and placed under house arrest at the Château Chazeron, a medieval castle-turned–country house a few miles outside Riom. He was eventually joined by Blum, Mandel, Reynaud, Gamelin, and the others. The defendants stayed in the drafty, poorly maintained chateau until October 15, 1941, when on the orders of Pétain they were transferred to the Fort du Portalet, an even more austere fortress in the rugged mountains of the Pyrenees near the Spanish border. Three months later Daladier, Blum, Gamelin, Jacomet, and La Chambre were transferred yet again, this time to a dilapidated country house at Bourassol, a few miles south of Riom. Reynaud and Mandel did not accompany the others, for Pétain had decided to withdraw the charges against the two. This did not gain them their freedom, however, for both remained in Vichy's custody until they were turned over to the Germans.

At Bourassol, Daladier and his codefendants continued preparing their defense. When the trial finally began at Riom's hurriedly renovated Palace of Justice on the afternoon of February 19, 1942, it must have been something of a relief for the five men to actually be able to answer the charges against them. They were under no illusions, of course, that their defense, however spirited, would actually prevent them from being found guilty. Indeed, four months earlier Pétain had made it perfectly clear how he expected things to go when he publicly announced the defendants' guilt. The Vichy government intended the Riom Trial, as it became known, to be a blistering indictment of those it loudly proclaimed to be the "men who betrayed France." And the fact that some two hundred French and foreign journalists would be permitted to observe the trial was a clear indication that Pétain and his supporters also meant the event to be a propaganda victory for Vichy, one in which Daladier and the others could be properly humiliated, discredited, and disgraced.

The details of the Riom Trial—as fascinating and historically important as they are—are outside the scope of this volume. Suffice it to say that things did not go at all as Pétain and his collaborationist government had intended. While Gamelin refused to recognize Vichy's authority to try him and sat silent throughout the trial, Daladier and Blum mounted what can only be called a brilliant defense. Daladier's knowledge of the events that transpired between the Popular Front's electoral victory in 1936 and the French capitulation in 1940 was encyclopedic, and he was able to categorically refute virtually each point made by the poorly prepared and far less articulate prosecutors. And Blum's eloquence and legal acumen—he was, after all, an extremely skilled lawyer as well as a brilliant politician—allowed him to conduct withering cross-examinations of government witnesses that soon revealed Vichy's case against the five defendants to be nothing more than a politically motivated sham.

As the trial dragged on, Vichy's German masters became increasingly frustrated with both the tribunal's slow pace and the foreign press's increasingly sympathetic portrayal of the defendants. Hitler himself expressed outrage that the court seemed incapable of shutting Blum and Daladier up, much less proving their culpability for "forcing" Germany to attack France in 1940. In order to avert any further excoriation of the Vichy regime—and, by extension, his own—in the world's newspapers and to halt what was quickly becoming a public-relations nightmare, Hitler ordered the trial to be halted. On April 14, 1942, the president of the court, Pierre Caous, dutifully announced that the proceedings were to be "temporarily suspended"—after twenty-four public sessions—so that prosecutors could gather "further information."

The temporary suspension of the Riom Trial lasted until May 21, 1943, when the proceedings were officially terminated. By that time, however, much had changed for both Daladier and France. Operation Torch—the November 8, 1942, British-American invasion of French North Africa— had prompted Hitler to order his forces into unoccupied France. Within days the entire country was firmly under German control, the Vichy regime was reduced to a true puppet government, and the position of Daladier and his fellow Riom defendants had become far more precarious. Though Jacomet and La Chambre were sentenced to continuing house arrest at Bourassol, Heinrich Himmler had ordered Daladier, Blum, and Gamelin moved to "secure locations" in Germany to prevent their "kidnapping" by Allied agents.[11]

The three men began their melancholy journey on March 31, 1943, when they left Bourassol under police guard in a five-car convoy. Their first stop was the small airport in nearby Clermont-Ferrand, where they were joined by labor leader Léon Jouhaux. By April 3 the four were at Paris's Le Bourget airport, where they and their Gestapo escorts boarded a Luftwaffe transport bound for Mannheim and, ultimately, Frankfurt. From there the Frenchmen and their minders again traveled by road, and just after dawn on April 4 they arrived at their destination: the sprawling Buchenwald concentration camp[12] near Weimar.

Compared with the horrific conditions endured by most of Buchenwald's inmates, Daladier and the other French VIP prisoners lived in relative comfort. They were assigned individual rooms within the SS compound, which was separated from the main camp and surrounded by pine trees.[13] Though the windows in their rooms were barred and their doors locked at night from the outside, the Frenchmen were well fed, were allowed to walk around the compound's fenced perimeter (with guards, of course), and could write and receive letters. Perhaps just as important for these gregarious and once-powerful men, they were allowed to gather for a few hours each evening after dinner to share a bottle of German-provided cognac, smoke hand-rolled cigarettes of cheap Croatian tobacco, and dissect—often heatedly—the causes of their nation's defeat.

Daladier's sojourn at Buchenwald did not last long. On April 29 the camp's commandant, Hermann Pister, told Daladier that he, Gamelin, and

Jouhaux were to be transferred the following day to a "special facility" in the northern Tyrol, not far from Innsbruck. Ominously, Léon Blum would not accompany them; as a Jew, he was destined for "special detention," Pister said. So, too, was Georges Mandel, who was to arrive at Buchenwald within a few days. Daladier was deeply troubled that his friend would be staying behind at the concentration camp, but Blum himself made light of it, saying that he and Mandel would "turn the place into a ghetto."[14]

Just after dawn on April 30, Daladier, Gamelin, and Jouhaux said their good-byes to Blum and then were escorted by SS troops to the compound's main gate. The plan soon changed, however, for Buchenwald's assistant commandant arrived with news that their departure for Tyrol had been postponed, though he gave no reason. Finally, on the morning of May 2, Daladier and his companions stepped into a Mercedes staff car and, with their SS escort, set off for Munich and, ultimately, Schloss Itter.

The drive south was an eye-opening experience for the three Frenchmen, for even after nearly four years of war the roads of central and southern Germany were alive with military traffic. Several times field police soldiers[15] waved the staff car and its escorts to the side of the road so long convoys of troop trucks, interspersed with vehicles towing artillery pieces and multibarreled rocket launchers, could move past unimpeded. Despite clear evidence of Allied air attacks—destroyed and damaged buildings, downed bridges, and vast stretches of heavily cratered landscape—it was depressingly obvious to the Frenchmen that Germany was far from beaten.

MAURICE GAMELIN WAS PERHAPS the most deeply affected by the seemingly endless display of the Wehrmacht's combat power. The diminutive general—he stood barely five feet four inches tall—had spent more than fifty of his seventy-one years as an officer in his nation's army, a force whose primary raison d'être for at least a generation had been to prevent the exact military catastrophe that had overtaken France in June 1940. And the fact that most of his countrymen seemed to believe that he was solely and personally responsible for France's defeat and capitulation would have been a bitter pill to swallow for the erstwhile supreme commander of all French armed forces.

Gamelin's rise to his nation's highest military post seems, in retrospect, to have been almost preordained. He was born on September 20, 1872, in his family's ornate home on Paris's Boulevard Saint-Germain, literally just across the street from the French ministry of war. His father, Zéphyrin Gamelin, was a general and the army's controller-general, or senior administrator.[16] The younger Gamelin was educated at an elite Paris school, where he developed a deep and lifelong interest in art and philosophy, and in 1891 he entered the École Spéciale Militaire de Saint-Cyr, France's foremost military academy. A gifted student, he graduated at the top of his 449-member class in 1893 and was commissioned a second lieutenant.

Over the following two decades Gamelin proved himself to be both an excellent staff officer and a tactical commander of rare skill. After his initial field assignment in French North Africa, he ascended steadily through the ranks, along the way acquiring such powerful mentors as General Joseph Joffre, commander in chief of the French army in the years leading up to World War I. By November 1913 he was a member of the General Staff's operations bureau. In that position Gamelin helped develop the mobilization plan the army would put into motion in the event of war, and in March 1914 he was tapped to join Joffre's personal staff.

While World War I was a bloody tragedy for France, it was a personal triumph for Gamelin. Alternating between important staff positions and field commands, he built a solid reputation as an innovative, highly capable, and politically astute officer who cared about his men and maintained his composure no matter what surprises were thrown at him. The best illustration of the latter attribute was his brilliant command of the 9th Infantry Division during the Germans' massive spring offensive in 1918. Initially confronted by six enemy divisions, Gamelin ordered a fighting withdrawal that saved his division and, ultimately, allowed him to stop the German advance along the River Oise.

By the time the war ended in 1918, Gamelin was a brigadier general with a chest full of medals—both French and foreign. His wartime successes ensured his continued ascent in the postwar world, and he burnished his already lofty reputation with a series of highly successful assignments. He led the French military mission to Brazil from 1919 to 1925, commanded all French forces in Syria from 1925 to 1928,[17] and in 1930 was named deputy to General Maxime Weygand, chief of the army general staff. Prime Minister André Tardieu intended Gamelin to be a forward-thinking and relatively liberal counterweight—and eventual successor—to the vastly more conservative Weygand. While the latter favored the complete overhaul and mechanization of the French army—and was especially fervent about the need to create independent armored units equipped with state-of-the-art tanks[18]—his notoriously abrasive personality and penchant for publicly belittling politicians foolish enough to disagree with him often negated his sincere efforts to improve his nation's military readiness.

The Gamelin-Weygand partnership began well; indeed, soon after the former became his assistant in 1930, Weygand referred to him as "a colleague of peerless value."[19] Both officers were extremely wary of Germany's growing military might, and they agreed wholeheartedly on the need to modernize the French army and construct a line of fortifications along the nation's eastern frontier. But the honeymoon didn't last long; in February 1931 Weygand became the army's inspector general, and Gamelin replaced him as chief of staff, and from that point on the two men clashed with increasing frequency over the course, and cost, of France's military rejuvenation.

For his part, the arch-conservative Weygand found it virtually impossible to deal with the series of leftist prime ministers who came to power from 1932 onward. He believed their internationalist and optimistic views of foreign relations to be naive and possibly subversive, and he strongly felt that their failure to adequately fund the large-scale weapon purchases he considered essential was making France increasingly vulnerable. Though Gamelin agreed with many of Weygand's proposals, he also knew that alienating the politicians would be counterproductive. Gamelin was thus conciliatory where Weygand was confrontational, hoping to achieve through logic, persuasion, and compromise what would almost certainly not be gained through acrimonious intransigence. This point of view put him at odds with Weygand, who increasingly saw Gamelin as a dangerously indecisive leader whose beliefs and methods—which Weygand saw as holdovers from Gamelin's World War I service—were perpetuating the army's weakness and vastly increasing its risks of defeat in any conflict with Germany.

Gamelin's point of view ultimately prevailed for the simple reason that in January 1935 Weygand reached the mandatory retirement age of sixty-eight. Upon his departure, Gamelin replaced him not only as army chief of staff but also as both army inspector general and vice president of the Supreme War Council.[20] The latter position made Gamelin the peacetime deputy to the minister of war, Louis Maurin. In wartime, the council's vice president automatically became the commander of all French field armies.

Unfortunately for France, when the time came for Gamelin to actually take up the latter position—often referred to as "generalissimo"[21]—he proved consistently unequal to the monumental task facing him. Despite his genuine and consistent efforts during the inter-war years to improve the quality of the French army and the cooperation between military men and politicians, he dithered during the first few months of war. He failed to strike aggressively into Germany and preferred a static defense along the border based on the forts of the impressive, but incomplete, Maginot Line. When the so-called Phoney War ended with the German invasion of France and the Low Countries on May 10, 1940, he was slow to grasp the importance of the German thrust through the Ardennes, a rugged and heavily forested area he firmly believed to be impassable to tanks.

As French defeats mounted, Gamelin reacted by dismissing several of his field commanders, blaming the nation's reversals on their "incompetence" rather than on his own strategic and tactical blunders. The man who had made a name for himself during the static, grinding bloodbath of World War I and in subsequent colonial wars ultimately proved incapable of responding effectively to Germany's fast-paced and flexible combined-arms assault. Completely overwhelmed by blitzkrieg warfare, Gamelin continued to flounder until May 18, when Prime Minister Paul Reynaud sacked him and—adding insult to injury—called back Weygand as generalissimo.

Contrary to widespread rumors that he'd killed himself or fled the country,[22] Gamelin spent the weeks between his dismissal and France's capitulation to Germany at his home in Paris, tending his roses and listening to the increasingly dire news from the battlefronts. He expected the Nazis to arrest him, of course, when they arrived in the capital; what he hadn't anticipated was that he'd be taken into custody by fellow Frenchmen. On September 6, 1940—the same day Daladier was seized—Gamelin was visiting his friend Léo-Abel Gaboriaud, editor of the journal *L'Ère nouvelle*, when agents of the Sûreté Nationale[23] appeared at the door. They explained that they were reluctantly working under orders from the Germans to arrest Gamelin and transport him to the Château Chazeron. Gaboriaud walked with his friend to the waiting car, and, as the officers were about to put him in the backseat, the editor looked at them sternly and said, "The man you have taken into custody and who is leaving with you is alive. I assume he will be alive when he gets to Chazeron."[24]

Though Gaboriaud's concern for Gamelin's continued well-being was understandable, the diminutive general made it to Chazeron—and through the Riom trial—unscathed. While his subsequent incarceration with Daladier and the others in Buchenwald cannot have been salutary, his daily ritual of vigorous calisthenics followed by a few brisk turns around the inside of the small VIP compound's perimeter ensured that upon his arrival at Schloss Itter he was in reasonably good health for a man his age.

Unfortunately, the same could not be said of the third man Zvonko Čučković saw step out of the Mercedes staff car in the castle's courtyard.

————

THOUGH JUST SIXTY-FOUR YEARS OLD, Léon Jouhaux looked a good deal older. The secretary-general of the Confédération Générale du Travail (CGT), one of France's largest trade unions, had for several months been suffering from a flare-up of the arthritis that had plagued him for decades. More seriously, any sort of stress or anxiety brought on increasingly significant chest pain.[25] Convinced his heart was beginning to fail him but lacking a diagnosis or any sort of medication, the stout labor leader could do little but stoically accept his worsening condition.

Such passive acceptance was a trait new to Jouhaux, for his had not been an easy life.[26] Born in a poor section of Paris in 1879, he'd always been a fighter: first against childhood illness and schoolyard bullies, and for most of his adult life against social injustice in general and the oppression of working people in particular. He'd learned his radical activism from his father, who in 1871 had taken to the streets during the popular uprising that came to be known as the Paris Commune. When Jouhaux was two years old, his father left his job in a central-city slaughterhouse and moved the family to Aubervilliers, a less-crowded suburb, where work in a match factory offered marginally better pay.

The conditions in the new workplace were no better than those in the slaughterhouse, however. Workers toiled long hours in dismal and dangerous conditions, unable to escape the pervasive, toxic, and highly explosive fumes produced by the white phosphorous that was the match heads' main ingredient. The elder Jouhaux ultimately became a leader in the factory's nascent labor union and several times led the workers out on strikes meant to force the bosses to improve safety and working conditions. When Léon was twelve, his father's activism finally led to yet another long-term suspension from the match factory, an event that forced his intellectually gifted son to leave school and find a job in order to help support the family.

The young Jouhaux first went to work at Aubervilliers's Central Melting House, a foundry where conditions were miserable. When his father regained his position at the match factory, Jouhaux was able to go back to school, but nine months later his father was again laid off, so the boy took a job at a soap works. At the age of sixteen Léon himself went to work at the match factory, where he immediately joined the union his father had worked so hard to create. From that point on—except for a single year he was able to spend at a vocational school—Jouhaux was, as he later said, "completely caught up in the hard life of the industrial worker."[27]

In 1900 Jouhaux exchanged that form of hard life for another when he was called up for military service. After initial training he was dispatched to Algeria, where he served with the 1st Regiment of Zouaves. However, he was sent home and released from service in 1903 because his father— who had lost and regained his job several more times—had gone blind as a result of his long exposure to white phosphorous. Jouhaux went back to work in the match factory, where in addition to laboring on the production line he also replaced his father on the union's leadership committee. Sincerely dedicated to improving the lot of all workers, he quickly proved himself to be both a natural leader and a tough negotiator who was not afraid to go toe-to-toe with the bosses and the thugs they hired to break strikes.

Indeed, so effective were Jouhaux's tactics at the match factory that he soon came to the attention of national labor leaders. He was invited to join the executive committee of the CGT in 1906 and was soon working full-time on issues important to workers throughout France. Though he continued to be known as a tough negotiator, he also developed a healthy pragmatism that allowed him to compromise when it helped to ultimately advance the cause of the CGT and its members. Following several early successes, in 1909 he was named the CGT's secretary-general, a promotion that made him, at just thirty years old, arguably the most powerful labor leader in France.

Among the most pressing problems Jouhaux faced in his first years as head of the CGT was the rising tide of militarism in Europe. Believing that wars made workers suffer solely to further enrich their capitalist bosses, Jouhaux joined with other European labor leaders to endorse disarmament and universal antimilitarism. Yet when Europe descended into war in 1914—despite what Jouhaux later called the labor leaders' "best efforts to build a dike against the onrushing sea of blood"[28]—union members in each warring nation rallied to the colors and enlisted in droves. The reality of war changed even Jouhaux's mind: he quickly came to see that a German victory could very well lead to the virtual enslavement of French workers, and thereafter he worked diligently to support the French war effort.

Despite that support, Jouhaux never lost the belief that the working people of the world could ultimately help make war obsolete if they banded together in an international trade-union movement, and he worked diligently to make such an alliance a reality. He was a major player in the post–World War I reconstitution of the International Federation of Trade Unions (IFTU) and in 1919 became the organization's vice president even while maintaining his role as head of the CGT. Throughout the 1920s and 1930s he tirelessly exerted his considerable influence to bring together Europe's disparate labor organizations. In November 1937 Jouhaux was one of three IFTU leaders who traveled to Moscow for talks regarding the affiliation of Soviet Russia's Central Council of Trade Unions with the IFTU. Despite being a staunch anticommunist, Jouhaux maintained that such an affiliation was logical as a reaction to the growing power of fascism in both Germany and Italy, but his recommendation that the IFTU establish close and pragmatic ties with the Soviet organization was rejected by the full board of the IFTU.[29]

Jouhaux's efforts to help avert another world war were ultimately in vain, of course. Following France's June 1940 capitulation, Vichy ordered the CGT dissolved, prompting many of its members to form a nascent resistance movement. Jouhaux's outspoken criticism of the Pétain regime ensured that his name soon ended up on an arrest list, and a warrant was issued for him in October 1940. He'd already gone underground, however, traveling within unoccupied France on false papers that identified him as a Czech named Bedrich Woves.[30] He was referred to as "Mr. Buvot" by the compatriots who helped him move from one safe house to another but signed his own name to the many pamphlets he wrote, urging all true trade unionists to support the Allied cause and pleading for unity among France's fractious left-wing groups. To pass his writings on to those who would reproduce and distribute them, Jouhaux relied on his secretary and longtime companion (and future wife), Augusta Bruchlen,[31] an Alsace-born

Frenchwoman whose fluency in German several times helped her escape detection as she was attempting to contact members of the resistance movement that had grown out of the now-banned CGT.

In January 1940 the IFTU's London-based executive committee decided that all of the major labor leaders in continental Europe should be evacuated to Britain, and Jouhaux was the first on their list. The organization initially approached the British Secret Intelligence Service (SIS),[32] which favored the IFTU's plan but was ultimately unable to put it into operation. Following Britain's July 1940 creation of the Special Operations Executive (SOE)—a quasi-military organization specifically tasked with undertaking clandestine activities in enemy-occupied territories—the IFTU approached its political head, Minister of Economic Warfare Hugh Dalton. A longtime socialist, Dalton wholeheartedly agreed that Jouhaux would be far more valuable to the Allied cause working in London than he would be rotting in a Vichy or German prison.[33] Dalton therefore used his considerable influence to ensure that Jouhaux's escape from France became a top SOE priority.

By early November 1941 SOE had arranged for the labor leader to be smuggled out of France into neutral Portugal, where he was to board a flight for Britain. A double agent within the CGT resistance apparently got wind of the attempted escape, however, and betrayed the plan to the Vichy secret police. Jouhaux was arrested at the port of Marseilles on November 26,[34] 1941, just as he was about to take ship—using his false papers—for Portugal.

After his arrest Jouhaux was driven to Vals-les-Bains, a small spa town nestled in the Rhône-Alpes, where he was held incommunicado as his Vichy captors pondered what to do with him. At the end of January 1942 he was moved to Cahors, a quaint medieval town some ninety miles northwest of Vals-les-Bains, where he lived under house arrest until the beginning of November. He was then moved yet again, this time to the spa town of Évaux-les-Bains in central France, in which the Vichy regime had established a centralized internment center for top-level political prisoners. The accommodations were relatively civilized—the captives were housed in the town's former Grand Hotel—and about a month after his arrival Jouhaux was permitted a visit from Augusta Bruchlen. In January 1943 she herself was arrested by the Sûreté, apparently because of her work as a courier between Jouhaux and the CGT resistance. Eventually interned in the same Grand Hotel, she was apparently no longer considered a major threat, because her captors allowed her twice-weekly visits with Jouhaux, albeit in the presence of a policeman.[35] These occasions did much to cheer the labor leader, who had for several months been suffering from a prolonged arthritis flare-up and increasingly severe angina.

Jouhaux's idyll in Évaux-les-Bains ended abruptly on the night of March 31, 1943. A squad of German soldiers hustled him from his room with little more than the clothes on his back, handcuffed him, and shoved him into the back of a waiting military ambulance. With a German guard sitting on either side of him, he was driven to the airport in Clermont-Ferrand, where he joined Daladier and Gamelin for the journey to Buchenwald and, ultimately, Schloss Itter.

———

FOR SEBASTIAN WIMMER, the arrival of the castle's first three honor prisoners marked the beginning of what he fervently hoped would be a very rewarding phase in his career. He was, after all, commandant of what was planned to be arguably the most important and high-profile subcamp in all of Nazi Germany's sprawling concentration-camp system and would be responsible for some of the Third Reich's most valuable captives. If Wimmer played his cards right, he could win promotion, decorations, and, with luck, even personal recognition from the führer. And, perhaps most important, if his performance in this key post managed to sufficiently please his superiors in both Dachau and Berlin, he'd be able to avoid returning to a vastly less comfortable life working in one of the death camps or, far worse, actual front-line combat duty.

Though a brutal thug by both nature and training, Wimmer understood that his success as commandant of Schloss Itter would result in large part from his ability to treat his important prisoners with a level of "correctness" that was wholly outside his realm of experience. Because the führer might have future plans for the VIP captives—perhaps handing them over to the Allies as part of some political accommodation or even releasing them as a gesture of magnanimity after Germany's ultimate victory—Wimmer would have to do his best to keep them healthy and secure. And though he was certainly not the most intelligent man in the SS, even Wimmer understood that a German victory was not guaranteed: the Fatherland had already suffered a string of battlefield reversals, and Allied aircraft were turning the nation's industrial centers into smoking rubble with almost monotonous regularity. Wimmer realized very clearly that should Germany lose the war, having a few French VIPs testify that he treated them well might be the only thing that would save him from an Allied firing squad.

Attempting to strike a balance between correctness and the proper level of stern aloofness he felt his position required, Wimmer nodded to Daladier, Gamelin, and Jouhaux as they walked toward him after alighting from the staff car that had brought them to Itter, but he did not attempt to shake their hands. Flanked by members of the castle's SS guard detachment, the three Frenchmen followed Wimmer through the arched portal in the center of the schlosshof and across the large enclosed terrace that led to the vaulted entrance[36] to the castle's main hall. Stefan Otto of the SD was waiting, and, as Wimmer looked on, the younger officer assigned each of the Frenchmen a room—Otto was careful not to use the word "cell"— Jouhaux in number 9 on the second floor, and Gamelin and Daladier in numbers 10 and 11, respectively, on the third floor.[37]

Otto then solemnly read the new arrivals the decidedly relaxed rules of their captivity. Breakfast, lunch, and dinner would be served in the ground-floor dining hall, and they could take the meals back to their rooms if they chose or, in good weather, eat at tables on the adjoining terrace. Each man would receive a hundred liters of wine per month, as well as a monthly allowance of 500 Reichsmarks with which to purchase tobacco, writing paper, pens, and other sundries from a small kiosk tucked beneath the stairs on the ground floor. The prisoners would be able to send mail to, and receive it from, members of their immediate families, though all mail would, of course, be censored. The men would have free access to the castle's library and would even be permitted to listen to the large radio that graced the main hall—though the device was tuned exclusively to Radio Berlin. And, finally, each man could exercise in the large courtyard to the rear of the castle, which encompassed a thirteenth-century garden and fountain, in the morning and afternoon.

Lest the three Frenchmen somehow forget that they were indeed prisoners, Otto then spelled out a few harder facts. They were under the absolute control of the Third Reich and would obey the orders of Commandant Wimmer immediately and without question or argument. The men would each be locked into their rooms from eleven at night until seven in the morning. They would not be permitted to leave the castle without an SS escort, and, if discovered outside the schloss alone at any time, they would be considered escapees and could be shot on sight.

With the reading of the regulations completed, the Frenchmen were escorted to their rooms and locked in so that Wimmer could gather all his troops in the 150-foot-by-100-foot rear courtyard. He wanted to make a brief but pointed announcement, one probably largely intended to ensure that none of the SS men inadvertently violated the correctness Wimmer hoped would either be good for his career or save his neck:

> The three people who have just arrived to be imprisoned in the castle are French. They will be joined by others. By command of the führer, these prisoners are to be viewed as hostages. Upon meeting one of them you should salute them with a regular military salute, and not with the führer salute. If one of these gentlemen should attempt to speak to you, your response should be the following: "Your Excellency, would you please speak to Commandant Wimmer?" Understood?[38]

The ground rules firmly established, the guards and their prisoners began settling into a daily routine. For the former this revolved around the usual on- and off-duty periods, interspersed with the occasional recreational foray into Itter or Wörgl. For the latter, the days were primarily built around mealtimes—breakfast at eight, lunch at two, and dinner at seven. The food—prepared by the guard detachment's supply sergeant, Oschbald, and two junior soldiers—was plain but plentiful and was the same as that served to the SS troops. Between meals the three Frenchmen passed the time reading, talking, or walking around the inner courtyard. After dinner the men would share a cognac—from a bottle presented to them by Wimmer in a transparent attempt to curry favor—and some conversation; then each would repair to his own room to work on the notes and journals intended to form the basis for their exculpatory postwar memoirs.

But Schloss Itter had not been converted into a high-security prison in order to house just Daladier, Gamelin, and Jouhaux. The bureaucrats at Dachau intended to fill as many of the cells as possible, and over time the Tyrolean castle welcomed an additional fifteen "honor" prisoners, each with his or her own story.

CHAPTER 3

LOVERS, FRIENDS,
AND RIVALS

PAUL REYNAUD, MAY 12, 1943

We can only imagine the depth of Édouard Daladier's dismay when, just ten days after his own arrival at Schloss Itter, one of his most bitter political enemies literally turned up on his doorstep. He would soon find that Paul Reynaud's journey to the fortress in Tyrol had in some ways been even more difficult that his own.

Right up until his June 16, 1940, resignation as prime minister following the success of Germany's attack on France, Reynaud had been following a carefully charted path to the pinnacle of French politics. Born in southeast France in 1878, he'd studied law expressly to prepare himself for a life in politics. His plans were only temporarily interrupted by World War I, in which he saw army service. In 1919 he won election to the Chamber of Deputies, where he aligned himself with the center-right Democratic Alliance Party. Reynaud held several cabinet posts under various premiers, and in April 1938 he became Daladier's minister of justice. When the latter resigned on March 19, 1940, Reynaud became premier.

His elevation came less than eight weeks before Germany launched Case Yellow, the first phase of its invasion of France and the Low Countries, on

May 10. Like most of his countrymen, Reynaud was stunned by the rapidity of the German advance and by the failure of his nation's armed forces—and the British Expeditionary Force—to mount an effective defense. Convinced that General Maurice Gamelin was incapable of reversing France's military fortunes, on May 18 Reynaud replaced him with General Maxime Weygand. That same day Reynaud brought the eighty-four-year-old World War I hero Marshal Philippe Pétain into the government as minister of state.

The military and political changes could not stop the Nazi juggernaut, however, especially after the Germans launched Case Red, the second phase of their assault, on June 5. After flanking the Maginot Line, the Wehrmacht was slowed only occasionally by successive defensive lines set up by the overwhelmed Weygand. Reynaud and his government left Paris on June 10 for Tours and, ultimately, Bordeaux. German troops occupied the undefended capital on June 14.

Though Reynaud was convinced France could carry on the fight from its North African colonies, the pressure on him to surrender was intense—and much of it came from his mistress, the allegedly pro-German countess Hélène de Portes.[1] When his cabinet voted on June 15 to ask Germany for peace terms, Reynaud resigned and was replaced by Pétain, who immediately announced his intention to seek an armistice.

Reynaud and de Portes stayed in Bordeaux until after the June 22 signing of the armistice and then left for Reynaud's summer home on the Mediterranean coast. On June 28 their car left the road and hit a tree; de Portes died instantly, and Reynaud suffered a serious concussion. During his recovery at a hospital in Montpellier, German troops occupied northern France, and the Pétain-led government in Vichy proclaimed the elderly marshal "head of state" and replaced the Third Republic with an increasingly fascist regime only too willing to be Berlin's lapdog. Pétain announced his intention to try members of the former government for their betrayal of France, and on September 6, 1940, agents of the Sûreté took Reynaud into custody.

Pétain ultimately decided that Reynaud and Mandel would not be part of the show trial and ordered them to remain imprisoned at the Fort du Portalet. They stayed there for just over a year, mostly in solitary confinement. Though cheered by visits from his adult daughter, Colette Reynaud Dernis, and his private secretary, twenty-eight-year-old Christiane Mabire, Reynaud knew that Vichy would turn him over to the Germans. That day came on November 20, 1942, when he and Mandel were transported to Berlin. The two Frenchmen were separated, and Reynaud was driven to Sachsenhausen concentration camp in Oranienburg.[2]

Reynaud spent five months in isolation at Sachsenhausen. In February 1943 he discovered that Mandel was being held in a nearby cell. The two were able to steal a few moments of whispered conversation when one or the other was taken to the shower room. Those moments with Mandel came to a halt in mid-March, when Reynaud was taken to a section of Sachsenhausen known as "the Bunker" and installed in a large hut surrounded by a high-voltage fence. After a few weeks in his new quarters, he was joined by the tennis player and former Vichy official Jean Borotra.

On May 10 the two men were told to pack their few belongings, and within hours they were on the road, headed south toward Austria. When he stepped from the staff car in Schloss Itter's front courtyard, Reynaud was shocked to see Daladier and Gamelin—both of whom he'd assumed had been executed after the Riom show trial—and Jouhaux, whom he'd known before the war. Looking around at his new home, Reynaud found it far more acceptable than his previous prison. As he later recalled, "Daladier, Jouhaux, and Gamelin had been there for some days. I fear that I must have shocked them when I cried out: 'This is paradise!'"[3]

It was an exclamation he'd come to regret.

JEAN BOROTRA, MAY 12, 1943

Though Borotra's initial impression of Schloss Itter was more restrained than Reynaud's, he, too, found the castle a vast improvement over Sachsenhausen. And for the tall, lanky tennis star—a man for whom daily strenuous physical activity was as necessary as food and water—the most appealing aspect of this new prison was the pathway that encompassed the rear courtyard just inside its surrounding wall. Borotra realized that if his captors allowed him to run several circuits every day he would soon be back in the superlative physical condition that would be necessary if he was to attempt what he thought constantly about: escape.

Fitness had been a key aspect of Borotra's life virtually from the day of his birth on August 13, 1898.[4] Born into a Basque family near Biarritz, he grew up walking the mountainous landscape of France's border with Spain. At fourteen he discovered tennis while spending the summer of 1912 in England. Fast, agile, and competitive, Borotra took to the sport immediately, though the outbreak of world war brought a temporary halt to his development as a tennis player.

Deeply patriotic, Borotra enlisted in September 1916. As a fit and obviously well-educated young man—he was fluent in Spanish, German, and English as well as French—Borotra was trained as an artillery officer. Following his commissioning in April 1917, he saw extensive combat, won the Croix de guerre, and ended the war as a battery commander. Upon his release from active duty in 1919, he returned to school, graduating with degrees in engineering and law.

Borotra continued playing tennis and began winning tournaments throughout France. His highly athletic style—lightening-fast volleys and crushing overhead smashes intermingled with almost balletic leaps and spins—earned him the nickname "the Bounding Basque," and he quickly became a crowd-pleasing favorite. And the crowds soon became international, as Borotra began representing both himself and his country in matches worldwide. By the late 1920s he'd won singles and doubles titles in most of the world's top championships, including Wimbledon.

His athletic success did not keep Borotra from looking for opportunities in the business world. He realized that professional tennis wouldn't provide a living wage and in 1923 secured a position as an engineer with a Paris-based firm. Over the next seventeen years his language skills, charm, social connections, business acumen, and celebrity allowed him to build a successful career as an international salesman. And by scheduling his international business trips to coincide with the major tennis tournaments, he was able to simultaneously pursue both his chosen careers.

Borotra also found time for politics. In the late 1920s he joined the Croix de feu ("Cross of Fire"), a far-right veterans' group led by Colonel François de La Rocque. Borotra admired the organization's espousal of a moral, Roman Catholic France, and his celebrity status was a boon to the group's recruiting efforts. When in 1936 de La Rocque transformed the Croix de feu into a somewhat more moderate political party called the Parti Social Français (PSF), Borotra remained a loyal member. In 1931 he met de La Rocque's chief of information, Edmond Barrachin, and his English wife. Borotra was smitten with the immensely attractive Madame Barrachin, and the tennis star was widely assumed to be the cause for her 1934 divorce. She and Borotra were married in 1937 and had one son, Yves.[5]

As if sport, business, and family did not keep him busy enough, Borotra also remained a reserve officer. His unit—5th Squadron, 232nd Divisional Heavy Artillery Regiment—was mobilized a few weeks before Germany's invasion of Poland. He and his men first saw combat on the Lorraine front but by June 16 had been cut off and completely surrounded. The following day Pétain told the nation of his intention to seek an armistice, an announcement that convinced Borotra he should escape to England to carry on the fight. When the 5th Squadron surrendered to the Germans, Borotra slipped off and made his way toward the French lines in the rugged Massif Central. He ultimately joined forces with a young French air force pilot who had access to a small civilian aircraft, and the two agreed to set off on their clandestine cross-Channel flight on the night of July 3.[6]

Borotra's escape to England never took place. Hours before the flight was to begin, Radio France announced that Britain's Royal Navy had attacked French warships in Algeria, an assault that killed more than 1,200 French sailors. Borotra understood the reason for the British strike—to prevent the warships from falling under German control—but was outraged by the destruction meted out by the Royal Navy in an unprovoked surprise attack. He decided to stay in France—though his wife and son were in London—and was determined to do whatever he could for his country. Unfortunately, Borotra's patriotism and his respect for, and admiration of, both Maxime Weygand and Phillipe Pétain soon led the tennis star to make the worst decision of his life.

Upon Vichy's 1940 creation, the minister of youth and family affairs, Basque right-winger Jean Ybarnegaray, asked Borotra to become commissioner for sports and help "morally re-educate" France's young people, to make them "better equipped for life and better prepared to answer all the calls"[7] their nation might address to them. Though Borotra's politics were not as conservative as his own, Ybarnegaray felt his fellow PSF member would be the ideal choice for the new post. Though Borotra expressed his misgivings about the job, on July 20 he assumed the post of director of the Commission of General Education and Sports.

Over the following twenty-one months the Bounding Basque sought to implement a national program to improve the physical and moral health of France's young people. But despite his zeal for the job and his status as a Vichy official, Borotra refused to be a lapdog for the Germans. Soon after the Nazis conducted their first roundup of Parisian Jews in

August 1941, he banned all French sports organizations from competing against German teams.

Borotra's lack of enthusiasm for the collaborationist policies of the Pétain regime and his disdain for the Nazis soon drew official attention. In early April 1942 he was summoned to the German embassy in Paris, where a functionary demanded that Borotra publicly announce his support for collaboration with Germany and exclude "undesirables" from all French sports. The tennis legend refused, adding that it was his job to bring France's young people together through sports, regardless of their race, religion, or politics. The German warned Borotra that he'd better change his tune or he'd suffer the consequences. Borotra refused to bow to German pressure, and on April 19, 1942, the Germans forced Vichy to fire him.

Borotra went back to work, but over the following months he decided to leave France and join the Allied forces. On November 22, 1942, he went to Paris's Gare d'Austerlitz intending to take a train south and cross into Spain on foot. Unfortunately, Borotra had told friends of his plan, and, as he was about to board his train, he was arrested by Gestapo agents.[8]

After questioning in Paris Borotra was taken to Berlin and from there to Sachsenhausen. He was kept in solitary in the same cell block as Reynaud and Mandel, though he was unaware of their presence. In late April 1943 he was moved to the Bunker, where Reynaud was already in residence. The two men had known each other for years but, given their differing politics, were not friends. That changed over the weeks they spent together in the Bunker, and on the eve of their departure for Schloss Itter Reynaud recorded in his diary that Borotra had become "an excellent companion."[9]

Borotra's first impression of Itter improved considerably when he realized that the rear courtyard would offer him the chance to run. Though still in good physical condition—especially for a man of forty-five—Borotra knew he would have to be far more fit if he were to have any hope of achieving what he'd dreamed about since the moment of his arrest: freedom.

AUGUSTA BRUCHLEN, JUNE 19, 1943

While Borotra hoped to escape from Schloss Itter, Augusta Bruchlen had done all she could to get into the fortress. From the moment she'd learned that Léon Jouhaux had been moved to the castle, she'd lobbied the German authorities to allow her to join him. She knew he was ailing physically and emotionally, and she was convinced that without her presence he would not survive his incarceration. She was determined that Jouhaux, the man she'd loved for many years, would not die in a German prison.

Born in 1899 in German-owned Alsace-Lorraine—it had been annexed following the 1870–1871 Franco-Prussian War—Bruchlen believed the region was rightfully French. But it was her fluency in German (and her reasonable command of English) that won her a job after she moved to Paris. In 1924 she was hired as Jouhaux's secretary and primary translator, a role that required her to accompany the labor leader on his extensive travels. They developed a romantic relationship, and by the early 1930s Bruchlen was widely acknowledged as Jouhaux's "companion" as well as his indispensable executive assistant.

When Jouhaux went underground following the outbreak of war, Bruchlen was a vital link between him and the CGT resistance movement. In addition to editing and passing on his pamphlets, she coordinated his movements. After Jouhaux's arrest in November 1941, Bruchlen heard nothing for a year. In November 1942 she discovered he was in Évaux-les-Bains and began visiting him whenever possible. That became easier following her own arrest in January 1943; Bruchlen was sentenced to "enforced residence" in the same Grand Hotel in which Jouhaux was being held.[10]

Though under house arrest, Bruchlen came and went from the Grand Hotel virtually at will—the only restrictions were that she sleep in the hotel and that she not leave Évaux-Les-Bains without police permission. Neither regulation proved difficult to follow until Jouhaux was moved at the end of March 1943. Fearing for her companion's life and not knowing where he'd been taken, Bruchlen left Évaux-Les-Bains—without permission—and set off for Vichy. There she demanded to be allowed to join Jouhaux, wherever he was. Told that the labor leader had been transferred to a concentration camp in Germany, this remarkable woman insisted on being allowed to join him.

On May 29 Bruchlen was summoned to Gestapo headquarters in Paris and informed that she could join Jouhaux—on one condition. She would have to agree, in writing, to accept indefinite imprisonment without privileges and to absolve Vichy and Germany of responsibility for any harm that might befall her while incarcerated. Having signed the documents, she was told to be at Paris's Gare du Nord on June 17. Two days later she was in a Gestapo car driving up the Itterstrasse, and when the castle came into view, Bruchlen felt a tremor of foreboding: the schloss looked to her like something from a Gothic horror story. Her outlook improved considerably, however, when the car pulled into the front courtyard and she saw Jouhaux, a smile on his face and a bouquet of flowers in his hand.

CHRISTIANE MABIRE, JULY 2, 1943

While Augusta Bruchlen's arrival at Itter was an answered prayer for both her and Léon Jouhaux, it was a call to action for Paul Reynaud. Soon after he was transferred to Sachsenhausen, he'd learned that Christiane Mabire had been arrested. Bruchlen's appearance emboldened Reynaud to demand that Wimmer find out if Mabire was still alive and, if so, have the young woman transferred to Itter. As Wimmer discerned, Reynaud's concern for Mabire's welfare was more than simple humanity.

Christiane Dolorès Mabire was born in Paris on February 17, 1913, to an upper-middle-class family. She received an excellent education and grew into what one observer called a "remarkably elegant" young woman, a "tall, slender girl with the hands and feet of a thoroughbred, a narrow face and aquiline nose" who "dressed with unusual care and good taste."[11] She was also intelligent and fluent in English. Reynaud appreciated all of the young woman's qualities when Mabire was introduced to him by his daughter, Colette, soon after he became prime minister. Indeed, so impressed was Reynaud that he hired the then twenty-seven-year-old Mabire as his secretary despite the opposition of the thirty-eight-year-old countess Hélène de Portes.

Mabire was among the staffers who accompanied Reynaud to Tours and then Bordeaux when the French government left Paris. But when the former prime minister suggested to de Portes that his secretary accompany them to the Mediterranean coast—in order to help him begin work on a book about France's defeat, he said—the countess refused to allow it. That refusal probably saved Mabire's life, since she was not in Reynaud's car when it struck the tree that injured him and killed de Portes.

Though Mabire was unable to see Reynaud in Montpellier, she and Dernis visited him in Le Portalet prison. While Mabire's presence was often in a professional capacity, it is clear from his diary entries that Reynaud was delighted every time she appeared. Those appearances increased considerably after Mabire took a room at a hotel in a nearby town, where she lived for most of the year that Reynaud spent in Le Portalet. Mabire's visits eased the discomfort of Reynaud's imprisonment, and the friendship between the former prime minister and his secretary evolved into something deeper, despite the thirty-five-year age difference.

Mabire was understandably alarmed when she arrived at Le Portalet on November 21, 1942, only to be told that Reynaud had been transferred the night before. The authorities would not tell her where he'd been taken, and she was herself arrested by Gestapo agents on November 22. Three days later Mabire arrived at Fresnes Prison. Immediately upon her arrival she was locked into a bare room and left alone for several hours.

After a brief interrogation Mabire was moved to a cell and remained in solitary confinement until December 10, when she was transported to Ravensbrück, a concentration camp for women some fifty miles north of Berlin, where she was to spend nearly six months. The young French-woman was assigned the cover name Frau Müller and confined, alone, in a cell block for high-value prisoners. Since she did not read or speak German and was not allowed to interact with other prisoners, her isolation was nearly complete.

Until, that is, the day when she was taking her usual fifteen minutes of exercise in the cell block's small courtyard. Lost in thought, she was startled by a woman's whispered voice calling "Madame!" in slightly accented French. The greeting came from another prisoner, the Polish countess Karolina Lanckoronska, speaking through the bars of her cell window. Lanckoronska had caught sight of Mabire and knew from her bearing that she must be French. A guard's inattentiveness allowed the women a few moments together two days after their first contact. They "chattered away" in French, said Lanckoronska, and over the following weeks the Polish countess and the elegant Parisienne quickly became close friends.

That friendship was interrupted, however, during the last weeks of June 1943, when Wimmer arranged to have Frau Müller transferred to his cus-tody. It was not an act of kindness, of course, for the SS-TV officer believed that having a former prime minister of France indebted to him might pay some future dividend.

Wimmer's intervention had an immediate effect on Christiane Mabire's life. On the last day of June two SS-TV men drove her south into Austria, and during the trip Mabire became convinced that Reynaud was respon-sible for her departure from Ravensbrück. As the miles passed she allowed herself to hope that she might be reunited with the man who had come to mean so much to her.

When that reunion occurred, just before noon on July 2,[12] Reynaud warmly embraced the gaunt but laughing Mabire as she stepped from the staff car, kissed her on both cheeks, and led her by the hand toward the castle's main entrance. Though still incarcerated, the elderly politician and his young companion could now face the uncertain future together.

MARCEL GRANGER, JULY 2, 1943

Barely an hour after Mabire's arrival a second car rolled into the castle's front courtyard bearing another "special prisoner." Bruchlen, Jouhaux, Gamelin, and Borotra drifted down through the schlosshof's arched gateway to see who their new companion might be. Though none of them recognized the man, they were all struck by his attire: riding breeches, knee-high leather boots, a cotton shirt with a North African motif, and—much to Borotra's delight—a Basque beret set at a jaunty angle.[13] Later, at lunch, the man introduced himself as Marcel Granger and then told his listeners how his brother's wife had saved him from death in Dachau.

Born in Toulon in 1901, Granger settled in French Tunisia and established a successful agricultural estate. He was a reserve officer in the French colonial forces, and upon the 1939 outbreak of war he'd been mobilized. He remained on duty after the French capitulation and Vichy's takeover of Tunisia, but by December 1940 he had joined a resistance cell. Granger's fluency in Arabic and his knowledge of the country and its people made him an ideal intelligence agent, and he was put in charge of establishing secret arms dumps to support Allied forces should they invade Tunisia.

The Allied landings in Morocco and Algeria in November 1942 seemed to indicate that Granger's hard work was about to come to fruition, but the Germans' decision to funnel reinforcements through Tunisia's ports and airfields made a swift Allied liberation unlikely. The infusion of Wehrmacht troops—and the increased vigilance of the Milice, Vichy's paramilitary anti-resistance force—further complicated Granger's task. In early April 1943 he was captured by Milice troops and handed over to the Gestapo. Within days he'd entered the living hell of Dachau.

Granger was put to work in the fields surrounding the camp, where between interrogations he labored eighteen hours a day with little food or water. Conditions were made worse for Granger by periodic beatings intended to loosen his tongue. In late June 1943 the Frenchman was summoned to the camp headquarters, where, to his amazement, an officer announced that Granger was to be transferred to a "special facility" where conditions would be far more to the Frenchman's liking. Granger asked the reason for his unexpected good fortune and was dumbfounded when the SS-TV man replied, "Because of your sister-in-law."

The Frenchman's brother, Pierre, was married to Renée, one of the daughters of French army general Henri Giraud, who had escaped from German captivity after the fall of France and was now cooperating with the Allies. Hitler ordered Himmler to arrest any members of Giraud's family who were within reach, the intent being to hold them hostage in an attempt to sway the general's allegiance to the Allied cause. Himmler's dragnet brought in seventeen members of Giraud's extended family, including Renée and her four children. The sweep missed Pierre Granger, however, who was serving as his father-in-law's aide. When a routine file review revealed the connection between Marcel Granger and the Giraud clan, Granger was marked for "special handling" and tapped for transfer to Schloss Itter.

Granger's story—told as he wolfed down as much food as he could—fascinated his small audience. Their fascination turned to horror, however, when Granger told them of the hellish scenes he'd witnessed at Dachau.[14] Though each of his listeners had endured the rigors of German captivity, none had experienced the horrific conditions described in Granger's grim recitation. It was a sobering reminder that the conditions at Schloss Itter could change in an instant and that none of them should forget what the hated Germans were capable of.

MAXIME AND MARIE-RENÉE-JOSÉPHINE WEYGAND, DECEMBER 5, 1943

Daladier's distress at Reynaud's appearance within Schloss Itter's walls was nothing compared to the horrified disbelief that Maxime Weygand's arrival generated in both Gamelin and Reynaud. While the source of Gamelin's discomfort was professional embarrassment—he had been replaced by Weygand at the most critical point in France's history—Reynaud's reaction was more visceral. Despite having elevated Weygand, Reynaud blamed the general more than anyone else for France's defeat in 1940. On seeing the former army chief and his wife striding through Itter's entrance hall, Reynaud muttered, quite audibly, "Traitor, collaborator!"

Stinging epithets were nothing new to the then seventy-six-year-old Weygand. Indeed, from the day of his birth in January 1867 the man had had to deal with derision. Born illegitimately in Brussels,[15] he was brought up in France as the ward of David de Léon Cohen, a wealthy, Italian-born, Jewish merchant. The young bastard became a staunch Roman Catholic and a fiery French nationalist, and he ultimately decided on a military career. Still officially Belgian, he entered the St. Cyr military academy as a foreign student, but following his adoption by Cohen's accountant—a paperwork-only event Cohen engineered to allow his ward to become "fully French"— the young man adopted the name Maxime Weygand.

Over the years following his commissioning, Weygand excelled in increasingly challenging assignments and along the way married Marie-Renée-Joséphine de Forsanz, with whom he had two sons. By the time World War I erupted, Weygand was a lieutenant colonel, and after a brief stint of front-line duty he became chief of staff to French XX Corps commander General Ferdinand Foch. Excellent staff work and the ability to adapt to military necessity ensured Weygand's rapid rise through the ranks. By the end of the war he was a major general.

Weygand's career following World War I was eventful and successful, and he became the army's chief of staff in 1930. This ushered in the period of his initial collaboration with, and eventual antagonism toward, Gamelin. Following his mandatory retirement in January 1935, Weygand took up a senior administrative position with the Suez Canal Company. But as the clouds of war again gathered over Europe, Weygand hoped to be called back into military service, and in August 1939 he was. Much to his surprise, his old nemesis Gamelin—at Daladier's prompting—asked if Weygand would take command of French forces in the eastern Mediterranean. He jumped at the opportunity and took up his new post within weeks.

Gamelin's ineffectual response to the 1940 German invasion prompted Reynaud to call Weygand back to Paris from Syria, and upon his arrival Weygand replaced Gamelin as commander in chief of all French military forces. Weygand realized that France had no hope of halting the German juggernaut and decided that the way to avert widespread destruction of the nation's infrastructure and of preserving some semblance of French sovereignty was to achieve an immediate armistice. Reynaud's June 16 resignation—and Pétain's appointment of Weygand as defense minister the following day—cleared the way for Weygand and others who saw a cessation of hostilities as France's only hope for survival.

While it can be said that the actions of Weygand and other armistice-minded French leaders saved their nation from further destruction and allowed half the country to remain unoccupied—at least initially—it is also obvious why many on both sides of the Channel considered France's capitulation to be premature. Nor is it difficult to understand how Weygand's participation in the Vichy government appeared to many as collaboration with the Germans, though the general later explained that he was simply attempting to preserve as much of the nation's military power as possible in order to fight "another day."

In September 1940 Weygand became commander in chief of French forces in Africa, but the perception in both Vichy and Berlin that the general was not a wholehearted team player ultimately led to his downfall. On November 17, 1941, he was recalled to France and removed from his position at the Germans' insistence. Weygand and his wife retired to the south of France, where the general set about writing his memoirs. But following the November 1942 Allied landings in North Africa and Germany's subsequent invasion of unoccupied France, Hitler ordered Weygand's arrest.

Taken into custody on November 12, Weygand was in Germany within days. He was ultimately moved to Schloss Garlitz, a VIP prison southwest of Hamburg. In January 1943 his wife was allowed to join him, and the couple settled into a relatively comfortable routine. That routine was disrupted on December 2, 1943, when the Weygands were told to pack their belongings. Three days later they walked through Schloss Itter's front gate, to be greeted by Reynaud's purposely audible mutterings.

MICHEL CLEMENCEAU, JANUARY 9, 1944

New prisoners next arrived at Schloss Itter on a Sunday afternoon in the middle of a heavy snowfall. The swirling flakes blotted out the view of the surrounding alps and muted the engine noise of the car that had transported Michel Clemenceau, François de La Rocque, and Wimmer from Wörgl's train station to the castle's front courtyard.

Reynaud and Borotra—both of whom were acquainted with the new guests—braved the snow to greet the men.[16] They were stunned, however, by de La Rocque's haggard appearance. Barely fifty-nine, he looked twenty years older and was having difficulty standing. The seventy-one-year-old Clemenceau, on the other hand, seemed to be both healthy and fascinated by his new surroundings. As he shook hands with Reynaud, Clemenceau smiled slightly and said, "So, Paul, another adventure, eh?"[17]

That Clemenceau could describe imprisonment in an Austrian castle as an "adventure" says much about his earlier life. Born November 24, 1873, in France's Pays-de-la-Loire region, he was the third child of physician-turned-politician Georges Clemenceau. Something of a hellion in his youth, Michel bounced from school to school in Paris until his exasperated father—who would ultimately twice be France's prime minister—finally had enough and packed his fifteen-year-old wild child off to study with a tutor in Zurich. The boy soon settled down and in 1894 graduated from the Swiss city's Agronomy Institute with an engineering degree and a remarkable fluency in German.

With lucrative interests in a variety of businesses, by 1914 the forty-one-year-old Michel Clemenceau seemed set to enjoy his early middle age—but then he became one of the millions of Frenchmen called up as World War I loomed. On August 21, 1914, his unit encountered a formation of German lancers; Lieutenant Clemenceau was hit by a bullet from an enemy's pistol but managed to kill the man before losing consciousness. After an extended convalescence Clemenceau was promoted to captain, and he finished the war as a decorated battalion commander.

By the late 1930s Clemenceau was a prosperous entrepreneur with his hand in a variety of profitable businesses. Following Germany's September 1, 1939, invasion of Poland, the sixty-five-year-old volunteered for military service. Clemenceau's distinguished World War I record and political connections won him a major's commission despite his age, and he was assigned to the army's foreign-intelligence branch, the Deuxième Bureau.[18] Briefly detained by the Germans following France's surrender, he was released and returned to Paris.

Though a longtime admirer of Pétain, Clemenceau opposed the aged general's collaboration with the Germans, and his views drew the attention of the Gestapo. In November 1940 Clemenceau convinced his wife to leave France for America, but he stayed. His political connections kept him safe from official retribution until May 1943, when Gestapo agents arrested him. He spent several months in French prisons, and, on August 31, 1943, he was transferred to Schloss Eisenberg, a castle-turned-VIP prison in Czecho-slovakia. Clemenceau held up well despite poor food and spartan condi-tions; unlike de La Rocque, he maintained a relatively optimistic attitude throughout his imprisonment. He was therefore able to accept the sudden transfer to Schloss Itter with a calm self-possession that prompted Reynaud to note that Clemenceau's arrival brought the castle's other VIP prisoners "the reassurance of his unshakable confidence."[19]

Sadly, Clemenceau's traveling companion, de La Rocque, could boast neither health, nor self-confidence, nor optimism.

FRANÇOIS DE LA ROCQUE, JANUARY 9, 1944

While Reynaud and Borotra were stunned by de La Rocque's appearance upon his arrival at Schloss Itter, they were even more shocked that he was a prisoner of the Germans.

Until his arrest ten months earlier de La Rocque had been a member of the Vichy government, a confidant of Pétain, and a man widely viewed both at home and abroad as one of France's leading fascists. While the fact that someone with de La Rocque's right-wing credentials could so quickly fall from political grace certainly surprised both Reynaud and Borotra, they would have been thunderstruck to learn that de La Rocque was also the head of a resistance movement that funneled information to Britain's in-telligence service.

Born October 6, 1885, in Lorient, Annet-Marie-Jean-François de La Rocque de Sévérac was the scion of one of France's noble families and, ac-cording to one biographer,[20] the hereditary viscount of Chateaubriand. The young man attended St. Cyr military academy and in 1907 was commis-sioned a lieutenant of cavalry. In North Africa he commanded a mounted company that saw action against Moroccan guerillas. Severely wounded during a 1916 battle with insurgents, he refused medical attention and con-tinued to lead his unit until a relief force arrived.

Cited for bravery and promoted, de La Rocque returned to France for convalescence. Once again fit, he was assigned to an infantry unit and spent the remainder of World War I on the Western Front. Twice promoted and much decorated, he ended the war as a lieutenant colonel. Upon his retire-ment from the army in 1928, he was lauded as a highly effective leader con-cerned with the welfare of his troops.

Given his strict Catholicism, aristocratic lineage, and intense patriotism, it's no surprise that de La Rocque's postwar politics veered toward the right. At thirty-eight he became the vice president of the extreme right-wing Croix de feu veterans' group, which advocated the replacement of France's admittedly chaotic form of parliamentary government with an authoritarian regime that would emphasize the "traditional French values" of work, family, and country.

As an articulate and decorated former soldier, de La Rocque soon became the Croix de feu's primary public spokesman, and in 1931 he became its president. Under his leadership the group's ranks swelled, and he was courted by every important right-wing politician in France. In 1936 the nation voted into office the broad left-wing coalition known as the Popular Front, and one of the new government's first acts was to outlaw the various right-wing organizations. De La Rocque shrewdly responded to the threat by transforming his group into a political party, the PSF, and announcing he would work within the very parliamentary system he had long criticized.

De La Rocque's decision to renounce the violent overthrow of the government put him at odds with other, overtly fascist groups. He was also excoriated by those organizations for his opposition to Germany's increasing military might and expansionist policies, as well as for his support for the modernization of France's armed forces. Right-wing and authoritarian de La Rocque might have been, but he also remembered the carnage France had endured at Germany's hands in World War I.

When war erupted in 1939, de La Rocque called for all PSF members to rally to the nation's defense. Even when it became obvious that the German blitzkrieg would result in a French defeat, de La Rocque opposed any armistice or outright surrender. But following France's fall, he concluded that Pétain was the only man capable of providing France with the postarmistice leadership and stability the nation so desperately needed. De La Rocque threw his support—and that of his PSF—behind Pétain's government. Nevertheless, de La Rocque's subsequent refusal to subjugate the PSF to Vichy's planned single-party system outraged the regime, and, as early as September 1940, he was telling his followers to respect Pétain but display "absolute reserve" toward the Vichy government.[21]

While de La Rocque remained politically active in Vichy, his increasing ambivalence about the regime trumped his respect for Pétain. Moreover, de La Rocque's belief that Germany was France's "ancestral enemy,"[22] coupled with his distaste for the Nazis, led him to be outspoken about his opposition to collaboration, and even before the Germans' November 1942 takeover of unoccupied France, de La Rocque had openly declared "no collaboration under the occupation."[23]

Given de La Rocque's dislike of Germany and less than wholehearted support for Vichy—and his politically savvy preference for keeping his options open—it's no surprise that he established a clandestine relationship with the Allied intelligence services. While some sources[24] indicate that he first began gathering information of potential value to the Allies in the summer of 1940, it was not until February 1942 that de La Rocque established contact with the Madrid-based Réseau Alibi, or Alibi Network, which had agents throughout France and reported directly to Britain's Secret Intelligence Service (SIS).

De La Rocque formalized the ad hoc intelligence-gathering effort he'd been leading and transformed it into an Alibi subnetwork known as the Réseau Klan (Klan Network), which used the PSF's social-services operations as a cover for intelligence gathering. While the extent and value of the information provided to the SIS by the Klan Network remains difficult to judge, there is no doubt that de La Rocque—a man maligned both during and after the war as a fascist collaborator—knowingly endangered himself, his family, and his followers to pass intelligence to the Allies.

De La Rocque's leadership of the Klan Network ended on March 9, 1943, when Gestapo agents dragged him from his home in Clermont-Ferrand. The PSF leader was held briefly in a local jail and then transferred to Fresnes Prison. Kept in solitary confinement in a cramped and filthy cell, he was denied the medications he'd been taking since being wounded in 1916, and his health quickly declined. Things did not improve following his August 31, 1943, transfer—along with Michel Clemenceau and others—to Schloss Eisenberg in Czechoslovakia. Indeed, so ill was de La Rocque that he was unconscious for much of the car journey that carried him and Clemenceau to Schloss Itter.

Though the Tyrolean fortress was still a prison, transfer to the castle—with its vastly better food and living conditions—would ultimately help save the PSF leader's life.

MARIE-AGNÈS AND ALFRED CAILLIAU, APRIL 13, 1945

The final prisoners to arrive at Schloss Itter were not incarcerated because of their own importance, but—as with Marcel Granger—simply because of a family relationship to someone in whom the Nazis were especially interested. In the Cailliaus' case, that someone was Marie-Agnès Cailliau's younger brother, Free French general Charles de Gaulle.

Born May 27, 1899, in Paris, Marie-Agnès was the second child—and only daughter—of Henri and Jeanne de Gaulle. Her father imbued his five children with an intense Roman Catholicism and a love for French history and culture, and Marie-Agnès—eighteen months older than Charles—was throughout her life "an ardent patriot and fervent Christian."[25]

After World War I Marie-Agnès and her Belgian husband, engineer Alfred Cailliau, settled in a suburb of Le Havre on the Normandy coast. Over the years the couple prospered, raising six sons and a daughter. Unfortunately, a resurgent Germany eventually cast a pall over the Cailliaus' life; four of their sons—Joseph, Michel, Henri, and Charles—fought the invading Wehrmacht in 1940. Joseph and Henri escaped to England to join the Free French effort, Michel was captured and sent to a POW camp in Germany, and twenty-four-year-old Charles was killed.[26] A fifth son, eighteen-year-old Pierre, ultimately made his way to Algeria and joined the Free French.

Understandably devastated by the death of one son and the uncertain fates of four others, Alfred and Marie-Agnès Cailliau did what they could to ensure the safety of their sixth son, ten-year-old Denys.[27] The Cailliaus moved in with their daughter, Marie-Thérèse, and her husband in the town of Roche-la-Molière, some thirty-five miles southwest of Lyon. When the area became part of Vichy, the Cailliaus stayed, renting a house in nearby Saint-Étienne. And they might have lived out the remainder of the war there in comfortable obscurity, had it not been for their son Michel's March 1942 escape from German captivity and their own desire to resist the occupiers of their beloved France.

During his time in the POW camp Michel Cailliau had joined the National Movement of Prisoners of War and Deportees, a fledgling resistance movement. Though not members of Michel's growing network, Alfred and Marie-Agnès hid documents and kept Michel informed about the activities of local German units. The elderly couple continued their low-level resistance work through the winter of 1942, and in April of the following year they moved back to northern France. The couple and their son Denys moved in with Alfred's sister, Madeleine, in a village southwest of Rouen. They had only been in their new home a few days, however, when disaster struck.

While eating a family lunch one day, Marie-Agnès saw two German military police officers getting out of a car in front of the house. The men knocked on the door, and when Marie-Agnès opened it, one of the agents politely told her that she and Alfred were to accompany them for routine questioning, though he declined to tell them the subject.

After initial processing in Rouen and Paris, Marie-Agnès and Alfred were sent to Fresnes Prison, where they were separated. While both had assumed that their arrests were the result of their resistance activities, it quickly became apparent that Marie-Agnès's relationship to the leader of the Free French was the real reason they'd been picked up. Though the Cailliaus were treated marginally better than most of the prisoners at Fresnes, neither had an easy time of it. Marie-Agnès was fifty-three, and Alfred was sixty-six; both suffered from the restricted diet and squalid living conditions, as well as from their forced separation. Alfred's conditions were destined to worsen—in January 1944 he was transferred to Buchenwald.

Marie-Agnès, on the other hand, saw a marked improvement in her own circumstances following her July 1944 deportation to the Rhinehotel Dreesen in a suburb of Bonn. The Nazis had converted the old lodge on the west bank of the Rhine into a VIP detention center, a satellite installation of Buchenwald. Though still prisoners, Marie-Agnès and the others slept in furnished rooms rather than cells, could walk in the large enclosed garden, and had access to decent food.[28]

Things changed dramatically when Allied forces neared Bonn in early 1945. On February 27 the German garrison herded the prisoners onto a barge and took them across to the east bank of the Rhine, where they boarded trucks that carried them to Buchenwald. There Marie-Agnès was reunited with Alfred, who was in poor health after his months in the camp. On March 8 they and about fifty other VIP prisoners were crowded into railway cattle cars and taken to Munich, where Marie-Agnès and Alfred—both now ill—were separated from the others and put in the back of a covered truck. Three young Wehrmacht soldiers climbed in with them, as did an older corporal. The truck drove through the night, with Marie-Agnès and Alfred sleeping on the hard metal floor of the vehicle's cargo area.

Then, on the afternoon of April 13, the truck halted before the sentry box at the foot of the short drive leading from Itter village to the castle's main gate. The corporal walked over to speak with the two soldiers standing guard, both of whom were wearing full combat gear and seemed surprised by the truck's arrival. When the guards refused to raise the barricade, the corporal demanded that they use the telephone in the sentry box to call for an officer.

Within a few minutes Stefan Otto appeared; he, too, was obviously surprised to see the French couple. Looking at their disheveled clothes and drawn faces, he barked, "We have no room for you," turned on his heel, and was about to start back toward the castle gate when Marie-Agnès called out, "But I am the sister of General De Gaulle!"

Otto turned and hurried back, his entire demeanor changed. "Madame, my sincere apologies, we weren't expecting you yet!" Taking Alfred gently by the arm, the officer led the French couple toward the castle gate. "Madame, you shall have my quarters this evening, and monsieur, you shall sleep in Colonel de La Rocque's room. At the moment he is away at a clinic. Tomorrow we will make other arrangements."[29]

Pleased at the change in Otto's attitude, Marie-Agnès was equally delighted by the realization that there was at least one other Frenchman resident in the castle looming before her. She knew who de La Rocque was and that he had served Vichy in some capacity. While their politics might differ, she believed that as French prisoners of the Germans, they—and any other of their countrymen held in the schloss—would put aside such petty concerns and draw together in solidarity, finding strength in each other's company and their shared nationality.

She would soon find out just how wrong she was.

———

DESPITE MARIE-AGNÈS CAILLIAU's hope that Schloss Itter's French prisoners would band together in the face of shared hardship and live in supportive camaraderie, just the opposite was true. For while all of the castle's prisoners were French[30] and all considered themselves patriots, they could not possibly have been more politically diverse, more determinedly irascible, or more obstinately quarrelsome.

The fault lines that developed among Schloss Itter's VIP prisoners were, in a sense, completely understandable. Reynaud and Daladier were bitter political enemies, and both detested Weygand, who, having replaced Gamelin as supreme commander of French forces in May 1940, surrendered to and initially collaborated with the occupying Germans. Following the December 1943 arrival of Weygand and his wife, Reynaud's snubs of the couple were so obvious and so continuous that at one point Weygand followed Reynaud down a corridor screaming, "Hooligan!" at him.[31] Gamelin, for obvious reasons, was not at all fond of Weygand and sided with Reynaud against Daladier. An authoritarian right-winger, de La Rocque could not abide the leftist Jouhaux. As a former member of the Croix de feu and of Pétain's Vichy government, Borotra was shunned by Daladier, Jouhaux, and Gamelin but embraced by Weygand and de La Rocque—and by Reynaud, despite their differing politics. And understandably, Schloss Itter's female prisoners—Marie Weygand, Christiane Mabire, and Augusta Bruchlen—reflected the opinions and prejudices of their male partners.

We can only imagine the heated exchanges that occurred among these once powerful and still resentful personages, and the perverse joy their German captors took in both the French prisoners' squabbling and the fact that they segregated themselves by political persuasion, avoiding each other as much as possible within the castle's confines. They even ate at separate tables in the dining room—the Weygands, Borotra, and de La Rocque at one; Reynaud, Mabire, Gamelin, and Clemenceau at another; and the "neutrals"—Daladier, Jouhaux, Bruchlen, and, later, the Cailliaus—at a third. And as Marie-Agnès Cailliau later noted, several of the "great men" incarcerated in Schloss Itter did more than just snub each other during meals; each spent hours every day penning the memoirs he hoped would explain his own wartime actions in the best light while vilifying those of his rivals.

There were, of course, activities other than the writing of self-aggrandizing memoirs in which the French prisoners could participate—activities that would have been incomprehensible to captives not fortunate enough to be classed as honor prisoners. The schloss's three-hundred-volume library was available to Itter's involuntary guests, and in good weather they could stroll much of the castle's walled grounds or pass the time playing ring tennis or, in Daladier's case, practicing solo nudism.[32] Those of a spiritual bent could attend Mass at St. Joseph's Church in Itter village—under guard—and the female prisoners were driven to nearby Hopfgarten for regular appointments with a hairdresser. Anyone requiring medical attention beyond what the garrison's medic could provide was transported to a suitable medical facility; Reynaud, for example, underwent eye surgery at the military hospital in Innsbruck, and Daladier had oral surgery at Dachau.

And then there was the food and drink. The prisoner-cook—a Czech named Andreas Krobot,[33] known to the French as André—used flour, fruit, vegetables, and dairy products from surrounding farms to turn out wholesome and plentiful meals for the captives. And there was even wine with which to wash down the food: each French prisoner was authorized two liters of local Austrian wine a week, one of red and one of white. To their credit, most of the VIPs ensured that André and Zvonimir Čučković passed on any leftover food and wine to the handful of far less fortunate female concentration-camp inmates—referred to as "number" prisoners because each had a number tattooed on her forearm—whom the SS had brought to work at Schloss Itter as servants.[34]

The French captives also had a link to the outside provided by Čučković, who organized—read "stole"—a small short-wave radio from one of the castle's guards.[35] Since the guard himself wasn't supposed to have the radio—its possession could have gotten him sent to the Russian Front, or worse—he couldn't report its theft. The radio was hidden in Reynaud's room, and Čučković and Christiane Mabire would keep watch while the former prime minister huddled under a blanket, listening to the BBC and other Allied stations. In a rare show of cooperation, Reynaud would share important news with his fellow captives via Mabire and Borotra.[36]

As cushy as life might have been for the French prisoners at Schloss Itter, Borotra remained determined to escape. From the moment of his arrival in May 1943, he exercised every morning, increasing the duration of his runs within the rear courtyard until he could do ninety circuits—roughly nine miles—nonstop. In addition to his physical preparations, Borotra tracked the movement and schedules of the guards and noted several areas where the barbed wire atop the schloss's walls seemed loosely secured.

The Bounding Basque made three escape attempts, each time going over the wall. While the dates of his first two tries are unclear, it appears that one occurred in the fall of 1943 and another in late March 1945. On both occasions he got several miles before being recaptured.[37] His only punishment following these first two excursions seems to have been a few days' confinement in his room.

Thanks to Daladier, we have more precise information regarding Borotra's third attempt, on April 29, 1945. At about six thirty that evening Daladier was strolling in the castle's rear courtyard when he encountered the tennis player, who greeted him with "Have a nice walk, prime minister." Borotra then ran to the closest section of the south wall, and as Daladier recounts:

> he scaled it and started running madly down the hill. The SS [guards] began firing at him from a few yards away. He took the barbed wire [rolls a few meters from the bottom of the castle's outer wall] in stride as more and more shots rang out and the SS began their pursuit. [At] 7:20 P.M. Borotra was brought back. He had probably twisted an ankle, given the way he was limping.[38]

Once again, Borotra's only punishment seems to have been a few days' house arrest. He was fortunate he'd been recaptured by castle guards sent out by Wimmer—by April 1945, the world outside Schloss Itter's gates had become a very dangerous place, crawling with Wehrmacht and Waffen-SS units to whom the life of a French honor prisoner meant absolutely nothing.

CHAPTER 4

A GROWING PERIL

THOUGH THE NAZI WAR EFFORT had already seen some significant reversals by the time Schloss Itter's first French prisoner arrived on May 2, 1943, the setbacks had largely occurred well beyond the borders of "greater" Germany, primarily on the Eastern Front, in North Africa, and in the Mediterranean. Over the next two years, however, the war got steadily closer to Itter. Allied armies approaching from several directions at once made the future increasingly uncertain for the castle's garrison troops and, ironically, decidedly more dangerous for its prisoners.

To the east, the Soviet Union's January 1943 victory at Stalingrad and destruction of the German 6th Army set the stage for the Red Army's seemingly inexorable advance westward. Soviet forces solidified their strategic advantage by crushing Germany's final large-scale attack on the Eastern Front—the assault on Kursk in July and August 1943. From that point on, the Germans could manage only local tactical successes, as they were forced to withdraw almost everywhere along a front stretching from the Baltic to the Black Sea. Having recaptured those parts of Ukraine, Belorussia, and Russia proper that had been occupied by German forces, by the spring of 1945 the Red Army had also taken Bulgaria, Romania, Poland, Czechoslovakia, Hungary, the Baltic states, parts of Yugoslavia, and much of eastern Germany. Of more immediate concern to Sebastian Wimmer and those he commanded at Schloss Itter, however, was the fact that by the last day of April 1945 elements of Marshal of the Soviet Union Fyodor Tolbukhin's 3rd Ukrainian Front[1] were rumored to be barely twenty-five miles to the east.

Nor was the military situation to the south of the Austrian Tyrol any less dire. After completing the ouster of German forces from North Africa, the Allies had captured Sicily in August 1943. The following month American and British troops had landed at Salerno on the Italian mainland and then began the hard slog north against determined German resistance. Despite that resistance, the Allied juggernaut rolled on, and Rome fell on June 4, 1944. Bologna was captured on April 21, 1945, followed by Milan six days later, and all German forces in Italy surrendered on April 29. That collapse cleared the way for Lieutenant General Geoffrey Keyes's U.S. II Corps to advance on the Brenner Pass—the most accessible of the traditional routes from northern Italy into Austria—just forty-seven miles to the southwest of Schloss Itter.

To the west and northwest, the most direct threat to continued German control of Tyrol came from Lieutenant General Alexander M. Patch's U.S. Seventh Army.[2] Having participated in the capture of Sicily[3] in July and August 1943, in August 1944 Seventh Army—with attached Free French First Army elements—undertook Operation Dragoon, the amphibious invasion of southern France. After fighting its way through the Vosges Mountains, Seventh Army moved north along the Swiss border toward Alsace and Lorraine, where it met stiff German resistance during the winter of 1944–1945. After crossing the Rhine River in the spring of 1945, the Seventh moved across southern Germany, in the process taking such major population centers as Worms, Saarbrücken, Mannheim, Nürnberg, and Munich. By April 30, lead Seventh Army elements had crossed into Austria, with the bulk of Patch's force arrayed along some eighty miles of the German-Austrian frontier. The closest American units were less than fifteen miles from Schloss Itter's front gate.

SEVENTH ARMY'S ADVANCE into Tyrol was in part a response to rumors Allied intelligence had been hearing since 1943 that spoke of an "alpine fortress" allegedly encompassing parts of southern Germany and northwestern Austria to which Hitler and his forces would retreat if the fortunes of war turned against them. There were stockpiles of weapons, ammunition, food, and fuel in vast underground storage complexes, so the rumors said, all protected by well-concealed and interconnected defenses that could hold off attackers for months or even years.

Though by January 1945 most senior Allied intelligence officials did not believe such a formidable and well-provisioned national redoubt actually existed, they realized only too well that Austria's alpine region—with its rugged mountains, fast-flowing rivers, and narrow, twisting roads—represented an easily defensible natural fortress even without the rumored underground complexes. Supreme Allied Commander General Dwight D. Eisenhower was concerned enough about the possibility of retreating German units making a final, bloody, and possibly protracted stand in the Alps that he made the blocking of all major passes into Austria—and especially those into Tyrol—a key part of his planning.[4]

Eisenhower's plans for securing Austria were built around two forces: General George S. Patton's Third Army and General Jacob L. Devers's 6th Army Group.[5] The former was to continue its eastward advance across southern Germany and into Austria near Salzburg, secure the city and the passes leading from it southwestward into Tyrol, and then continue northeastward to link up with the advancing Soviets near Linz. Devers's task was to capture all the other routes into Austria from the northwest and north. These included the pass at Bregenz, east of Lake Constance, which led into the Voralberg, Austria's westernmost region; those near the Bavarian cities of Füssen and Garmisch-Partenkirchen leading, respectively, toward Landeck and Innsbruck; and at Kufstein, in the Inn River valley.

Devers had at his disposal the eleven divisions of General Jean de Lattre de Tassigny's French First Army and the twelve U.S. divisions of Patch's Seventh Army. The operational boundary between Devers's two armies ran generally from northwest to southeast, roughly centered on Füssen, three miles from the Austrian border. This meant that the capture of the more easterly passes from Germany into Tyrol—including the one at Kufstein—became Seventh Army's responsibility generally, and of Patch's XXI Corps specifically. Commanded by Major General Frank W. Milburn, by April 30 the corps consisted primarily of the 3rd and 36th Infantry divisions and the 12th Armored Division.[6]

By this point in the war, XXI Corps's usual mode of advance was for the armored division to lead, followed by the infantry divisions. Milburn therefore ordered the tankers of the 12th AD to advance southward along the Munich-Salzburg autobahn to the Bavarian city of Rosenheim, at the confluence of the Mangfall and Inn Rivers. After securing the city, the 12th and its accompanying infantry divisions were to cover the roughly twenty-two miles directly south to Kufstein with what Milburn termed "the utmost dispatch."

Though the German army was in disarray throughout Bavaria, Patch and his subordinate commanders were under no illusions that the move into Austria would be a cakewalk. Intelligence reports indicated that the several German garrison units and training schools in Tyrol were well manned, relatively well equipped, and apparently ready to fight despite their general lack of combat experience. More disturbing, however, were reports that the battered remnants of several battle-hardened Wehrmacht and Waffen-SS units were withdrawing into Austria; their presence could significantly stiffen the resistance offered by the garrison and school troops. While the advancing Allied armies were in one sense a noose tightening around Tyrol, they were also inadvertently forcing a buildup of German military strength in a region ideally suited to be Nazism's last bastion.

In assessing the threat XXI Corps would face during the advance into Austria, Milburn's intelligence staff first concentrated on known enemy facilities and garrison units. And unfortunately for the Americans, most of the German formations believed to be stationed in and around the Inn River valley were specialized mountain-warfare units known as gebirgstruppen, comprised of soldiers who were used to maneuvering in—and making excellent tactical use of—the region's rugged terrain. Worse still, most of these units were former Bundesheer organizations absorbed into the Wehrmacht after the 1938 Anschluss, meaning the majority of their members were native Austrians who would literally be defending their homes and families.

Kufstein, the first major Austrian city XXI Corps would enter, was believed to be garrisoned by a battalion of front-line gebirgsjäger, or mountain infantry, and was also thought to house several replacement battalions for other infantry and artillery units. Further south, Wörgl had long been home to two mountain-infantry replacement units and, of possibly greater concern, the Wehrmacht training center for noncommissioned officers assigned to mountain-warfare units. The school's staff and instructors were all combat veterans, as were many of its several hundred students, and all could be expected to put to good use the skills they had so ably demonstrated in the mountains of Norway, Russia, and the Ukraine.

Then, of course, there were the frontline units thought to be retreating into Tyrol. The XXI Corps intelligence staffers were most worried by reports that elements of two Waffen-SS panzer-grenadier divisions[7]—the 12th "Hitlerjugend" and 17th "Götz von Berlichingen"—were thought to be operating to the east, west, and south of Kufstein. In addition, the remnants of at least one infantry division—its designation unknown—were rumored to be moving northeastward from Innsbruck along the Inn River valley. If the units were actually present, they and the garrison and school troops could number upwards of ten thousand men. And if the divisional units retained even limited numbers of armored vehicles, antitank guns, and artillery, they would pose a serious threat, not only to XXI Corps's ability to seize and hold the pass at Kufstein, but also to the Americans' plans to secure all of Tyrol.

Fortunately for XXI Corps, the actual number of German troops in the Inn Valley was far smaller than Allied intelligence estimates indicated. When Lieutenant General Georg Ritter von Hengl took over as commander of Alpine Front, Northwest, on April 20, he was ordered to defend the mountain passes along a seventy-mile sector anchored in the east at Lofer, in the center at Kufstein, and in the west at Innsbruck.[8] To accomplish that task he had barely three thousand men—a number roughly corresponding to a single regiment.

While this force did indeed include several hundred battle-hardened Wehrmacht infantrymen (whom von Hengl identifies as belonging to Panzer-Grenadier Division Grossdeutschland[9]) and about two hundred highly motivated Waffen-SS troops (likely from "Götz von Berlichingen"), the majority of von Hengl's ad hoc force consisted of rear-area support personnel, stragglers from various units, and even deserters rounded up by field police. Though relatively well provided for in terms of small arms and ammunition, von Hengl's new command had no aircraft, no armor, few wheeled vehicles, and just nine 88mm anti-aircraft guns that could be used as direct-fire artillery.[10] When von Hengl complained about his lack of men and firepower to his higher headquarters—in this case, Major General August Winter on the Oberkommando der Wehrmacht (OKW) command staff at Führungsstab B in Berchtesgaden[11]—he was told that he would also be

nents of the German 1st and 19th armies as they re-
..stria.[12]

gn, highly decorated, Bavarian-born professional soldier of aristo-
..ic lineage, von Hengl had led mountain troops in combat in Poland, Finland, and Russia. Though he privately believed his mission to defend the
alpine passes into Austria was ultimately hopeless, he was determined to
do what he could to slow the Allied advance into Tyrol. Having established
his headquarters in Wörgl, von Hengl quickly set about organizing five
kampfgruppen, or battle groups, each of which was named after its commander. Four of the units would each be responsible for a different pass
leading into the Inn Valley, with the fifth held in reserve. All of the battle
group commanders—Colonels Buchner,[13] Schirowski, Drück, and Forster,
and Lieutenant Colonel Johann Giehl[14]—were combat-proven gebirgsjägers.

Since Innsbruck itself was to be defended by Brigadier General Joannes
Böhaimb's Division Group North,[15] von Hengl established his most west-
erly task force, Battle Group Drück, at Schwaz. Jenbach, five miles to the
northeast, was to be the base of operations for Battle Group Schirowski.
Twenty-three miles downriver,[16] Battle Group Buchner was centered on
Kufstein, and seven miles almost directly north from there, just over the
German border in Neideraudorf, Battle Group Giehl established itself on
both banks of the Inn. The reserve task force, Battle Group Forster, remained in the armory at Wörgl.

Because intelligence reports indicated that the main American advance
into the Inn Valley would be through Kufstein, von Hengl ensured that
battle groups Buchner and Giehl were the most robust of his five task
forces. The two groups shared four hundred crack troops from Grossdeutschland;[17] one hundred Waffen-SS soldiers (again, most probably from
"Götz von Berlichingen"); several dozen officers and men from the NCO
school in Wörgl; four hundred gebirgsjägers; two hundred field police;
sixty combat engineers; and two of the 88mm flak guns, each with thirty
rounds of ammunition.[18] Since Giehl's mission was to slow the American
advance using hit-and-run tactics, his was the slightly smaller and more
mobile of the two battle groups.

By April 30 von Hengl's four frontline battle groups were deployed in
or near the Alpine passes. The Buchner and Giehl task forces were astride
both routes into Kufstein—the major highway leading almost directly south
from Rosenheim, just over the border and some eighteen miles downriver,

and the two-lane road leading southeast from Bavaria's Schliersee (Lake Schlier) toward Landl, Austria, and on to Kufstein. Though von Hengl was still understandably concerned about his insufficiency in men, armor, and artillery, he was confident that Alpine Front, Northwest, was as ready as it would ever be to resist the American advance into the Inn River valley.

Unfortunately for von Hengl, it wasn't just the Americans he had to worry about.

———————

As NOTED EARLIER IN THIS VOLUME, many Austrians had no desire to become citizens of "greater" Germany, and nascent anti-Nazi resistance cells began coalescing in Austria soon after the Anschluss. As in other occupied countries, these groups spanned the political and philosophical spectra: nationalists, monarchists, Socialists, Communists, Jews, even organized criminal groups. Though all shared a desire to oust the Nazi invaders from Austrian soil, their reasons for wishing to do so varied widely and were often at odds.[19]

In addition, the burgeoning Austrian resistance faced challenges with which the anti-Nazi movements in other nations—save that in Germany itself—did not have to contend. Because they had the same culture, the same language, and much of the same history as their oppressors, most Austrians did not experience the resistance-inducing brutality and radical social and ethnic changes that occurred in France, Poland, or Russia. And, of course, the unfortunate fact that a huge number of Austrians were ardent Nazis who fully supported the beliefs and goals of the Third Reich—and enthusiastically participated in their implementation—made it extremely difficult for the resistance-inclined to establish effective cells or avoid betrayal by friends, neighbors, or even family members.

Those Austrians who nonetheless chose to oppose the Nazis also faced daunting operational challenges. Since there was no Austrian government in exile, well into 1944 there was no conduit through which to gain Allied recognition and support. The various movements that did evolve therefore did not initially receive the weapons, money, or guidance provided to underground groups in France and the Low Countries. Poorly armed, isolated, and under constant threat of exposure and arrest, Austrian resisters thus originally avoided the type of armed guerilla warfare practiced by their French, Dutch, and Norwegian counterparts.

The various Austrian resistance groups instead adopted a pragmatic approach that emphasized nonviolent measures, including the distribution of anti-Nazi propaganda and the gathering of intelligence they hoped would be of value to the advancing Allies. At the same time, the groups sought to recruit and train new members—activities that became easier as Germany's military fortunes declined—and patiently worked to build the command structures necessary to make the disparate cells militarily effective. This latter effort received a significant boost with the December 1944 establishment of the Provisional Austrian National Committee (POEN),[20] a loose confederation of the leaders of the various resistance groups. POEN was able to make contact with the U.S. Office of Strategic Services (OSS)[21] station in Bern, Switzerland. This quickly led to a mutually rewarding partnership; the resistance groups—now collectively referred to as the O5[22] organization—provided OSS with valuable intelligence about German military operations and dispositions throughout Austria, and in return OSS provided weapons, funding, and liaison officers.[23] Given their proximity to Switzerland, the various resistance groups in Tyrol were among the earlier recipients of the OSS's largesse.

As elsewhere in Austria, the Tyrolean groups were of varying ideological and political slants. The cells had evolved both in the Innsbruck-Hall urban region and in small rural communities scattered in the river and mountain valleys. Though initially focused on local, rather than regional, activities, most of the groups had been brought into the POEN-O5 fold by mid-1944. While they were increasingly well armed, in order to avoid prompting savage German reprisals aimed at the civilian population, the Tyrolean groups did not generally undertake direct attacks on German forces. Instead, they focused their energies on planning and preparing for a popular uprising intended to coincide with the arrival in Tyrol of Allied forces. Their goals included preventing retreating German units from destroying key bridges and other structures, capturing and disarming enemy troops whenever possible, and, most important, protecting Austrian civilians from revenge attacks by the Gestapo and SS.

The resisters in Tyrol came from all walks of life—educators, students, farmers, housewives—and, not surprisingly, their ranks also included Austrian-born Wehrmacht officers and enlisted soldiers. The majority of these latter men were assigned to garrison, reserve, and replacement units, such as the Gebirgsjäger-Ersatz-Bataillon (Mountain Troops Replacement

Battalion) 136, whose companies were based in Landeck and Wörgl and whose senior commanders were all members of the resistance; the Reserve-Gebirgsjäger-Bataillon 137 in Kufstein; and the Gebirgs-Artillerie-Ersatz-Abteilung (Mountain Artillery Replacement Detachment) 118, also in Kufstein. In addition, several Austrian-born instructors and students at the mountain troops' NCO school in Wörgl were also sympathetic to the resistance.

Austrian-born military personnel who supported the anti-Nazi resistance did so for the same panoply of reasons—political, moral, and cultural—that motivated civilian resisters. But those in uniform were often in far better positions than their nonmilitary counterparts to undertake concrete, meaningful acts against the Third Reich. Among the earliest and most effective resisters, for example, was Friedrich Würthle. A prewar liberal journalist, he was called up for army service in 1940 and assigned to the main Military Registration Office in Innsbruck. As a noncommissioned officer in the organization's administrative office, he was able to provide fellow anti-Nazis serving in the Wehrmacht with doctored identity cards and travel documents, allowing them to move more freely throughout Tyrol and even into Germany itself. In addition, Würthle was able to help establish communications and forge alliances among the various nascent resistance groups, in the process becoming a key resistance leader himself.[24]

As happened elsewhere throughout Austria, the anti-Nazi Austrians serving in Wehrmacht units in Tyrol established strong—though obviously covert—ties to local civilian resistance groups. These were mutually beneficial alliances; the military resisters supplied their civilian counterparts with weapons, ammunition, and information about German troop dispositions and operations, while the civilians in turn provided shelter for Austrian deserters, safe houses for clandestine planning sessions, and intelligence on those local citizens who were most likely to betray resistance members to the Gestapo.

The Kufstein-Wörgl area had produced several early anti-Nazi resistance cells, some of which even predated the Anschluss.[25] Though several of these groups were broken up by the Gestapo after 1938, Germany's declining military fortunes from 1942 onward—combined with an increasingly meaningful resurgence of Austrian nationalism—spurred the renewed growth of civilian resistance groups. That these cells not only survived but flourished is especially noteworthy given that their members had to contend with both the threat posed by the Gestapo and the very real danger that they would be killed by Allied air attacks. From 1943 on, the H. Krieghof munitions factory in Kufstein and the major railroad marshaling yard in Wörgl were frequent targets for U.S. 15th Air Force B-17 and B-24 bombers flying from bases in Italy, and strafing attacks by P-38 and P-51 fighters made road and rail travel in the Inn Valley increasingly hazardous. Civilian casualties were inevitable; in a particularly tragic incident, many of the bombs intended for the Wörgl yards during a raid on February 22, 1945, instead hit the town center, killing thirty-nine civilians, injuring more than a hundred, and severely damaging or destroying scores of buildings.[26]

Despite the death and destruction caused by the Allied air attacks, the resisters in the eastern Inn River valley continued to organize and plan for the arrival of advancing U.S. forces. By March 1945 the various cells in and around Wörgl totaled some eighty people, including local government and business leaders, craftsmen, clergy, laborers, police officers, physicians, and homemakers. The titular leader of the combined movement was a well-to-do Wörgl business leader named Alois Mayr (who steadfastly maintained his pro-Allied stance despite the fact that his fifty-three-year-old sister and seventeen-year-old niece had been killed in the February 22 bombing). Mayr's deputy, and the head of the civilian movement's twenty to thirty armed fighters, was thirty-one-year-old local politician Rupert Hagleitner.

He and his fighters faced a daunting task. Not only were they supposed to prevent the retreating Germans from destroying key bridges, buildings, and other infrastructure, they were also charged with protecting the local civilians against reprisals by the Gestapo and SS. Though initially armed only with hunting rifles and fowling pieces, close cooperation with anti-Nazi Austrians in the various local military units eventually allowed Hagleitner and his men to begin adding the occasional Wehrmacht-issue Kar-98 rifle to their secret armory in the basement of Wörgl's Neue Post Inn.

While the accurate and mechanically reliable bolt-action Kar-98s were a welcome addition to the resisters' arsenal, Hagleitner and his fighters desperately needed more significant weaponry if they were to have any hope of surviving a firefight with frontline Wehrmacht or Waffen-SS units. Though Austrian deserters from the German forces provided one or two

MP-40 submachine guns and the odd hand grenade, it was not until early March 1945 that Hagleitner and the Wörgl resistance cell were contacted by someone in a position to provide both advanced weapons and men trained and experienced in their use. Much to the resisters' surprise, that man was a highly decorated German major named Josef Gangl, and he was destined to play a pivotal, heroic, and ultimately tragic role in the events soon to unfold at Schloss Itter.

———

AT FIRST GLANCE, JOSEF GANGL—known to friends and family by the nickname Sepp—seems an unlikely anti-Nazi resister. Indeed, a review of his Wehrmacht service record, his personalakten,[27] portrays a dedicated career soldier, one who worked his way up from the enlisted ranks to company-grade officer and was highly regarded by both his superiors and the men he led. On the fourth page of his personnel file a grainy black-and-white photo taken in May 1940 depicts him as a newly commissioned thirty-year-old second lieutenant, the very model of a steely-eyed, square-jawed, ramrod-straight German officer. What the image cannot show us, of course, are the events and experiences that led a man to ultimately betray his nation and violate his solemn oath, all in the service of a far greater good.

Sepp Gangl was born September 12, 1910, in Obertraubling, a small Bavarian town on the southeast outskirts of Regensburg.[28] His origins, if not exactly humble, were certainly not exalted, either: at the time of Gangl's birth his twenty-four-year-old father had just secured a job as a low-level bureaucrat in the Regensburg regional office of the Royal Bavarian State Railways, and his twenty-three-year-old mother—until her pregnancy— had worked part-time in a shop near their modest home. A few years after Sepp's birth, his father was transferred to a railway facility in Peissenberg, some thirty-five miles southwest of Munich. The Gangls had more children after the move;[29] all had strictly conventional upbringings, attending local secular schools despite their parents' nominal Roman Catholicism. Though the elder Gangl's work for the railways was deemed important enough by the government to keep him out of the kaiser's army during World War I, the stagnant economy and high unemployment rate in postwar Germany ensured that military service was one of the few job choices available to Sepp when he finished his formal education. On November 1, 1928—less than two months after his eighteenth birthday—Gangl did what young men with no other viable prospects have done throughout history: he joined the army.

Known at that time as the Reichsheer, the German army was one half of the Reichswehr, the unified military that also included the navy, the Reichsmarine. Neither was the mighty force it had been during World War I. The 1919 Treaty of Versailles severely restricted the size of both services, with the Reichsheer limited to no more than one hundred thousand men. There were also significant restraints on the number and types of weapons the army could possess and the sorts of operations it could undertake. While these restrictions guaranteed that soldiers would spend the vast majority of their careers trapped in the cyclic, mindless drudgery of peacetime garrison life—training, drilling, cleaning weapons, maintaining uniforms and barracks, training some more—enlistment in the Reichswehr offered young men like Sepp Gangl several advantages that were becoming increasingly important as the worldwide Great Depression began to pummel an already battered Germany: a roof over their heads, a small but steady income, and regular meals. And it could well be that Gangl—like many who grew up amid the social and political chaos that wracked Germany in the decade after the war—craved the discipline, order, and camaraderie inherent in military service.

Whatever his reasons for enlisting, Gangl quickly proved himself to be a motivated and highly competent soldier. Assigned to the artillery—whether by his choice or the army's isn't clear—he underwent initial training with the Nürnberg-based Artillerie-Regiment 7. He remained with that unit until September 1929, garnering the first of many glowing efficiency reports, and over the next ten years rose steadily in the ranks while serving with, successively, Artillerie-Regiment 5 in Ulm and Artillerie-Regiment 25 in Ludwigsburg. By November 1938 Gangl was a master sergeant and had been tapped to attend officer candidate school. He was also a husband and father: he'd married the former Walburga Renz, a Ludwigsburg shopgirl, in 1935, and the first of two children,[30] daughter Sieglinde, was born the following year.

While the initial years of Gangl's military career had followed the dull peacetime cycle, Germany's clandestine rearmament during the 1930s and the Nazi Party's rise to power ensured that by the time he became a senior noncommissioned officer, the Heer—as the Reichsheer had been renamed in 1935, at the same time the Reichswehr became the Wehrmacht—was a far larger and more active force. It was also a vastly more political one, in that promotions and choice assignments for enlisted men and officers alike tended to go to those who embraced, at least publicly, the führer and the party. Like many German soldiers of his generation, Gangl was politically adaptable. While we don't know how he truly felt about Adolf Hitler or the rise of Nazism in his native land, we do know that from 1935 onward Gangl's efficiency reports referred to him as "a dedicated National Socialist" with "correct political views."

Those views may well have contributed to his selection for officer candidate school, which he was initially scheduled to begin in October 1939. The outbreak of World War II the preceding month disrupted that timetable, however, because, in the weeks before Germany's September 1 invasion of Poland, Gangl's entire regiment deployed from Ludwigsburg to the Saarpfalz region bordering France. Attached to the 25th Infanterie-Division, Gangl's Artillerie-Regiment 25 dug in several miles behind the frontier and prepared to help repulse any Allied invasion of the Reich. That attack came on September 7, when eleven French divisions crossed the border on a twenty-two-mile front. The invasion was intended to help relieve the pressure on Poland by forcing the Germans to shift forces to the west, but the attack was poorly planned and timidly executed. Though the invaders managed to advance about five miles into Germany and occupy some small towns from which German troops had already withdrawn, the incursion was a dismal failure, and the French forces withdrew within two weeks—without forcing the transfer of any German units from Poland to the west.

The brief conflict, which marked Sepp Gangl's first combat action, was soon followed by a period of military stalemate on the Western Front that became known as the Phoney War and the *sitzkrieg*.[31] The phase, roughly from mid-September 1939 until the May 1940 German invasion of France and the Low Countries, also marks something of a mysterious time in Gangl's life. Though his personnel file makes no mention of a wound or injury received during the brief French incursion, it does clearly indicate that from September 13, 1939, through March 13, 1940, Gangl was assigned to four successive military hospitals—in Landau, Ludwigshafen, Schrobenhausen, and Ludwigsburg. While there are only a few possible reasons for this unexplained interlude—Gangl had been wounded in some way, had fallen ill or was injured in a noncombat accident, or was serving in some undisclosed administrative capacity—we simply can't be sure why the Bavarian artilleryman spent some six months in military hospitals. We do know, however, that Gangl returned to his regiment on March 14, 1940. Less than two months later he was commissioned a second lieutenant, and in the photo taken immediately after that event he looks hale and hearty.

Within days of his promotion Sepp Gangl was putting his leadership skills to work in combat. Artillerie-Regiment 25 under Brigadier General Hermann Kruse took part in Case Yellow, the German invasion of Belgium and the Netherlands that opened what soon became the Battle of France. Gangl spent the entire campaign as the leader of a forward-observation team attached to one of 25th Infanterie-Division's assault regiments, calling in artillery fire on enemy troop concentrations, fortifications, and any other target the advancing infantrymen deemed a threat. Constantly on the move and always far forward of the guns he was directing, Gangl's initial combat performance as an officer won him praise from his superiors, who cited his "excellent gunnery knowledge" and "calmness under fire."

Though the German conquest of France and the Low Countries was both rapid and brilliantly executed, it was not without cost to the invaders. The Allied armies managed to inflict significant casualties on the advancing German units, and Gangl's Artillerie-Regiment 25 was no exception. The replacement of the regiment's dead and wounded with properly trained troops was the task of Artillerie Ersatz Abteillung (Artillery Replacement Battalion) 25, and within weeks of France's capitulation Gangl was tapped to join the unit for temporary duty as a training officer. It was a position for which he was obviously well suited: as a combat-proven officer who'd spent most of his military career as an enlisted man, he would presumably have been able to connect with the young replacement troops in a way that other, more hidebound officers might not have. Moreover, coming up through the ranks, he had mastered virtually every aspect of the gunner's art, and his unusually comprehensive skill set would have been especially valuable to neophyte artillerymen, who would almost certainly have to put their training to combat use sooner rather than later. Gangl left France on August 7, 1940, and, after a few brief days at home with his family, traveled on to Artillerie Ersatz Abteilung 25's base in Taus in the Protectorate of Bohemia and Moravia, a section of occupied Czechoslovakia administered by the Nazis as part of the greater Reich.[32]

After spending roughly three months with the replacement battalion—and in the process garnering still more highly complimentary efficiency reports from his commanders—Sepp Gangl went back to school himself. On November 25, 1940, he started a monthlong course at the Artillery School in Jüterbog, some forty miles southwest of Berlin. The training qualified him to serve as a battery commander, and upon completion of the course Gangl returned to his home unit. By that point the regiment had been withdrawn from France to Ludwigsburg to reorganize with a larger number of motor vehicles, after which it had been redesignated Artillerie-Regiment (Motorisiert) 25. The unit's increased mobility would soon come in handy, for Gangl and his comrades were about to become part of Operation Barbarossa, Germany's invasion of Soviet Russia.

While the larger details of that massive onslaught—and its eventual, catastrophic failure—are beyond the scope of this volume, Gangl's nearly four years on the Russian Front are not. And yet we know frustratingly little about a period that was undoubtedly crucial in shaping the man who would later play so important a role in the events at Schloss Itter. Though the basic outlines of his service are contained in his Wehrmacht personnel file, the exacting detail with which that document chronicled the first fifteen years of his military career is missing. The reason isn't hard to fathom: as the war progressed, one of the many aspects of Wehrmacht efficiency that declined was the keeping of accurate, complete, and up-to-date personnel records. In Gangl's case the result is akin to watching a full-color portrait fading to black and white before our eyes.

So, what do we know about his time in Russia?

When Operation Barbarossa kicked off on June 22, 1941, Artillerie-Regiment (Motorisiert) 25 was attached to General Ewald von Kliest's Panzergruppe 1, which attacked into Ukraine as part of Army Group South. For the following ten months Gangl commanded a battery of 10.5 cm (105mm) howitzers in the regiment's 3rd Battalion during the advance to and capture of Kiev. The fighting was fierce and constant, as the Germans sought to destroy the several Russian armies they'd managed to encircle. Gangl's battery was constantly on the move, employing a tactic that is known in the U.S. Army as "shoot and scoot": stopping to unlimber the guns and fire hurried barrages on targets either preplanned or called in by forward observers, reattaching the guns to their tow vehicles, then moving on. This tactic ensures that the spearhead units—in this case tanks and motorized infantry—always have supporting artillery as they advance, and it also prevents the enemy from undertaking effective counterbattery fire. By the time the Russians had determined the location from which the German howitzers were firing, Gangl and his men had packed up and moved on.

Despite the huge losses in men and materiel the Germans inflicted on the Soviet forces opposing them, the advance into Ukraine was not a walk in the park. Though many Russian units quickly disintegrated when subjected to the Germans' overwhelming combined-arms[33] attack, others held their ground and fought furiously. German artillery units were often instrumental in breaking up Soviet counterattacks, and, during one such Russian push in July 1941, Gangl and his battery prevented an enemy unit from overrunning a company of German infantrymen. While details of the fight are scarce, we know that for his actions that day Gangl was awarded—on August 20, 1941—the Iron Cross Second Class. Five months later he was promoted to first lieutenant, and, on February 12, 1942, Gangl was awarded the Iron Cross First Class. Though the reasons for the second medal are apparently lost to history, we can assume that the young artillery officer was decorated for having demonstrated the requisite "extraordinary bravery" in combat. From that point on he wore the black, white, and red ribbon of the first award in a buttonhole of his tunic, and the iconic silver and black medal of the second centered on his breast pocket.

Just over two months after pinning on his second Iron Cross, Sepp Gangl underwent a career change that probably seemed relatively unimportant at the time but would prevent him from dying in Russia and ultimately result in his presence at Schloss Itter. That change was his reassignment from traditional, single-barrel artillery to his regiment's independent werfer[34] battery. The unit consisted of six Nebelwerfer 41 six-barreled rocket launchers, each mounted on a two-wheeled carriage and pulled by a half-track. The weapon could ripple-fire all of its spin-stabilized, unguided rockets in seconds, and a full-battery barrage could saturate a target area with high-explosive or incendiary projectiles.[35] The Nebelwerfer 41 had its drawbacks—primarily its limited range and a telltale smoke signature that made it unusually vulnerable to counterbattery fire—but when properly employed, it was a devastating weapon more than capable of decimating Soviet troops and soft-skinned (nonarmored) vehicles. While it is unclear whether Gangl had had any previous experience with the weapon, on April

24, 1942, he was put in command of the werfer battery, a job he held for the remainder of his time with Artillerie-Regiment (Motorisiert) 25.

And that time was all too eventful. Though the Germans were initially able to capture vast swaths of Russia—in the process destroying entire Soviet armies and taking millions of prisoners—by the time Gangl took command of the werfer battery, things had already begun to turn against the Wehrmacht. German forces had been unable to capture Moscow, begun an ultimately unsuccessful siege of Leningrad, and suffered through their first ferocious Russian winter. Soviet resistance stiffened as German supply lines lengthened, and units like Gangl's found themselves increasingly on the defensive. Artillerie-Regiment (Motorisiert) 25, like virtually every other German unit on the Russian Front, was steadily ground down by two years of constant combat. The wounded and dead were not replaced, supplies were inadequate, and by February 1944 the unit was on the verge of collapse.

Fortunately, Captain Gangl—he'd been promoted the previous April—did not have to participate in the unit's inexorable disintegration. In November 1943 he'd been assigned to a werfer-related position on the staff of 4th Army, a post in which he helped develop policy and tactics for the wider and more effective use of the multibarreled rocket launchers. Gangl again impressed his superiors with his knowledge and capabilities, so much so that in January 1944 he was tapped to take command of one of the new werfer battalions then being formed in Germany. That selection proved to be his ticket out of Russia and away from the Götterdämmerung the Soviets would soon inflict on the Wehrmacht's Eastern Front armies.

Gangl's first stop was in Höchstädt an der Donau, some sixty miles northwest of Munich. The city was home to Werfer Ersatz Ausbildungs Abteilung (Werfer Replacement Training Battalion) 7, and for almost two months the Russian Front veteran shared his expertise with soldiers who in far too many cases had been civilians just weeks earlier. On weekends Gangl was able to travel to Ludwigsburg to spend time with his wife and children, though Allied bombing attacks on Germany's rail hubs often made the two-hour train ride a far longer ordeal. In early February he was on the move again, this time headed to Belgium for a month of training at the Army School for Battalion and Detachment Leaders in Antwerp.

Upon his March 4 completion of the course, Gangl traveled to Celle, in north-central Germany, where he joined the then-forming Werfer-Regiment

83. The unit consisted of three battalions, two of which (1st and 2nd) were each equipped with eighteen 15cm Nebelwerfer 41s divided among three firing batteries; the 3rd Battalion had eighteen of the larger 21cm (210mm) Nebelwerfer 42s. The regiment also included sixteen armored half-tracks, known as Maultiers[36] ("mules"), each of which carried a 15cm launcher. The vehicles were evenly divided between the 1st and 2nd Battalions; those in the former were designated "21. Batterie" and those in the latter as "22. Batterie." Gangl was given command of one of the 3rd Battalion's Nebel-werfer 41 batteries, apparently with the understanding that he'd take over the entire battalion in due time. Gangl's organization and a second identi-cally equipped unit, Werfer-Regiment 84, made up Werfer-Brigade 7.[37]

By this point in the war it was clear that the Allies would soon attempt the invasion of western Europe, most probably on the Normandy coast of France, and after several weeks of training Gangl's new brigade began moving west to become part of the force the German High Command hoped would repulse that offensive. It wasn't an easy journey: because the rail networks of western Germany and northern France were subject to in-creasingly frequent strikes by Allied heavy bombers, Werfer-Brigade 7's troop trucks, tow vehicles, launchers, and Maultier half-tracks had to make the trip by road. Not only did this expose them to the very real threat of at-tack by low-flying Allied fighter-bombers, it imposed severe mechanical strains—especially on the Maultiers' tracks—and breakdowns were fre-quent. And there were other hazards as well: as part of the buildup to the invasion, French resistance groups were stepping up their activities. These ranged from the relatively benign, such as switching road signs to lead Ger-man convoys astray, to such decidedly more violent activities as sniping attacks and full-blown ambushes.

Despite the difficulties and potential hazards, Werfer-Brigade 7 man-aged to reach its initial forward-assembly point in Beauvais—some fifty miles northwest of Paris—on May 18. Over the following weeks the brigade's troops did what they could to prepare for the coming battle: load-ing ammunition and fuel, maintaining the vehicles, and trying their best to avoid the attention of Allied aircraft. While no documents survive that might give us insight into Sepp Gangl's frame of mind during this period— was he frightened? resigned? sick to death of the war?—we can safely as-sume that he did his best to prepare the men in his battery for the storm that was about to engulf them.

That storm arrived early on June 6, of course, in the form of some 156,000 airborne and seaborne Allied troops. The next day Werfer-Brigade 7 was ordered to move toward the Normandy coast, where British and Canadian forces were threatening the city of Caen. The 116-mile trip took three days and Allied aircraft inflicted losses on both men and materiel. Upon arrival in Caen the brigade was subordinated to the 12th SS Panzer Division "Hitlerjugend," and for the next two months the two werfer regiments were constantly in action. Though Gangl and his fellow gunners were able to play a key role in the stubborn German defense of Caen, by the third week of August Werfer-Regiment 7—along with virtually all of Field Marshal Walter Model's Army Group B—had been squeezed into the Falaise Pocket south of Caen. Some 100,000 German troops were in danger of being completely encircled by American units advancing from the south and British-Canadian-Polish forces from the north, but the surviving members of Gangl's brigade were among the 25,000 to 45,000 who were able to escape before the jaws of the trap snapped shut on August 20.

While Werfer-Brigade 7 managed to escape to fight another day, it did so only by leaving all of its launchers and vehicles behind. The unit was reassembled and partially reequipped in Prüm, in the Eifel region of western Germany, and in mid-November it was redesignated Volks-Werfer-Brigade 7. On December 16 both its regiments contributed to the massive barrage that immediately preceded the last-ditch German offensive that quickly became known as the Battle of the Bulge. As the attacking forces surged forward, Volks-Werfer-Brigade 7 followed to provide fire support for 5th Panzer-Armee and eventually settled on the eastern outskirts of St. Vith, Belgium. But as American resistance stiffened on the ground and clearing weather allowed Allied attack aircraft to once again range freely over the snow-covered battlefield, the brigade joined the general German withdrawal eastward.

In January and February 1945 Volks-Werfer-Brigade 7 took part in the ultimately futile defense of Saarbrücken against Alexander Patch's U.S. Seventh Army, a fight during which Sepp Gangl was again cited for extreme bravery in combat. Though the details of his heroism are lost to history, we know that he was awarded the German Cross in Gold[38] on March 8. Days later Gangl was promoted to major and given command of his regiment's 2nd Battalion, though by that point the battalion could muster barely enough men to constitute a single battery. Gangl wouldn't have had

much time to savor the promotion, for by that point the battered brigade—
at barely half strength and with few working vehicles and no remaining
launchers—was engaged in almost constant retreat. Moving only at night
in order to avoid roving Allied aircraft, Volks-Werfer-Brigade 7 headed
steadily southeastward, and by the first week of April what was left of the
unit was spread across several miles of Bavaria in the area of Peissenberg,
the town where Gangl had grown up. The regiment was no longer a coherent fighting force, and its commander, Brigadier General Dr. Kurt Paape,[39]
broke it up into independent battalions, ordering the commanders of each
to take their remaining men into the Austrian Tyrol and offer their services
to whoever was organizing the defense of the Alpine Fortress.

While we're not certain of the route Sepp Gangl and the thirty or so men
that by now constituted his entire battalion took on their journey into Austria, it seems likely that the rapid advance of American forces across lower
Bavaria would have dictated an initial move directly east from Peissenberg
toward Bad Tölz, then a turn south down the Isar River valley. Some twelve
miles on, where the Isar flows north out of the Sylvensteinsee, Gangl and
his men would have turned east and crossed into Austria. Once across what
until 1938 had been the frontier, they would have headed south through
the Achental Valley, along the east side of the Achensee and into the Inn
Valley at Jenbach. Immediately upon their mid-April arrival within von
Hengl's Northwest Alpine Front, Gangl and the few surviving members
of his 2nd Battalion were dragooned into service with Battle Group Giehl,
whose headquarters' elements were by then in Wörgl.

We will likely never know with any certainty whether Sepp Gangl took
his remaining soldiers into Austria seriously intending to join the last-ditch
fight against the Americans or was simply looking for a quiet backwater
where he and his men could safely wait out the last weeks of the war. Nor
can we be sure whether the Wehrmacht artillery officer—a career soldier
three times decorated for bravery in combat against his nation's enemies—
had ever actually believed in the führer to whom he'd sworn a solemn oath
of obedience. But we can infer much about Gangl's true character from the
fact that within days of his arrival in Wörgl, he made contact with Alois
Mayr's resistance cell and offered to provide both weapons and his unre-
served assistance. It was a blatant act of treason against both führer and
fatherland, one punishable by death not only for Gangl[40] but by that point
in the war for his wife and children as well.

And yet, despite the risks to himself and his loved ones, Sepp Gangl ultimately made the decision that within weeks would lead him to put his life in even more direct peril in order to help save a querulous group of French VIPs locked away in a fairytale castle.

———

WHILE WE DON'T KNOW how Gangl made initial contact with the Wörgl resisters, we can make a few educated guesses.

The first is that upon joining the staff of Battle Group Giehl, Gangl gained access to intelligence reports that identified Mayr, Hagleitner, and other key members of the organization and, acting on his own, sought them out. This is the least likely scenario, given the simple fact that had the resistance members' identities been known and recorded in any official file, they would almost certainly already have been arrested. Even during the last weeks of the war SS and Gestapo units were active throughout Tyrol, summarily executing real or suspected anti-Nazis and "defeatists" in the military and civilian populations. Von Hengl's Alpine Front, Northwest, staff included (quite possibly against the aristocratic general's will) members of both organizations, and they would have demanded and received access to any information that might identify resisters.

Another possibility is that in the course of his work on Giehl's staff, Gangl somehow learned the identity of one or more of the Wörgl resistance members and reached out to them. While plausible, this is also doubtful. Given the continuing predations of the SS and Gestapo, no resister in his right mind would have considered the advances of a highly decorated, non-Austrian Wehrmacht officer to be anything but a fairly clumsy attempt at entrapment. In the best-case scenario Gangl would have been politely brushed off with fulsome protestations of innocence; in the worst, he could well have ended up floating down the Inn River with a bullet in the back of his head.

The most likely way that Gangl made contact with Mayr's cell, then, was through a trusted intermediary. As noted earlier in this chapter, key Austrian-born officers in several of the second-line Wehrmacht units in the Kufstein-Wörgl area—including Gebirgsjäger-Ersatz-Bataillon 136, Reserve-Gebirgsjäger-Bataillon 137, and Gebirgs-Artillerie-Ersatz-Abteilung 118—are known to have been active in, or at the very least sympathetic to, the resistance. Since those organizations, and for that matter the mountain troops' NCO school, were expected to provide men or materiel to von Hengl's battle groups, it's entirely possible that Gangl came into contact with one or more of their anti-Nazi members during the course of his official duties. Did Gangl make the first move, or did someone approach him? While we can't know who reached out to whom, we can be certain that the initial contact would have constituted a tremendous leap of faith: an ill-considered overture to the wrong person could very well have ended in front of a firing squad.

However Gangl gained an introduction to the Mayr-Hagleitner resistance organization, we know that his position as one of Battle Group Giehl's senior officers made him extremely valuable to the anti-Nazi movement. In the course of his official duties Gangl moved freely throughout the Rosenheim-Kufstein-Wörgl area, ostensibly coordinating with the other battle groups and overseeing the Organization Todt's[41] construction of roadblocks and placement of demolition charges on key roads and bridges. He made careful notes on the location of the obstacles and the strength and armament of Wehrmacht and Waffen-SS units deployed in the region, which he passed to Hagleitner for transmission up the POEN-O5 chain. In addition to providing the resisters with weapons and ammunition, Gangl supplied details on which of his fellow battle-group officers were die-hard Nazis and which could be trusted to aid the resistance when the time came. In the latter category were a dozen of the former Werfer-Regiment 83 comrades—both officers and enlisted soldiers—who'd accompanied Gangl into Austria and who he'd determined shared his views.

In the days since his initial contact with the Wörgl resistance cell, Gangl had shown himself to be both a dedicated anti-Nazi and a highly competent soldier, and, at a meeting on Monday, April 30, Alois Mayr put the Wehrmacht officer in charge of the group's military operations.[42] Gangl's first decision was that the resisters would have to prevent the execution of two orders issued by Giehl.[43] The first command dictated that Wörgl be vigorously defended against the advancing Americans, and the second that all of the town's bridges and its major roads be obstructed or destroyed with explosives.

Gangl's second decision concerned the French prisoners being held at Schloss Itter, whom he'd been told of shortly after his initial contact with the Wörgl resisters. The VIPs obviously had to be secured, he said, but any attempt to rescue them would have to be carried out covertly to avoid a full-scale battle with Waffen-SS and Wehrmacht troops still loyal to the führer. Gangl ordered that weapons and ammunition for the rescue be cached somewhere outside Wörgl, and the following day Mayr and a local mechanic named Hans Scheffold removed two carloads of the necessary items from the basement of the Neue Post Inn and drove them via back roads to an abandoned farmhouse in Kelchsau, some six miles southeast of Wörgl.

Though Gangl had intended to secure the French prisoners sooner rather than later, the rapidly changing military situation in the Inn Valley kept him from launching an immediate rescue. On Tuesday morning, May 1, even as Mayr and Scheffold were on their way to cache the weapons, Giehl ordered Gangl to inspect those elements of the battle group deployed on either side of the main road leading south from Rosenheim to Kufstein. The next day Gangl was tied up in meetings all day with Colonel Forster, the commander of the Wörgl-based reserve task force. And any hopes Gangl might have had of securing the French VIPs on Thursday, May 3, disappeared when elements of Battle Group Giehl came under attack by the U.S. 12th Armored Division in and around Niederaudorf, Germany, seven miles north of Kufstein.[44]

The appearance of American forces just over the German border sparked a flurry of activity in and around Wörgl. In the early afternoon von Hengl dispatched Forster's reserve task force to Schwaz to help block the Inn River valley, but the unit was decimated by American air strikes and artillery fire before it had gone five miles. By late afternoon those elements of Battle Group Giehl north of Kufstein had been effectively destroyed, and by early evening von Hengl had decided to pull his remaining forces—now totaling fewer than 1,400 men—out of Wörgl to new positions east of Schloss Itter. His order didn't affect the various independent Waffen-SS units that had retreated into the area, however, and they filtered into Wörgl and the surrounding area as von Hengl's men moved out.

It was the appearance of large numbers of these die-hard Waffen-SS troops that prompted Gangl to make his final break with the Wehrmacht. Late on Thursday evening, even as Giehl and his other staff officers were jumping into their vehicles and roaring out of Wörgl, Gangl was meeting with a very concerned Alois Mayr. The resistance leader was understandably concerned that the withdrawal of von Hengl's troops would allow the newly arrived Waffen-SS units to wreak havoc on the local people, many of whom had already started putting out white flags in anticipation of the Americans' arrival. It wasn't an idle worry: barely ten days earlier, Heinrich Himmler had issued an order stating that "all male persons inhabiting a house showing a white flag will be shot. No hesitation in executing these orders can be permitted any longer. 'Male persons' who are to be considered responsible in this respect are those aged 14 years or over."[45] Gangl, fully aware that he and those soldiers who had chosen to join him, as well as Hagleitner's armed resistance members, were the only force capable of providing any protection for Wörgl's civilians, decided on the spot to remain in the town as the rest of Giehl's battle group withdrew.

But on Friday morning, May 4, the artillery officer and newly minted resistance leader was unexpectedly handed another task, one arguably as important as organizing the defense of Wörgl. Just after eleven AM, as Gangl was handing out automatic weapons and hand grenades to Hagleitner and some of his men, other resisters appeared, accompanying a disheveled man on a battered bicycle. Walking directly up to Gangl, the new arrival said, in heavily accented German, that his name was Andreas Krobot and he was the bearer of important news from Schloss Itter.

CHAPTER 5

AN UNCERTAIN FUTURE

THAT ANDREAS KROBOT had managed to make it safely from Schloss Itter to Wörgl was nothing short of miraculous. Despite von Hengl's withdrawal of his battered forces to positions east of the castle, the roads along which the Czech cook had ridden west were not free of danger. Die-hard Waffen-SS troops were increasingly active in the area, setting up roadblocks, searching for deserters, and engaging any Austrian resisters they encountered. Through a combination of good luck and extreme caution Krobot had nonetheless managed to evade the obstacles, arriving in Wörgl with a tale of French honor prisoners in need of immediate rescue.

———

THE CONDITIONS THAT ULTIMATELY made such a relief mission necessary had been developing for many months. Though the French prisoners had certainly fared far better than the vast majority of the Nazis' captives, the essentially benign routine at Schloss Itter began to change as Germany's military fortunes steadily deteriorated throughout the latter half of 1944. Food became increasingly scarce for both the prisoners and their guards, and a growing shortage of fuel for the castle's generators meant that candles and lanterns ultimately replaced electric lights. More ominously, the members of the castle's guard force began taking the threat of enemy action more seriously. On October 7, 1944, Édouard Daladier witnessed an example of this higher level of readiness and recorded in his diary that he'd

> watched the SS go rushing about the castle. Red flares went off. It was all either preparation to ward off a commando raid or a positioning exercise in anticipation of an attack from the village or from down in the valley. The maneuvers lasted two hours, and enlisted men and officers alike went through them in dead seriousness.[1]

Just ten days later, Daladier noted, the decidedly second-string guards—most of whom had never fired a shot in anger—were reinforced by twenty-seven combat-experienced Waffen-SS troops, who arrived at Schloss Itter bearing several additional machine guns and crates of ammunition. The newcomers immediately began reinforcing the castle's defenses with what the elderly Frenchman described as "speed and discipline,"[2] setting up sand-bagged firing positions and felling trees to be used to block the approach roads. And there were other measures as well. On October 27 Wimmer announced that he was instituting a defensive alarm system. One type of siren would indicate an Allied air attack; when it sounded, the French prisoners could decide for themselves whether to take shelter in the castle's cellars, with the understanding that if they didn't, it was at their own risk. The other alarm would sound if a ground attack were imminent; in that case the prisoners were to move immediately to the cellars. If they didn't, Wimmer said, they would be taken there by force.[3]

While the danger of the French prisoners being killed or injured by an errant Allied bomb was real, they were in many ways more vulnerable to the increasingly erratic behavior of Sebastian Wimmer. The castle's commandant had always been mercurial and subject to fits of unreasoning anger, but his personality swings had become far more pronounced following a mid-July 1944 trip to Munich to attend the funeral of his brother, who had been killed days earlier in an Allied bombing raid. The city had been subjected to another massive air attack the day before Wimmer's arrival, and on reaching the city the SS-TV officer couldn't find a taxi or working streetcar. As he was walking through rubble-filled streets toward the makeshift morgue that held his brother's remains, the air-raid sirens wailed yet again, and falling bombs obliterated the building. Wimmer, Daladier recalled, "returned to Itter totally demoralized."[4]

Schloss Itter's commander increasingly sought to alleviate his demor-alization with alcohol, often drinking steadily from morning until late at night. Prisoners and guards alike tried to avoid Wimmer anytime after noon: though he was usually calm for the first few hours after opening a bottle of Asbach Uralt,[5] later in the day his true nature would reveal itself in screaming rages and random violence. While the SS-TV officer generally didn't focus his alcohol-fueled anger on his VIP charges, he had no com-punctions about tormenting the number prisoners. One of his favorite tar-gets was Zvonko Čučković; while Wimmer would occasionally treat the Croat handyman with something approaching kindness,[6] his more usual attitude is illustrated by two incidents that occurred during the winter of 1944–1945.

In the first, Čučković was working on Wimmer's staff car in the small courtyard between the castle's front gate and the schlosshof when the SS-TV officer staggered up to him and without saying a word punched the Croat in the face. Knowing well that any reaction would only further en-rage the drunken Wimmer, Čučković said nothing and quickly snapped to attention. The castle's commandant nevertheless hit him again and was about to punch the Croat a third time when he realized that Maurice Gamelin—out for his daily constitutional—had walked up behind him. Wimmer saluted the French general, who returned a withering glare and said, "You cannot beat a prisoner," before turning his back and walking away. Wimmer staggered off, muttering to himself, and didn't leave his suite for two days.

The second incident was potentially more dangerous for Čučković. Just after a particularly heavy snowfall, a seriously inebriated Wimmer sum-moned the Croat to the guardroom and began screaming at him for not re-pairing a leaking toilet in the commandant's suite. Čučković tried to explain that he'd ordered the necessary rubber washer from the supply depot at Dachau, but it hadn't yet arrived. Wimmer shrieked that he wasn't inter-ested in excuses and ordered the Croat to spend the next two nights shov-eling snow in the rear courtyard from six PM until six AM. Had it not been for the occasional help provided by the two SS enlisted men who'd been tasked to watch him—their assistance most probably an attempt to curry favor as Germany spiraled ever closer to defeat—Čučković might well have died of exhaustion or exposure.

Wimmer's outbursts increased in both frequency and virulence as the Allied armies got closer to Schloss Itter. Fortunately for Čučković, one of the worst wasn't aimed at him. On March 20, 1945, the Croat was again working on the commandant's staff car when Gertrud, one of the female number prisoners, ran up to him with the news that Wimmer was about to shoot Andreas Krobot. Rushing to the castle's scullery, Čučković found a scene of pandemonium: An obviously drunken Wimmer was pointing his Walther P-38 pistol out an open window at the terrified Czech cook, who was standing in the middle of the castle's small vegetable garden. All of the female prisoners who worked in the kitchen were standing to one side, sobbing loudly, as Wimmer screamed at Krobot, "You dog, come one step forward and one to the left," apparently trying to line up a better shot. Čučković grabbed a large knife from a nearby rack, determined to kill the commandant if he shot Krobot, but the sudden appearance of Wimmer's wife defused the situation before any blood was spilled.[7]

By the first month of 1945, the Waffen-SS troops who'd temporarily bolstered Schloss Itter's defenses had moved on, leaving behind a guard force infected with what Daladier called "utter consternation" because of Germany's clearly terminal military condition. In a January 30 diary entry, the Frenchman wrote:

> This is the twilight of the gods. . . . All the radios have been locked up in the Commandant's office for the last few days, probably to keep the garrison's morale from caving in, but in spite of all the precautions, disastrous news reports continue to filter through. The SS [men] can see the clenched jaws and the faces of [Wimmer and Otto]; their strained and downcast looks tell them just as much as they could ever learn from listening to the field communiqués. . . . I could see the dejection on the faces . . . of the soldiers. . . . [Čučković] told me that we had to be on our guard. Some of the SS troops were talking about suicide. Others planned to seize all the food supplies . . . get drunk and shoot us.[8]

The last possibility was of real concern to Daladier and his fellow honor prisoners, for they knew all too well that their lives might not be worth much to Nazis intent on covering up their crimes. Reynaud was seen as especially vulnerable, and during the last days of April, Clemenceau—who spoke fluent German—took it on himself to summon Wimmer to a meeting with Reynaud and Gamelin. In their presence, Clemenceau reminded the castle's commandant that the lives of Reynaud and indeed all the French prisoners were in the SS officer's hands.

"It is possible that you may shortly be told to hand over President Paul Reynaud," Clemenceau said. "If President Reynaud is taken away, you know for what purpose it will be. You also know the Allies will hold responsible all those who help in an action of this nature. What do you mean to do?"

Recounting this conversation in his memoirs, Reynaud said that Wimmer replied that he was only accountable to his conscience (an attribute, it must be said, that was completely absent during the SS-TV officer's time in Poland and at Majdanek and Dachau). Wimmer also said, however, that the deaths of Reynaud and the other prisoners would not be compatible with Germany's postwar interests and that he would aid in their escape if it became necessary.[9]

Despite Wimmer's pledge, the arrival at the castle of a nearly constant stream of senior SS-TV officers kept the French on edge. Often accompanied by their families and always loaded down with weapons, baggage, and booty, the SS men used Itter as a way station as they attempted to escape the advancing Allies.[10] Most of the fleeing Nazis stayed only long enough to requisition what food and water they could, but on the night of April 30 SS-Lieutenant Colonel Wilhelm Eduard Weiter, the last commander of Dachau, settled in with a retinue of his subordinates and their wives and children.

It was not Weiter's first visit to Itter; he had inspected the castle and its prisoners in October 1943 and at that time had spoken with Reynaud and several of the other French captives. On this, his final visit, Weiter—whom Daladier later described as "obese and apoplectic, with the face of a brute"[11]—drunkenly bragged to Wimmer that he had ordered the execution of some two thousand prisoners before leaving Dachau for the last time. Hearing of Weiter's boast, the French captives at Itter were therefore understandably concerned that his arrival signaled their own executions. As it turned out, however, the only death Weiter had on his mind was his own. As Reynaud later recounted, early on the morning of Wednesday, May 2,[12] "I heard in the room next to mine a couple of shots: [Weiter] had just shot himself near the heart, and then finished himself off with a second shot behind the ear."[13]

A group of Weiter's SS minions slapped together a pine box and hauled it up to his room but found that it was too large to fit through the door. Improvising, they dragged his corpse into the hallway and manhandled it down several flights of stairs and into the garage in the schlosshof.

There they unceremoniously dumped the body into the pine coffin, and one of them left to speak with the priest of Itter village's small parish church of St. Joseph. At that point Reynaud, Gamelin, Jouhaux, and Clemenceau—wanting to positively identify the dead man as the senior Dachau officer who had inspected Itter months earlier, so as to allow the Allies to cross him off any list of wanted war criminals—demanded to see the corpse. As Reynaud later recalled: "It was a frightful sight. Soldiers had stolen the dead man's boots. His bloodstained shirt was half opened to show his breast; his head was thrown back; his mouth was wide open and his eyes staring. This torturer looked like one of the damned."[14]

Once the Frenchmen had agreed that the corpse was indeed that of Weiter, SS men carried the crude coffin out the castle's front gate and started toward the village, only to encounter the soldier who had gone off to speak to the priest at St. Joseph's. The clergyman, to his credit, had categorically refused to let Weiter be interred in holy ground, so the SS men hurriedly buried the "butcher of Dachau" in an unmarked grave in a small clearing just outside the castle's walls. His only monument was a heap of brush meant to hide the patch of newly turned earth.[15]

Weiter's suicide seemed to galvanize Wimmer. Early on May 4—after first asking several of the VIPs to sign a statement saying he had treated them "correctly" and then assuring Reynaud and Daladier that he would find a way to protect the French prisoners against reprisal by the roving bands of Waffen-SS troops active in the surrounding hills—the SS-TV man abruptly fled the castle with his wife. Wimmer was only marginally true to his word, however, since all he did to ensure the promised "protection" for the VIPs was to enlist the aid of an acquaintance, a war-wounded officer recuperating at home in Itter village. And in what Wimmer may have intended as a final irony, the man he tapped to be the French VIPs' surrogate savior was himself a decorated member of the Waffen-SS.

———

AT FIRST GLANCE SS-CAPTAIN Kurt-Siegfried Schrader appears to be the very archetype of all the evil Nazis who have goose-stepped across cinema screens for the past seventy years. He peers with frightening intensity from the official photo attached to his personnel file, the highly polished death's head totem on his peaked officer's hat almost pulsating with menace and the double lightning-stroke SS runes on his collar obviously worn with arrogant pride. But it is not simply the uniform and facial expression that speak of his dedication to the cause: the man portrayed in the personalakten—and in Schrader's own postwar writings[16]—was for most of his military career the personification of the dedicated Waffen-SS officer.

Born in Magdeburg in August 1916, Schrader was the third and youngest child of a minor prewar judicial official who at the time of his son's birth was a soldier serving in France. With the end of World War I Schrader Senior returned to his former post, his position and influence increasing considerably over the years, even as his politics veered sharply to the right. In 1930 the elder Schrader attended a Nazi rally in Leipzig and upon his return proclaimed to his family that Adolf Hitler would be the "savior of Germany."[17] Kurt-Siegfried was soon drawn into his father's politics, and at the age of fourteen he joined a pro-Nazi youth group. The organization was still illegal in what at the time was the federal state of Prussia, and, when young Schrader was caught handing out Nazi propaganda stickers to his fellow students, he was expelled and thereafter prohibited from attending public schools. Undaunted by the expulsion, Schrader enrolled in a right-wing private school and joined the Hitler Youth movement. He participated in several large Nazi rallies, and, when Hitler was named Germany's chancellor in January 1933, Schrader remembered that it was as if a bright light had suddenly illuminated what had been a dark and forbidding horizon.

In 1934 Schrader's considerable intelligence—and his father's political connections—led to the eighteen-year-old's admission to a two-year program at an elite military-political school in Berlin. Following his graduation the young man spent a compulsory six months in the civilian Reich Labor Service,[18] after which he had expected to do his required two years of military service with the Nürnberg-based Artillerie Regiment 7. When that unit turned down his application, a former teacher suggested that Schrader apply to one of the military units then being formed within the SS. He did, and in April 1937 he joined the field telephone company of the SS-Nachrichtensturmbann (signals battalion).[19]

As a junior enlisted man in the communications unit Schrader took part in both the March 1938 Austrian Anschluss and the annexation of the Czech Sudetenland the following October. Upon the conclusion of the latter operation Schrader was tapped to attend four weeks of infantry training provided by the SS regiment Germania, and in April 1939 he entered the SS officer candidate school in Braunschweig. Schrader enjoyed both the military and political aspects of his officer training, later remembering that it was at Braunschweig that he "really got serious" about his professional life.[20] And it was after his graduation and commissioning as a second lieutenant that the young officer got serious about his personal life: in January 1940 Schrader married his girlfriend, Annaliese Patales.

The war didn't initially intrude on the newlyweds. For the first year of their marriage Schrader was assigned to various staff positions in eastern Germany, and in January 1941 he took up a three-month posting to Prague as the adjutant in a replacement battalion. He and Annaliese apparently enjoyed their time in the former Czech capital, for Schrader recalled that they "had everything their hearts could desire."[21] In April the young SS officer received a plum assignment as adjutant in Heinrich Himmler's newly formed guard unit, the Begleitbataillon Reichsführer SS. After organizing and equipping in Berlin, the battalion moved to Wolf's Lair, Hitler's field headquarters near Rastenburg in East Prussia, where it provided perimeter security.

That relatively safe assignment didn't last long. Soon after Germany's June 1941 invasion of Soviet Russia, Schrader's unit was sent to join the forces besieging Leningrad. In late November Schrader, the battalion commander, their driver, and two escorting motorcyclists were ambushed by Russian partisans while inspecting unit dispositions. The Waffen-SS[22] men escaped with their lives, but Schrader was wounded in the ankle. He was first sent to a military hospital in Tosno (a Leningrad suburb) and then evacuated west by hospital train. It was a slow trip, mainly because Russian partisans kept blowing up sections of the track. He finally arrived in East Prussia and was put on another hospital train to Prague, where he was reunited with his wife in mid-December. Within days of that reunion the Schraders welcomed their first child, a daughter they named Heidi. Because of his wounds, in early 1942 Schrader was temporarily released from active duty and allowed to enroll in Berlin's Humboldt University; for two semesters he studied biology and geography while living with his wife and daughter.

Schrader put his uniform back on in October 1942, when he was assigned as the battalion adjutant in the 7. SS-Freiwilligen Gebirgsdivision (volunteer mountain division) "Prinz Eugen," which was fighting partisans near Pancevo, in the southern Banat area of Serbia. In February 1943 he was tapped to be the adjutant of the 22nd SS-Panzergrenadier Regiment, part of the 10th SS-Panzer Division "Frundsberg," then being formed in Angoulême, in France's Charente department. While he was thus engaged, Annaliese gave birth to their second child, daughter Birgit, in Berlin. Concerned for the safety of his family, he took advantage of a proclamation by Reichsminister Josef Goebbels that mothers with small children could leave the capital to avoid the increasingly heavy Allied bombing. Annaliese and her daughters first moved in with her parents near Bielefeld, some 200 miles southwest of Berlin; when the bombing got worse there, they moved to Augsburg, another 350 miles to the southeast.

At the end of 1943 Schrader decided to move his family yet again, this time to a place he assumed was unlikely to attract the attention of Allied bombers—the Austrian Tyrol. He had heard that an officer he'd known in Prague, none other than "Wastl" Wimmer, had just taken command of the Special Prisoner Facility at Schloss Itter. Schrader contacted Wimmer, who offered to find a place for Annaliese and the girls in Itter village. The castle's commandant obtained a small but comfortable house (probably by requisitioning it from its rightful owners), and Schrader was apparently able to get time off to move his family from Augsburg to Itter. Soon after that move, in January 1944, the Schraders' Berlin apartment was destroyed by an Allied bomb.[23]

In March 1944 "Frundsberg" was deployed to Ukraine, and in April it underwent its baptism of fire near Tarnopol. The division was rushed back to France in response to the Allied landings in Normandy in June and immediately went into action southwest of Metz. Beginning on June 29 "Frundsberg" took part in the German counteroffensives near Caen, and the fighting was intense—Schrader called it "an inferno" and "murderous."[24] His unit was subjected to constant attack by Allied aircraft, naval gunfire, and artillery, and within just a few weeks 22nd SS-Panzergrenadier Regiment had been effectively destroyed. In early July Schrader himself fell victim to Allied aircraft: a fighter-bomber strafed the kübelwagen[25] in which he was riding, and he suffered severe wounds to his head and right leg. Indeed, so grievous were his injuries that at the field aid station where he was initially treated, someone crossed out his name on the first page of his soldbuch (the twenty-four-page personal identity document carried by all German soldiers) and then rewrote it in very black ink, an indication that he was not expected to live.

Schrader did survive, however, and was transferred first to a field hospital in Dijon and then by train to a larger hospital in Munich. Within days of his arrival there, word came of the July 20 attempted assassination of Hitler. Apparently already disillusioned with Nazism, the bedridden Schrader had lots of time to think. He ultimately came to a conclusion that was especially momentous, given his SS oath: he "mentally broke" with the führer, the Nazi Party, and the Third Reich. His only goal now was to protect his family and make it through the rest of the war unscathed.[26]

While Annaliese Schrader was able to visit her husband once a week, taking the train from Wörgl to Munich, Allied air attacks on Germany's rail networks were making the trip increasingly time-consuming and significantly more dangerous. In January 1945 Schrader was able to get himself transferred to the small military hospital in Wörgl, and within days of his arrival in Austria he had convinced his doctors to let him live with his family in Itter village. This marked the start of a time of relative peace for Schrader: he had no military duties, wore no uniform, and was able to spend quality time with his wife and young daughters. Indeed, his only official task during this time was to make twice-weekly trips to the Wörgl hospital for examinations and consultations with his doctor.

Schrader made the journeys as a passenger in a staff car provided by his old comrade Wimmer. In order to exercise his damaged leg, the injured Waffen-SS man would walk the several hundred yards from his home in the village to Schloss Itter, where the guards would usher him into the courtyard. While waiting for the staff car to be readied, Schrader would often fall into conversation with some of the German-speaking French VIPs, to whom he apparently made known his disgust with the Nazi regime. His views earned him such a warm welcome among the schloss's French guests that Schrader began making regular social visits to the castle, sharing cigarettes and rough Tyrolean red wine with the likes of Clemenceau, Jouhaux, and Bruchlen during wide-ranging discussions of politics and philosophy. Schrader would sometimes bring his wife and daughters along during his visits to the castle, and the children made such an impression on Andreas Krobot that he would make small cakes, torts, and other sweets for them. The Czech cook's kindness to Heidi and Birgit touched Schrader, and the unlikely friendship that developed between the political prisoner and the Waffen-SS officer would ultimately save the latter's life.

As pleasant as it was, Schrader's Tyrolean idyll couldn't last. Germany's horrendous casualty rates in the last months of the war meant that virtually any soldier who could fog a mirror and hold a weapon would be put into the front line. In March 1945 Schrader—despite being far from recovered and still needing a cane—was declared fit for duty and assigned as the adjutant in SS-Feldersatz Brigade 502. Though officially a replacement unit intended to provide trained infantry troops to field units, the brigade was put directly into the line to help prevent the American capture of the Ludendorff Bridge over the Rhine River at Remagen. The German defense failed, and Schrader barely escaped capture. What remained of Feldersatz Brigade 502 was withdrawn to Nabburg, some fifty miles east of Nürnberg. There Schrader received orders assigning him to a unit near Budapest, Hungary, but when he reached Vienna in mid-April, the local Waffen-SS commander told him that Budapest had already fallen to the advancing Russians. He was ordered to instead present himself for duty at the SS-Führungshauptamt, the operational headquarters of the SS, which had moved from Berlin to Bad Tölz, Bavaria, just thirty-four miles northwest of Itter. But again enemy action forced a change in plan. The train[27] Schrader boarded in Vienna on April 24 was attacked by Royal Air Force fighter-bombers near the city of Melk, Austria, destroying the engine and forcing all the passengers to seek shelter in the nearby woods. The British aircraft returned repeatedly to strafe the train's occupants in what Schrader called a "rabbit hunt"; when the attackers eventually departed, a replacement locomotive appeared, several undamaged rail cars were attached, and Schrader's trip west continued.

That journey ultimately took the train to the major railway junction at Wörgl, and Schrader, in no hurry to get to Bad Tölz and hoping for a chance to see his family at Itter, took the opportunity to go in search of an officer he thought might be able to change his orders. That man was none other than Lieutenant Colonel Giehl, commander of both the mountain troops' NCO school and the newly constituted battle group that bore his name, with whom Schrader had become acquainted during his convalescence in Wörgl. The Waffen-SS officer was in luck; Giehl told him it was no longer possible to get to Bad Tölz, because American forces had already taken Munich and were moving rapidly south. Instead, on April 28 Giehl added Schrader to the battle group staff as a supply and logistics officer.

While pleased to again be stationed close to his family, Schrader had no intention of participating in Germany's obviously terminal war effort. For several days after joining Giehl's staff the twenty-nine-year-old Waffen-SS officer carefully sounded out the battle group's other staffers on their feelings about continuing the fight. It must have been a very delicate investigation indeed, for the wrong word to the wrong person could well have put Schrader in front of a firing squad. Moreover, the officers Schrader cautiously approached—all of whom were Wehrmacht—would certainly have had their own serious misgivings about sharing their true beliefs with a highly decorated member of the Waffen-SS, the same organization whose troops were even then hauling "defeatists" out of their homes and shooting them or hanging them from lampposts simply for displaying white flags.

Perhaps it was a genuine desire to end the war without further bloodshed and destruction, or possibly it was a less honorable (though no less understandable) wish to simply survive the conflict: for whatever reason, Schrader and several of his Wehrmacht colleagues on the battle group staff overcame their mutual suspicion and decided to trust one another. Then, having revealed themselves to be in favor of immediate peace instead of continued war, the officers went to Giehl and convinced him that further combat was pointless. On May 2 the battle-group commander ordered his troops to stop fighting and surrender to the advancing Americans as the opportunity arose; he also told his staff officers to make their way home as best they could. Knowing that roving bands of Waffen-SS troops and Gestapo men were summarily executing as deserters any soldiers caught on the road without orders officially releasing them from duty, Schrader asked Giehl for a signed discharge statement. Written hurriedly on a sheet of scrap paper, the document read:

CONFIRMATION

SS Captain Schrader from the Reserves reported for duty on April 28, 1945, to serve his country. As he is of no use in battle due to his injury, he was released from my staff to return to his hometown, Itter.

In lack of an official seal, signed

Giehl,
Lieutenant colonel and commander[28]

While the document was something less than a full discharge—to protect himself should Schrader be arrested, Giehl wrote that he'd "released"
the Waffen-SS officer from duty because of his injuries rather than discharg-
ing him from the military altogether—it was well phrased. And it worked:
though stopped several times between Wörgl and Itter by Waffen-SS troops
and Gestapo men manning hastily erected roadblocks, Schrader was not
detained. He made it safely home and put away his uniform, assuming his
war was over.

———————

THOUGH EDUARD WEITER'S suicide in the early hours of May 2 was apparently the trigger for "Wastl" Wimmer's ultimate departure from Schloss Itter, the castle's commandant was also unnerved by an event that occurred
the following day. Zvonko Čučković, whom Wimmer had assumed he'd
browbeaten and bullied into cringing obedience, had disappeared without
a trace. The SS-TV officer was convinced—rightly, as it happened—that
the Croat handyman had left the castle and gone in search of Allied troops
he intended to guide back in order to rescue the French prisoners.

Čučković's flight on May 3 was the result of rare agreement between
Paul Reynaud and Édouard Daladier. The news pouring from the clandestine radio hidden in Reynaud's room clearly indicated that American forces
were advancing into Tyrol, with Innsbruck as their initial objective. Knowing that the breakdown of German military discipline in the area would
only increase the vulnerability of themselves and their fellow honor prisoners, the two decided that someone should leave the castle and go in
search of the closest Allied unit. Čučković seemed the ideal choice, in that
the Croat often left the castle to do errands for Wimmer. Indeed, for several
days Zvonko had been biking back and forth the two miles between Schloss
Itter and the farmhouse in Mühltal[29] in which the Wimmers were apparently intending to hide out, working to install electric lights. When the elderly Frenchmen approached Čučković with their plan, he readily agreed.
Christiane Mabire wrote a letter in English explaining the prisoners' plight,
which Čučković was to present to the first Americans he encountered. All
that remained was to find a plausible reason for the Croat handyman to
leave the castle.

Ironically, Wimmer himself provided the reason. Just before noon on May 3 Čučković was in the schlosshof's garage when the commandant walked in and asked him if he had enough parts to finish installing the electric bedside lamps in the farmhouse.

"Sir," Čučković replied, "I have enough material."

"Good, you will accompany Sergeant Euba on foot this afternoon and ensure that there is electricity in those two lamps."

Understandably concerned that the presence of one of the castle's guards would prevent his escape, Čučković responded that he could accomplish his task more quickly if he were allowed to bike to Mühltal by himself. After peering intently at the Croat for a few moments, Wimmer turned and walked off. Not knowing whether he'd somehow given himself away, Čučković remained rooted to the spot, trying to decide what to do next. Before he reached a decision, Wimmer returned with a bicycle.

"I've put your tools in the basket," the commandant said. "Let's go."

Čučković pushed the bike to the front gate, which Wimmer unlocked and pulled open. Glancing at his watch, the Croat noted that it was one thirty, just as Wimmer said, "Be quick about it."

"I will be, Captain," Čučković replied and started pedaling up the schlossweg, the short access road, toward Itter village. As he passed the small St. Joseph's Church, the Catholic handyman muttered a quick prayer: "Dear Lord, please help me get to the Americans today."[30]

Čučković headed northeast out of the village and covered the distance to Mühltal in less than twenty-five minutes—and kept right on going. He intended to make first for Wörgl and then turn southwest on the road along the south bank of the Inn River. He calculated that he could travel the thirty-five miles to Innsbruck in less than three hours, passing through Kundl, Jenbach, Schwaz, and Hall. What he hadn't counted on was the presence along his route of so many armed German soldiers. The main road between Wörgl and Mühltal was busy with troop trucks and kübelwagens carrying men of Battle Group Forster east to take up blocking positions near Söll, and when Čučković reached Wörgl, he noted scores of Waffen-SS troops going door to door, apparently searching for deserters. The Croat managed to cycle through the town without being stopped, but, as he turned onto the road leading to Kundl, some four miles on, a commanding voice shouted "Halt!"

Čučković stopped instantly and looked around. A squad of men of the Grossdeutschland division had emplaced four MG-42 machine guns to cover the road junction, and one of the soldiers was walking forward, his machine pistol pointed straight at the handyman. Mindful that the letter in his pocket—written in English and asking American forces to rush to Schloss Itter—could condemn him to a quick death if discovered by the Wehrmacht troops, Čučković put on his most ingratiating smile and bowed his head slightly as the soldier approached.

"Who are you, and where are going?" the man barked.

"Sir, I am on the way to Kundl,"Čučković replied carefully.

"What do you want there?"

"Sir, Captain Wimmer at Schloss Itter ordered me to install some electric lights," the Croat said. "He told me it was very important that I do the work and return quickly."

The mention of Wimmer's name and rank seemed to ease the soldier's suspicion, and, after a quick look at the tools in the bicycle's basket, he waved his hand dismissively and grunted, "On your way, then."

Čučković remounted and pedaled on. Just west of Kundl he was forced to the side of the road as two Tiger tanks rumbled by, headed east toward Wörgl. The men in the commander's hatches were wearing black Waffen-SS tunics, and daubed on the turret sides in white paint were the slogans "Loyal to the Führer!" and "People to Their Weapons!" The tankers stared at Čučković but didn't stop, and, as soon as they passed, the Croat resumed his journey west. He'd gone only a few miles when a Waffen-SS trooper guarding a small bridge near Jenbach halted him. Čučković gave him a variation of the story he'd earlier told the Grossdeutschland soldiers, this time saying Wimmer had ordered him to Schwaz to do some unspecified electrical work. The tale was apparently just as convincing, for the SS man allowed him to pass. A few hundred meters along the road the Croat stopped to rest, and he noticed a military truck coming toward him from the west. The vehicle roared past and then stopped briefly to pick up the soldier on the bridge. Seconds after the truck moved on, a huge explosion demolished the span. The unexpected detonation startled Čučković, who jumped back on his bike and set off quickly down the road, exhorting himself, "Forward, Zvonko, you're in no man's land!"

Zvonko was indeed between the lines and passed through Schwaz and Hall without seeing anyone; the only movement in either town was the fluttering of white and red-white-red (Austrian) flags from upper-floor windows. Čučković could hear occasional gunshots in the distance and was shocked by the sight of a dead civilian lying in the road as he reached the outskirts of Innsbruck. Pedaling toward the center of the city, he rounded a corner and was suddenly confronted by more tanks. Skidding to a halt he fully expected to be riddled by gunfire but then realized that the vehicles all bore large white stars. Čučković's long, lonely ride was over: he'd found the U.S. Army.

The Croat had literally run into the lead elements of Major General Anthony C. McAuliffe's 103rd Infantry Division. The famed paratrooper[31] and his men were completing their largely unopposed capture of Innsbruck, and the roadblock Čučković encountered marked the most easterly edge of the American line. A soldier wearing a brassard and with "MP" lettered in white on his helmet walked up to the Croat and spoke to him. Gesturing to indicate that he spoke no English, Čučković handed the man the letter written by Christiane Mabire. The soldier scanned it quickly and then motioned the Croat to follow him.

The MP led Čučković to Innsbruck's town hall, which had been turned into the division's makeshift headquarters. The building was crowded, and the MP called out to a civilian wearing a colored armband. The two spoke for a moment; then the civilian turned and, in German, asked Čučković where he was from.

"Yugoslavia," the Croat replied.

The civilian's face lit up as he responded in Serbo-Croatian: "Brother, why didn't you say so earlier? I am a Yugoslav myself, but born in America!"

Thrilled at the chance to speak his native tongue, Čučković poured out the story of his ride from Schloss Itter, adding that they needed to rescue the French VIPs as soon as possible.

"Brother, please listen to me," the civilian[32] said. "We are the first group to arrive here; we just got here an hour ago. We are not allowed to leave Innsbruck until our commanders arrive. They won't get here until midnight, so it is best if you get some rest because you look like you are very tired. Come back tomorrow at seven AM, and we will find a solution."

Though not pleased at the delay, Čučković saw the wisdom of getting some sleep. He'd ridden for nearly seven hours and was bone tired, and he didn't protest when his newfound friend led him to a nearby hotel that had been commandeered for use as a barracks. The Croat was given food, water, and cigarettes, then led to a private room. Within minutes of walking in the door he was sprawled across the bed, dead to the world.

———

EVEN AS ČUČKOVIĆ WAS ENJOYING his well-earned sleep, events at Schloss Itter were continuing to unfold. Sebastian Wimmer's sudden, predawn departure had convinced the castle's SS-TV guards that it was also time for them to leave, and, by daybreak on May 4, the French notables and number prisoners had the schloss all to themselves. At the urging of generals Maxime Weygand and Maurice Gamelin, the now-free VIPs broke into the unguarded weapons room and equipped themselves with a variety of pistols, rifles, and submachine guns.

Suddenly liberated and newly armed, two of the Frenchmen decided—somewhat inexplicably, given their still-precarious situation—that their first free act would be to stroll the 150 yards into Itter village. Paul Reynaud and Michel Clemenceau walked calmly through the castle's now unmanned front gate, past the small inn at the foot of the access road and, further on, the building housing the offices of St. Joseph's Church, before reaching the small square in front of the church itself. While the two men saw Austrian and white flags flying from many windows, they were surprised and alarmed to see German troops and vehicles on the roads to the northeast of the village. Though a quick glance through the binoculars he'd "liberated" from the arms room showed Reynaud that many of the retreating soldiers were just "boys in uniform, who seemed to be hardly more than 10 years old,"[33] the sight of so many troops—and the weapons they carried—convinced the Frenchman that while he and his fellow ex-prisoners might be free, they were certainly not yet safe.

Reynaud and Clemenceau hurried back to Schloss Itter and called the French VIPs together to tell them what they'd seen. Putting their personal and political differences aside for the moment, they all agreed that the continuing presence of German military units in the area meant that no one in the castle would be truly safe until Allied troops arrived in strength. Given that Zvonko Čučković had not been heard from since his departure the day before, and that his perilous ride toward Innsbruck had so far not

resulted in the appearance of an Allied rescue force, the gathered VIPs de-
bated their next move. The discussion was surprisingly brief and unusually
free of acrimony, and the former prisoners unanimously agreed on three
courses of action.

First, they would fashion a huge French tricolor banner from whatever
materials they could find and then suspend it from the top windows of the
keep to prevent attacks on the castle by Allied aircraft and let advancing
friendly forces know of the VIPs' presence. Second, they would summon
Kurt-Siegfried Schrader from the village and formally ask him to take responsibility for their safety—not because Sebastian Wimmer had indicated
that the decorated Waffen-SS man was his choice to be the VIPs' guardian,
but because the French themselves had come to know and trust Schrader
over the course of his many visits to the castle. And third, realizing that it
was more than likely that Čučković had been captured or killed trying to
reach Innsbruck, they decided to send another bicycle-borne emissary out
to contact the nearest American unit. As they were debating who that mes-
senger should be, Andreas Krobot stepped forward. He and several other
number prisoners had been listening to the discussion from the sidelines,
and he calmly explained that it would make no sense for one of the VIPs
to attempt the trip, only to be caught and executed on the spot. Far better
for him, a mere cook, to undertake the potentially hazardous ride. Though
Jean Borotra insisted that he should be the one to make the attempt, the
logic of Krobot's argument carried the day.

The first task, summoning Schrader to the castle, was carried out by
Léon Jouhaux and Augusta Bruchlen, at their insistence. The labor leader
and his German-speaking companion had spent perhaps the most time
with the Waffen-SS man and his family during their visits to Schloss Itter,
and Jouhaux apparently felt that he and Bruchlen would be able to relieve
any last-minute qualms Schrader might have about throwing in his lot
with the French. Despite his still-frail health, Jouhaux insisted the walk
into the village would do him good. The couple covered the short distance
at a steady pace, hand in hand and with Jouhaux carrying an MP-40 submachine gun slung over his shoulder. Schrader, dressed in civilian clothes,
answered their knock immediately and agreed to accompany them back
to Schloss Itter. When the trio returned to the castle at about one PM, they
found most of the French VIPs gathered in the front courtyard waiting for
them. Clemenceau, speaking in German, formally asked Schrader to accept

responsibility for ensuring the safety of the former prisoners until American troops arrived. Though the Waffen-SS officer knew beyond doubt that his presence would do nothing to prevent German troops from taking the castle if they decided to do so, he believed that in the case of an attack he might be able to negotiate some sort of deal that would save the VIPs' lives. Schrader thus accepted "command" of Schloss Itter, with the proviso that his wife and daughters be allowed to join him within its walls.[34]

At the same time Jouhaux and Bruchlen set out to summon Schrader, Krobot had embarked on his own journey. Provided with an English-language plea for help—again penned by Christiane Mabire—and riding a bicycle that had formerly belonged to one of the castle's now-vanished guards, the Czech had set out for Wörgl. The French VIPs felt the town must surely have already been captured by the Americans; Krobot wasn't so sure, and his reservations were quickly borne out. Cycling into Wörgl along the same route Čučković had traveled the day before, and, barely thirty minutes after leaving Schloss Itter, the Czech saw Waffen-SS troops in the streets. The soldiers were firing at any window from which a white or Austrian flag fluttered. Turning down a narrow side street, Krobot encountered a man in civilian clothes standing in a doorway, peering carefully in the opposite direction as though on lookout duty. Taking a huge chance, the Czech asked the man for help. After looking searchingly into Krobot's eyes, the man pulled the end of a small red-and-white Austrian flag from his pocket and smiled.[35]

Minutes later, the Czech cook was talking to Sepp Gangl.

ANDREAS KROBOT'S SUDDEN appearance in Wörgl with the letter from the French VIPs put Gangl in something of a predicament.

The Wehrmacht major had intended for several days to mount a Schloss Itter rescue operation, of course, but had hesitated because he hadn't wanted to fight a pitched battle against Sebastian Wimmer and his guard force. While Krobot's news that the commandant and his minions had fled was welcome, Gangl knew that, even if he and his dozen or so men were able to reach the castle without running into Waffen-SS units, they would almost certainly not be able to hold it against a determined attack by troops wielding machine guns and shoulder-launched panzerfaust antitank rockets.

And if those troops were backed by artillery or armor, defending Schloss Itter and its VIPs would be virtually suicidal.

Moreover, as the new head of the Wörgl resistance, Gangl had to worry about protecting the town—and his troops—from the continuing depredations of the Waffen-SS soldiers still active in the area. The threat was demonstrated all too clearly shortly after Krobot's arrival. As Second Lieutenant Blechschmidt[36]—one of Gangl's trusted compatriots—was meeting with Alois Mayr about the need to protect Wörgl's warehoused food supplies from marauding bands of deserters and the thousands of refugees choking the roads of north Tyrol, firing broke out inside the Neue Post Inn. A platoon of Waffen-SS troops had somehow discovered the resistance group's arsenal in the building's basement; though the resisters guarding the structure had fled, an SS officer wildly fired his MP-40 in the building's main room and threatened to kill Frau Lenk, the proprietor, and several other women who had been drinking tea in the guesthouse dining room. As the Waffen-SS troops carted off the weapons they'd discovered, Blechschmidt could do little more than watch from a safe distance and send one of Mayr's men to let Gangl know what was happening.

The news convinced the Wehrmacht major that the only way he'd be able to ensure the safety of both the townspeople and the VIPs at Schloss Itter would be to speed the arrival of American forces. And since the Americans might not pay sufficient attention to a note-bearing civilian on a bicycle, the best way to accomplish the task, Gangl decided, was to go in search of them himself. He was, in effect, the German military commander of Wörgl, and, as such, he could officially surrender to the Americans all remaining Wehrmacht troops in the town.

Having made his decision, Gangl huddled with his deputy, Captain Dietrich, and Mayr's deputy, Rupert Hagleitner. Dietrich would be in command until he returned, Gangl said, assisted by First Lieutenant Höckel and second lieutenants Blechschmidt and Wegscheider. Knowing that American units had reached the outskirts of Kufstein the previous evening, the men agreed that Gangl should head there instead of attempting the longer and potentially more dangerous drive west toward Innsbruck. He would make the roughly seven-mile trip in a kübelwagen, accompanied only by his enlisted driver, Corporal Keblitsch. They would take a white flag with them, but, given the number of Waffen-SS troops still in the area, they would not raise the banner until they were relatively close to the American lines.

With plans made and assignments given, just before three o'clock Gangl shoved the letter Krobot had brought from the castle into the pocket of his tunic, grabbed his MP-40, and strode to his vehicle. As Keblitsch started the kübelwagen moving, Gangl turned in his seat to shout some last-minute instruction to Dietrich, who was standing with Höckel, Blechschmidt, and Wegscheider. The sentence died in the Wehrmacht major's throat when he realized that all four men were standing at attention, saluting him.

While we don't know how Gangl and Keblitsch felt about their chances of actually making it to the American front line, we can safely assume that both men well understood the extreme risk they were taking. The seven miles separating Wörgl from the leading U.S. units were crawling with bands of Waffen-SS and Wehrmacht troops still loyal to the now-dead führer, and they had thrown up hastily constructed roadblocks at several points on the main Wörgl-Kufstein road. Though Gangl would have tried to bluff his way through on the strength of his rank and the combat decorations adorning his tunic, or possibly by producing Battle Group Forster documents and declaring he was on his way to rally the defense against the oncoming Americans, the discovery of the letter in his pocket or the white flag concealed somewhere in the vehicle would have been enough to get him and Keblitsch executed on the spot. Nor were die-hard German troops the only danger: There were also groups of Austrian resistance fighters in the area who might well open fire on the kübelwagen without bothering to determine if the men it carried were friend or foe. And, of course, there were all the other common World War II perils: random mortar or artillery barrages, attack by enemy aircraft, and land mines laid on unpaved side roads.

Whether Gangl and Keblitsch stuck to the main road and bluffed their way through roadblocks or avoided them by going cross-country on forest tracks is unclear. All we know is that despite the myriad potential dangers of their journey, the two men made it to the outskirts of Kufstein unscathed. But then they faced a hazard of a different kind. They would be driving into a city newly occupied by American troops—soldiers wary of ambush, of snipers, and of all the other hazards common to warfare in built-up areas. And Gangl was likely aware of recent events that made their approach to the American lines even more risky, despite the large white flag now flying from the kübelwagen's antenna: For several days the Allied radio stations to which Gangl's resistance colleagues listened had been reporting the unspeakable horrors discovered by the American units that liberated Dachau and other concentration camps near Munich. As a seasoned combat veteran who had undoubtedly seen his share of horror on the Russian Front, Gangl would have realized that if the GIs moving into Kufstein had been among those who had witnessed the gruesome conditions inside the camps, they might not be in any mood to accept the surrender of two Germans, white flag or not.[37]

Some forty-five minutes after leaving Wörgl, Gangl and Keblitsch rolled into the southern end of Kufstein and found . . . no one. The streets were deserted, and white bedsheets and red-white-red Austrian flags hung from shuttered windows. Driving slowly toward the center of town with their own white flag flying high, the two men rounded a corner and found themselves barely thirty feet from four American M4 Sherman tanks, two parked on either side of the street. Keblitsch stopped the kübelwagen immediately, and both men slowly and carefully raised their hands in the air. GIs wearing padded tanker helmets appeared from behind the armored vehicles and moved forward, their M3 submachine guns pointed at the Germans. Dropping to their knees in response to yelled commands from the advancing Americans, Gangl and Keblitsch—their hands still in the air—must have wondered if they were about to be gunned down in the street. Instead, both men were quickly frisked, told to stand, and with their hands still in the air hustled toward the rear of the nearest Sherman. Waiting there was a squat, powerfully built man wearing a wrinkled khaki uniform and a .45-caliber automatic pistol in a shoulder holster, his teeth clenching a well-chewed but unlit cigar.

Assuming the man to be in charge, Gangl introduced himself in passable English, said he wished to surrender the German garrison in Wörgl, and added that he had information about important French prisoners. After motioning toward his tunic pocket and getting a nod from the officer in return, Gangl carefully retrieved Christiane Mabire's letter and proffered it to the American. The man unceremoniously ripped the envelope open and quickly scanned the letter, then hoisted himself aboard the Sherman, and dropped into the turret. Minutes later he reappeared and climbed onto the tank's rear engine deck, a wide smile on his face.

Looking down at the German major, the American said his name was Lee and that it looked like they were all going on a rescue mission.[38]

CHAPTER 6

TANKERS ON THE MARCH

THAT JACK LEE WAS SMILING at the thought of roaring off behind German lines on what might well have been the last day of World War II in Europe gives a fair insight into the then twenty-seven-year-old tanker's personality. The five-foot-ten, 190-pound former high school and college football star from New York was by all accounts a rough-talking, hard-drinking, and hard-charging bull of a man who'd found his niche in war. And, as with many men—in many wars—to whom that description has applied, Lee's early life gave clear indications of the warrior he would eventually become.

———————

JOHN CAREY LEE JR. WAS BORN in Nebraska on March 12, 1918, the first of four children of Dr. John C. Lee Sr. and Mary Agnes (Fleming) Lee. Both parents were natives of rural New York and had moved to Nebraska a year before Jack's birth, apparently so the elder Lee could accept his first position after graduating from medical school. The young couple returned to New York sometime in the mid-1920s and settled in Norwich, a small town in the south-central part of the state, where Dr. Lee established what soon became a thriving private practice. Jack and his three younger siblings— brothers William and David and sister Mary—grew up in solidly upper-middle-class comfort. The family was Roman Catholic, though it seems

Jack didn't let the church's precepts unduly cramp his style. He grew up adventurous and independent, with a quick grin and a devil-may-care attitude that made him increasingly popular with girls but occasionally got him in minor trouble both at home and at school.

Bright and inquisitive, Jack was a better-than-average student who also excelled in athletics. Football became his game of choice, and he was a star player during his four years at Norwich High School. He took those gridiron skills with him when he entered Vermont's Norwich University in 1938, earning letters in the sport each of the four years he spent there. Far more important, however, was the new skill the brash young man from New York mastered at Norwich: he became a cavalryman.

Founded by Captain Alden Partridge[1] in 1819 as the American Literary, Scientific and Military Academy, by the time of Lee's arrival Norwich had evolved into one of the nation's premier private military colleges, combining a traditional four-year civilian education in such fields as engineering and the social sciences with training in military subjects that prepared graduates for service as reserve officers.[2] Among the martial skills to which the student-cadets were exposed were those of traditional cavalry: horsemanship, saber drill, and mounted tactics. As the soldiers-to-be wheeled and galloped and surged across the training fields, many of them discovered within themselves an innate affinity for the spirit of cavalry: a delight in the lightning advance, the rapid encirclement, and the chance to ruthlessly exploit any weakness in an enemy's defenses. It comes as no great revelation that Jack Lee, who so obviously loved the team spirit, intricate maneuvering, and broken-field running of football, took to cavalry training with almost obsessive enthusiasm. Nor is it a surprise that his enthusiasm was more than matched by his mastery of every facet of the training—a mastery rooted in the same athleticism, intelligence, competitiveness, and self-confidence that stood him in such good stead on the football field. Indeed, the cavalry so well suited Lee's temperament and capabilities—and, we can safely assume, ideally complemented what many who knew him called his "swashbuckling" personality—that during his last year at Norwich he listed "Cavalry" as the army branch to which he wanted to be assigned following his postgraduation commissioning.[3] Lee understood, of course, that the cavalry in which he would actually serve would be mechanized rather than hoofed, but he obviously felt that a tank was a perfectly acceptable substitution for a horse.[4]

The United States' December 1941 entry into World War II ensured that Jack Lee and his fellow Norwich graduates were called to active duty shortly after their May 11, 1942, graduation. To his immense delight, the newly commissioned Second Lieutenant Lee received orders directing him to report to the Armored Force School at Fort Knox, Kentucky, to attend the basic armor officer course. He lingered in New York state only long enough to marry a woman named Virginia[5] and then headed south by train. During the ninety-day program Lee soaked up the fundamentals of tank gunnery, armor tactics, communications, and vehicle maintenance, and during the concluding three-day field exercise he demonstrated what one of his instructors called "a natural talent" for armored warfare.

Upon completion of the Fort Knox course, Lee received orders assigning him to the 12th Armored Division, which was then forming at Camp Campbell, Kentucky, a newly established installation[6] straddling the Kentucky-Tennessee border. The 12th AD was initially constituted as a heavy armored division consisting of six tank battalions, three armored-infantry battalions, three armored-artillery battalions, and supporting engineer, reconnaissance, medical, and supply units. However, the initial combat experience of U.S. armored units in North Africa and Sicily showed the heavy armored division structure to be unwieldy and overly complex, and in November 1943 the 12th began reorganizing on the light armored division model then being adopted army-wide. This structure was built around three combat commands—A, B, and R (reserve), each of which had a tank battalion, an armored-infantry battalion, and an armored-artillery battalion, plus support units. The 12th AD undertook this metamorphosis even as it was moving to a new post: Camp Barkley, near Abilene, Texas.[7] By the time the reorganization was completed, Lee—now a first lieutenant—was the executive officer (second in command) and leader of the five-tank 1st Platoon in Captain Donald Cowan's Company B, 23rd Tank Battalion.

Lee's company was equipped with early models of the M4 Sherman medium tank, a robust vehicle armed with a single turret-mounted 75mm cannon, two .30-caliber machine guns (one in the lower hull and the other mounted coaxially[8] with the main gun), and one .50-caliber machine gun (on a swivel mount atop the turret for air defense). Each tank was crewed by five men—the driver and assistant driver/machine gunner in the lower hull, and the gunner, loader, and vehicle commander in the turret. Though the Sherman was inferior in both armor and armament to the German tanks it was meant to engage—a fact Lee and his comrades wouldn't become aware of until they entered combat—it was mechanically reliable and surprisingly nimble for a vehicle with an average combat weight of some thirty-five tons.

Given Jack Lee's temperament, it comes as no surprise that during the 12th AD's training in both Kentucky and Texas he personally demonstrated the "mental alertness and aggressiveness, and ability to think, act and quickly take advantage of tactical opportunities"[9] that the army considered to be the essential qualities of an armored corps officer. Lee worked doggedly to mold his platoon into an aggressive, determined, and cohesive group. Indeed, he and his twenty-five men soon developed a reputation as Company B's rough-and-tumble, "Hell for Leather" platoon,[10] always eager to push themselves to the limit during field maneuvers—and equally ready to raise a little hell in Abilene's bars and clubs when they got the chance. Lee himself was no slouch when it came to having fun; he pushed himself and his men hard during the workday, but off duty he was known as a man who thoroughly enjoyed a drink and a laugh. His frequent companion on his forays into Abilene was First Lt. Harry Basse, Company B's motor officer—the man responsible for managing the maintenance program for the company's tracked and wheeled vehicles. Though the thirty-three-year-old from Pomona, California, was in many ways Lee's exact opposite—tall, lanky, soft-spoken, and contemplative[11]—the two men formed a lifelong friendship that was initially based on mutual respect for each other's military skills and on a shared desire to put those skills to work killing Germans.

In July 1944 Lee, Basse, and the roughly 10,750 other men of the 12th AD learned that they would soon have the chance to put all their training to good use: The division was alerted for overseas movement. Leaving their tanks and other vehicles behind in Texas, in August the troops boarded trains for the slow trip to Camp Shanks, New York, twenty miles north of Manhattan. Arriving in groups between September 8 and 13, the GIs underwent several days of predeployment processing—physical exams, inoculations, equipment issue, and the sobering act of updating wills and GI life-insurance forms—and on September 18 and 19 were back on the rails, this time for the short ride to the port of embarkation at the Brooklyn Navy Yard. The men of the division were allocated among several vessels, with the 23rd TB embarked on *Empress of Australia*, a twenty-five-year-old Canadian Pacific Steamships passenger liner converted for troopship duty.[12] After eleven days at sea—largely spent sleeping, playing seemingly endless games of poker, and attempting to stave off seasickness—the men of the 23rd TB gratefully disembarked at the southern English port of Southampton. They and the rest of the division were then moved north by train and bus to Tidworth Barracks, a vast staging area on Salisbury Plain, where they spent the remainder of September and the first weeks of November gearing up for war.[13]

The major part of that task consisted of drawing new tanks, trucks, half-tracks, and "peeps"—the latter being the name by which tankers referred to the Willys-built four-wheel-drive vehicle everyone else in the U.S. Army called a "jeep." Lee and his men were happy to see that the Shermans being issued to the 23rd TB were examples of the upgraded M4A3 variant powered by liquid-cooled Ford GAA V-8 engines, which were more powerful and reliable than the Continental-built radials that had propelled the tanks they'd trained on in Texas. Lee and his men named their new Sherman *Besotten Jenny*[14] and over the following weeks ensured that both they and the vehicle were as prepared as possible for the battles to come.

Transported from England to France aboard U.S. Navy LSTs[15] in November 1944, the 12th Armored Division—now commanded by Major General Roderick R. Allen and assigned to Lieutenant General Alexander M. Patch's U.S. Seventh Army—underwent its baptism of fire in early December in a series of sharp fights in France's Alsace-Lorraine region. These initial battles in and around the German-occupied forts of the Maginot Line were sobering for the men of the 12th AD, and especially so for Lee and his colleagues in the 23rd TB. The battalion fared reasonably well in its first combat action, on December 9, when it supported the 17th Armored Infantry Battalion's attack on a line of enemy-held buildings called the Bining Barracks, but that night Company B commander Captain Donald Cowen was killed when the peep in which he and Company C's Captain James P. Fortenberry were riding hit a mine. Cowan's death elevated Jack Lee to command of Company B, and on December 11 battalion commander Lieutenant Colonel Montgomery C. Meigs tasked Lee and his men to spearhead the unit's support for an infantry assault on several pillboxes blocking the line of advance. The Shermans were engaged by well-sited German anti-tank guns, and in the ensuing melee two of Lee's platoon leaders were killed and the third seriously wounded.[16] Battalion commander Meigs was also killed.[17]

The war didn't get any easier for Jack Lee and Company B in the months following their combat debut. Hardly had the 23rd TB made good its initial losses in men and equipment when in mid-January 1945 it and the rest of the 12th AD were engulfed in a battle that came to be known as Bloody Herrlisheim: the attempt to route German forces that had crossed the Rhine into Alsace in an attempt to recapture Strasbourg. Fought in winter snows over poor terrain against determined enemy forces that included the crack 10th SS-Panzer-Grenadier Division, the battle resulted in the virtual destruction of the 12th AD's 43rd Tank and 17th Armored Infantry battalions, and by the time the division was relieved on January 20, seventy-two men of the 23rd TB had been killed and Lee's Company B had lost half its Shermans.[18]

The only positive outcomes of the 12th AD's mauling at Herrlisheim were, first, that the 23rd TB's destroyed tanks were replaced by the M4A3 (76)W variant—referred to as the "Easy 8"[19]—fitted with 76mm guns that were said to be more effective against German tanks than the 75mm. And though Lee didn't think much about it at the time, the vehicles had another feature that would later prove extremely important: a "wet" ammunition-stowage system that was intended to prevent the Sherman's 76mm rounds from detonating if the tank's hull was breeched by enemy fire.[20] And, second, the men who survived Herrlisheim came out of the battle as seasoned veterans. As the war rolled on, they—and the replacements with whom they shared their expertise—demonstrated their prowess as the Seventh Army swept across southern Germany and, eventually, into Austria.

Along the way, Jack Lee sharpened his skills as a combat leader and was awarded the Bronze Star for his "superior leadership ability . . . cool and aggressive handling of the platoon . . . and his courage and his ability to meet any situation that confronted him."[21] By the time the 23rd TB— which along with the 17th Armored Infantry and 495th Armored Field Artillery battalions constituted the 12th AD's Combat Command R (CCR)—crossed the Austrian frontier late on the evening of May 3, 1945, the unit was arguably among the most experienced and successful tank battalions in the U.S. Army and Lee one of its ablest officers.

And it was because 23rd TB commander Lieutenant Colonel Kelso G. Clow considered Lee to be one of the best tank officers in the 12th AD that Lee spearheaded the division's move into Austria. Weeks earlier Clow had

Sited atop a hill that commands the entrance to Austria's Brixental Valley, Schloss Itter is first mentioned in the historical record in 1241. Damaged, rebuilt, and enlarged over the centuries, before its 1941 conversion into a VIP prison it had served successively as a military fortress, a private home, and a boutique hotel. *(Author's collection)*

German police march into Tyrol following Germany's March 12, 1938, annexation of Austria. The Anschluss led directly to Schloss Itter's transformation from fairytale castle and hotel into something decidedly more sinister. *(National Archives)*

The network of "special prisons" maintained by the Nazis grew from Adolf Hitler's belief that important prisoners might prove of value in negotiations with the Allies. *Ehrenhäftlinge*—honor prisoners—were housed in reasonably good conditions in castles, hotels, and similar facilities throughout the Reich, though their continued good health relied solely on the führer's whim. *(National Archives)*

Though Hitler fully supported the work of the Schloss Itter–based "Alliance for Combating the Dangers of Tobacco," Reichsführer der SS Heinrich Himmler believed the Austrian castle was ideal for more nefarious purposes. On November 23, 1942, he got Hitler to sign an order to begin the process of acquiring the castle outright for "special SS use," and Schloss Itter was officially requisitioned by the SS in February 1943. *(National Archives)*

SS Major General Theodor Eicke, the director of the Nazis' concentration camp system and originator of the "inflexible harshness" doctrine applied to KZ prisoners, directed that Sebastian Wimmer and the commanders of other honor prisoners' facilities treat their prisoners well but stand ready to execute the VIPs at a moment's notice, without compunction and without remorse. *(National Archives)*

Plans for Schloss Itter's conversion from an anti-smoking administrative center into a high-security honor prisoner facility were apparently overseen by no less a personage than Albert Speer, Hitler's minister of armaments and war production. *(National Archives)*

By the time he arrived at Schloss Itter, General Maurice Gamelin had spent more than fifty of his seventy-one years as an officer in his nation's army. His career was marred, however, when his poor response to Germany's May 1940 invasion of France led Prime Minster Paul Reynaud to replace him as supreme military commander with arch-rival General Maxime Weygand. *(National Archives)*

Stocky, barrel-chested, and pugnacious, sixty-one-year-old Édouard Daladier was the youngest of the three VIPs whose arrival at Schloss Itter on May 2, 1943, marked the castle's official opening as a prison. *(National Archives)*

Seen here during a prewar visit to the United States, labor leader Léon Jouhaux and his colleague and longtime companion Augusta Bruchlen both ended up imprisoned in Schloss Itter; Bruchlen's incarceration in the Tyrolean fortress was voluntary, Jouhaux's was not. *(National Archives)*

Sent to Schloss Itter in May 1943, Paul Reynaud was horrified to discover that his arch political rival Édouard Daladier had preceded him but was relieved to find conditions at the castle far better than those he'd experienced at Sachsenhausen concentration camp. *(National Archives)*

Though Jean Borotra—the famed "Bounding Basque"—willingly joined Marshal Philippe Pétain's collaborationist Vichy government following France's capitulation, the tennis star's less-than-discrete disdain for the Nazis led to his dismissal and ultimate arrest. Borotra encountered Paul Reynaud at Sachsenhausen, and the two remained friends at Schloss Itter despite their differing politics. *(National Archives)*

Upon his December 1943 arrival at Schloss Itter, General Maxime Weygand encountered immediate vituperation from Paul Reynaud and only less obvious hostility from Maurice Gamelin; the former considered Weygand a traitor to France, and the latter burned with professional embarrassment. *(National Archives)*

Though Michel Clemenceau had been a longtime admirer of Pétain, he became an outspoken critic of what he saw as the aged general's willingness to collaborate with the Germans. Clemenceau's views quickly drew the attention of the Gestapo, and he was arrested in May 1943. His calm self-possession upon arrival at Schloss Itter prompted Reynaud to note that the castle's other VIP prisoners were reassured by Clemenceau's "unshakable confidence." *(National Archives)*

Until his arrest by the Gestapo in 1943, François de La Rocque had been a key member of the Vichy government, a confidant of Pétain, and a man widely viewed as one of France's leading fascists. His arrival at Schloss Itter was thus a surprise to the other VIP prisoners, who would have been further astounded to learn that de La Rocque led a resistance movement that provided valuable information to British intelligence. *(National Archives)*

SS-Lieutenant Colonel Wilhelm Eduard Weiter, the last commandant of Dachau, arrived at Schloss Itter with his retinue on April 30, 1945. His suicide just 48 hours later prompted Sebastian Wimmer and his troops to abandon the castle and its VIP prisoners. *(National Archives)*

During his four years at Vermont's Norwich University, John Carey Lee Jr. was known for both his football skills and his equestrian abilities and is seen here following his May 11, 1942, graduation and commissioning as a second lieutenant of cavalry. *(Photo courtesy Robert D. Lee)*

Upon his graduation from Norwich, Lee received orders to attend the basic armor officer course at Fort
Knox, Kentucky, and lingered in New York only long
enough to marry a woman named Virginia, the first
of his eventual three wives. *(Photo courtesy Robert D. Lee)*

Taken about two months before the battle at Schloss Itter, this image depicts
Company B commander Jack Lee (at right) with, from left, 2nd Lieutenant
John Powell, one of Lee's platoon leaders, and 1st Lieutenant Harry Basse,
Company B's motor officer and Lee's closest friend in the unit. Within weeks
Powell was dead and Lee and Basse had both been lightly wounded. *(Photo
courtesy Robert D. Lee)*

Following the 23rd Tank Battalion's mauling during the January 1945 Battle of Herrl-isheim, Jack Lee's Company B was reequipped with the improved M4A3(76)W version of the Sherman tank. Also referred to as the M4A3E8, the variant was widely known as the "Easy Eight." By the time of the Schloss Itter mission, the second *Besotten Jenny* would have appeared virtually identical to the well-worn 10th Armored Division vehicle shown here. *(U.S. Army photo, courtesy Steven Zaloga)*

A tanker stows main-gun rounds in the "wet" ammunition-stowage racks in the floor of an "Easy Eight." The system was intended to prevent the Sherman's 76mm rounds from detonating if the tank's hull was breeched by enemy fire. It was a feature that would prove extremely important for *Besotten Jenny* during the battle for Schloss Itter. *(U.S. Army photo courtesy Steven Zaloga)*

Black soldiers of Company D, 17th Armored Infantry Battalion, clear German civilians from a recently captured town. Though most secondhand accounts of the Schloss Itter action state that Jack Lee tapped several Company D troops to take part in the rescue mission, the author's research has shown that the four U.S. infantrymen who rode aboard Lee's tank and helped defend the castle were actually drawn from the all-white 2nd Platoon, Company E, 2nd Battalion, 142nd Infantry Regiment. *(U.S. Army photo courtesy Steven Zaloga)*

Soldiers of the crack 17th SS Panzer Grenadier Division "Götz von Berlichingen" take a break from the intense hedgerow fighting that followed the June 1944 Allied landing in Normandy. Less than a year later elements of the Waffen-SS unit would besiege Schloss Itter. *(National Archives)*

A career soldier three times decorated for bravery in combat against his nation's enemies, Wehrmacht Major Josef "Sepp" Gangl willingly chose to put his life in even more direct peril in order to help Jack Lee save a querulous group of French VIPs locked away in a fairytale Austrian castle. *(National Archives)*

For most of his military career the personification of the dedicated Waffen-SS officer, Hauptsturmführer Kurt-Siegfried Schrader nonetheless threw in his lot with Lee, Gangl, and Schloss Itter's French prisoners. *(National Archives courtesy John Moore)*

Maj. John T. Kramers (seen here in a postwar photo), a German-speaking former artilleryman assigned to the 103rd Infantry Division's military-government section, was unaware of Jack Lee's rescue force and launched his own effort to secure the French VIPs at Schloss Itter. *(Photo courtesy John T. Kramers)*

A Seventh Army military policeman chats with (from left), Léon Jouhaux, François de La Rocque, Jean Borotra, and Marcel Granger following their rescue. *(National Archives)*

Major General Anthony C. McAuliffe, commander of the 103rd Infantry Division, poses for a photo at his Innsbruck headquarters with former Schloss Itter honor prisoners (from left) Paul Reynaud, Marie-Renée-Joséphine Weygand, Maurice Gamelin, Édouard Daladier, and Maxime Weygand. *(National Archives)*

Though Jack Lee is smiling in this 1947 photo taken outside Hand's Inn in Norwich, NY, where he found employment after his plans for a profootball career fell through, his life went into a slow but seemingly inexorable downward spiral after World War II. The hero of "The Last Battle" died on Jan. 15, 1973, at the age of 54. *(Photo courtesy James I. Dunne)*

tapped the aggressive young tanker to lead Task Force (TF) Lee, a mixed group of Company B Shermans and half-tracks bearing black GIs of the 17th AIB's Company D.[22] TF Lee was "on point" for both the battalion and CCR, punching ahead of the main force to clear enemy roadblocks, secure key bridges and road junctions, and reconnoiter the towns and villages on the line of advance.

While the task-force mission ideally suited Lee's aggressive and piratical nature, we can safely assume that at least some of the men serving under him were not quite so enthusiastic about being "out front." Hitler's suicide on April 30 and the obvious disintegration of the German armed forces clearly indicated to most GIs that the end of the war in Europe was imminent, and no one wanted to be the last man killed in "Krautland." The men of TF Lee were thus heartened by news their brash young captain—he'd been officially promoted on May 1[23]—passed around soon after he halted the unit in Kufstein at 3:25 PM on May 4. Upon radioing battalion commander Clow that the task force was in the town and had encountered no opposition, Lee was told to "hold in place" because CCR was in the process of turning over responsibility for Kufstein and the surrounding region to the 36th Infantry Division. A theater-wide cease-fire was possible at any time within the next twenty-four hours, and Lee was ordered to establish defensive positions, engage German forces only if fired on, and await relief by elements of the 36th ID's 142nd Infantry Regiment.

When Lee passed the news on to the men of his task force, they were jubilant. The war was apparently over for all intents and purposes, and they were still alive. Though Lee cautioned them not to let their guard down, more than a few of his men pulled "liberated" bottles of schnapps or wine from their packs or from hiding places within their vehicles and began toasting each other. There was much laughing and backslapping throughout the column as the "Joes" began setting up defensive positions, but up forward, around Lee's tank, the sudden arrival of a Wehrmacht officer waving a white flag quickly stifled the levity. News of the German's appearance rippled up and down the American column, and, when Jack Lee ducked into the turret of his tank to use the radio, those GIs in the immediate area who best knew the young American captain collectively held their breath.

When Lee reappeared with a wolfish smile on his face, they knew with sinking hearts that their war wasn't over quite yet.

———

EVEN AS GANGL AND LEE were meeting in Kufstein, a Schloss Itter rescue operation of which neither was aware was already in motion—thanks to Zvonko Čučković.

After spending the night in the hotel-turned-barracks, promptly at seven o'clock on the morning of May 4—even as Reynaud and Clemenceau were setting out on their stroll through Itter village—the well-rested Croat handyman had returned to the Innsbruck town hall. The Yugoslav-American civilian he'd met the day before introduced him to Major John T. Kramers, a German-speaking former artilleryman now assigned to the 103rd's military-government section.[24] Having read Christiane Mabire's letter, Kramers realized that a rescue mission to Schloss Itter was urgent. He called in one of the division's French army liaison officers (who also happened to be a good friend), Lieutenant[25] Eric Lutten, and together the two men poured over maps of the northern Tyrol and plotted out a route that would take them to the castle via the same roads Čučković had ridden. Kramers took the plan to his boss, who authorized the mission and arranged for three M4 Shermans of the 103rd's attached 783rd Tank Battalion to provide the necessary firepower.

The would-be rescuers set out just after noon, with Kramers, Lutten, Čučković, and a sergeant named Gris leading in a jeep. They rolled through Hall, Schwaz, and Jenbach without difficulty, but just east of Rattenberg they were stopped by GIs of Lieutenant Colonel Hubert E. Strange's 409th Infantry Regiment. The Joes told them that what appeared to be at least a hundred Waffen-SS troops were deployed in the town. The Germans were using panzerfausts, several MG-42s, and at least one antitank gun to cover the road, and they had already knocked out one U.S. Sherman and two M3 half-tracks. When the infantrymen estimated that it would be dark before they could root out the SS men and clear the road, Kramers reluctantly had to order his small force back to Innsbruck. Given the uncertainty of the tactical situation in Tyrol, division policy forbade small-unit, nontactical road movements at night.

As Jack Lee was informing his battalion commander of Gangl's arrival in Kufstein, Kramers was busy in Innsbruck putting together a larger rescue column he felt confident would be able to deal effectively with almost anything the Germans might throw at them while still being small enough to move rapidly. His new task force would consist of four M10 tank destroyers from the 824th TD Battalion, three jeeps equipped with .50-caliber machine guns, a truck bearing a platoon of infantrymen from the 3rd Battalion of the 409th, and an empty truck intended to carry the French VIPs and their baggage. As Kramers was putting the finishing touches on his plan, two civilians—U.S. war correspondent Meyer Levin and French photographer Eric Schwab—asked his permission to accompany the rescue force. Kramers agreed and told them the column would set out for Schloss Itter at dawn.[26]

It would prove to be an eventful journey.

———

IN HIS RESPONSE TO JACK LEE'S radio message regarding Sepp Gangl's appearance in Kufstein, 23rd TB commander Kelso Clow had directed Lee to deal with the situations in Wörgl and at Schloss Itter as he saw fit. Apparently not wanting to put the bulk of his task force in danger until it became absolutely necessary, Lee made what can only be described as a characteristically gutsy decision: He told Gangl that he wouldn't move the column into Wörgl or mount a full-blown rescue mission to Schloss Itter until he'd undertaken a personal reconnaissance to both places. And Lee, in an obvious test of Gangl's good faith and veracity, said they'd make the trip together in the major's kübelwagen. We don't know how Gangl felt about Lee's ultimatum, but we can be fairly certain that the GI whom Lee tapped to join him on the jaunt behind enemy lines—his twenty-nine-year-old gunner Corporal Edward J. "Stinky" Szymczyk[27]—probably wasn't too pleased to be "volunteered" for the mission.[28]

After passing temporary command of the task force to his executive officer, Lee wedged himself into the kübelwagen's cramped rear seat, with Szymczyk beside him and Gangl in the front passenger seat. As Corporal Keblitsch put the vehicle in motion, the two Americans settled back, their helmets most probably on the floor so as not to attract undue attention and their M3 submachine guns almost certainly laying cocked and ready on their laps. The party didn't encounter any hostile troops on the road to Wörgl, and the Wehrmacht soldiers they did meet were all loyal to Gangl. Lee checked several small bridges for demolition charges, and those he found Gangl ordered his men to remove. The kübelwagen rolled into Wörgl at approximately four thirty in the afternoon, and within minutes Lee had formally accepted Gangl's surrender of the town and its remaining garrison. In what can only have been both an obvious gesture of trust and a pragmatic acknowledgment that Gangl and his men were the only force capable of fighting off Waffen-SS units that might assault the town, the American tanker allowed the Germans to keep their weapons.

Formalities over, Gangl introduced Lee to Rupert Hagleitner and other key Wörgl resisters. The American officer told the Austrians that they were responsible for the town's administration until U.S. troops arrived and that Gangl's now-surrendered Wehrmacht soldiers would provide security. Then, turning to the matter of Schloss Itter, Lee asked Hagleitner to map out what he thought would be the safest route to the castle. Hagleitner instead offered to show him the way, and just before five thirty Lee, Gangl, Hagleitner, and Szymczyk set out in the kübelwagen, followed by Blechschmidt and several men in a small truck.

Though the distance to the castle was little more than five road miles, the need to take narrow dirt tracks and make several detours to avoid Waffen-SS roadblocks meant it took the party nearly forty-five minutes to reach Itter village. When they entered the small square in front of St. Joseph's Church, they encountered Kurt-Siegfried Schrader, who was on his way home after his drawn-out meeting with the French VIPs. Schrader told Lee he'd taken responsibility for the former prisoners' safety, and Gangl, seeing Lee's obvious skepticism, vouched for Schrader, whom he knew from Battle Group Giehl. Lee then told the Waffen-SS officer to return to the castle with his family and explained that a U.S. rescue force would arrive soon.[29]

This latter statement was a bit misleading, of course, in that Lee would have to return to Kufstein to assemble the relief column. And before he could do that, he had to ensure that the situation at the castle was in fact as Gangl had represented it to be. He thus directed Hagleitner, who was driving, to continue the 150 yards on to the castle. As the kübelwagen slowly approached the gatehouse—presumably with one of its occupants waving a white flag—two armed Frenchmen[30] stepped forward and leveled their weapons. Their understandable chagrin at the arrival of a German military vehicle would quickly have dissipated when Lee slowly stood up in the rear seat and announced himself to be an American officer.

Quickly ushered before the gathered French VIPs, Lee introduced himself and declared that he would return very soon with a sizable rescue force. While the tanker's exact words were not recorded, we can be certain that they were greeted with relief and enthusiasm. But we can also be fairly sure that Lee expressed himself in his typically brash, straightforward way, and, while he impressed Reynaud as having the "fine figure of a football player,"[31] he didn't make a particularly good impression on at least one of the other former prisoners. Though Édouard Daladier found Sepp Gangl to be "polite" and "dignified," the American captain struck him as "crude in both looks and manners," and the former French premier sniffed that "if Lee is a reflection of America's policies, Europe is in for a hard time."[32]

Daladier's disdain was the least of Lee's concerns, of course; he had a rescue to organize. Less than twenty minutes after arriving at Schloss Itter, and, after having directed Blechschmidt and his men to remain, Lee, Szymczyk, Gangl, and Hagleitner started back toward Wörgl in the kübelwagen, retracing their earlier route and again encountering no resistance. After dropping Hagleitner off, the other three continued on to Kufstein, where Lee sought out his battalion commander. Clow told him to proceed with the rescue effort but said that because CCR was already turning the area over to elements of the 36th Infantry Division, the only 23rd TB assets available to Lee were his own tank and one other—any additional men and vehicles would have to come from the 36th ID.

With Gangl in tow Lee rushed back to where he'd left his task force earlier in the day. He first informed his own crew—Szymcyk, driver Technician Fourth Grade William T. Rushford, loader Technician Fifth Grade Edward J. Seiner, and assistant driver/bow machine gunner Private First Class Herbert G. McHaley—of their new mission. He then asked his friend Harry Basse to take command of the second tank, Second Lieutenant Wallace S. Holbrook's *Boche Buster*, whose crew included sergeants William E. Elliot and Glenn E. Sherman.[33]

Still needing additional firepower, Lee was able to dragoon five Shermans from the incoming 3rd Platoon, Company B, 753rd Tank Battalion. Lee then went in search of Colonel George E. Lynch, commander of the 142nd Infantry Regiment, which was moving in to assume control of the area. Fascinated by Lee's tale of French VIPs in need of rescue, Lynch tasked three squads of infantrymen from 2nd Platoon, Company E, of Lieutenant

Colonel Marvin J. Coyle's 2nd Battalion to accompany the column. Lynch also pointed out that his regiment's planned axis of advance would take it toward Itter and pledged that the bulk of his battalions would be "right behind" Lee and his column.

That column rolled out of Kufstein just before seven PM. Lee and *Besotten Jenny* took the lead, followed by *Boche Buster* and the five 753rd TB Shermans. The infantrymen from the 142nd were spread among the tanks and riding atop the rear engine decks, and taking up the rear of the column was Gangl in his kübelwagen, the white flag on its radio antenna now supplemented by large white stars crudely painted on either side. Despite the apparent ease with which Lee and the others had managed to drive to and from Schloss Itter earlier in the day, the young officer was under no illusions that his considerably larger column would go unnoticed or unchallenged. Die-hard Waffen-SS and Wehrmacht units remained throughout northern Austria, and they could be expected to be well-equipped with the lethal panzerfaust antitank rockets that Allied tankers had learned to fear.

It quickly became obvious that panzerfausts were not the only thing the American tankers had to worry about. Almost immediately after leaving Kufstein, the relief column had to cross a small and obviously old bridge over an Inn River tributary known as the Brixentaler Ache. Lee's two tanks and two of the 753rd TB Shermans made it over the span without difficulty, but the structure began to collapse when the fifth tank attempted to cross. Lee had no choice but to order the last three 753rd vehicles to return to Kufstein with their embarked infantrymen.[34]

Further complications awaited the rescue force when it reached Wörgl at about eight PM. The same roving bands of die-hard troops that worried Lee were also of great concern to Rupert Hagleitner and his fellow resistance leaders, and they pleaded with the young officer to bolster their defenses. For reasons that aren't entirely clear, Lee agreed to leave the two remaining 753rd TB tanks and their accompanying infantrymen in Wörgl. However, Gangl offered to make up the deficit with more of his men, and when Lee agreed, the Wehrmacht officer called together two of his officers—Captain Dietrich and Lieutenant Höckel—and several additional enlisted men. When the relief column left Wörgl to continue the journey to Schloss Itter, Lee commanded two Sherman tanks, fourteen American soldiers, and a kübelwagen and small Mercedes truck carrying a total of ten Germans. It was certainly a first for an American officer in World War II.

The rescue force initially headed due east out of Wörgl but turned southeast when they hit the village of Söll-Leukental and then followed the two-lane Brixentalerstrasse south along the west bank of the Brixentaler Ache. At the small hamlet of Bruggberg they found a bridge that Lee determined would bear the weight of the tanks as they crossed to the other side of the small river, but it had already been wired with demolition charges. Realizing the span might be the only route back to U.S. lines with the evacuated French VIPs, Lee decided to leave *Boche Buster* and its crew—minus Basse—to disarm the explosives and protect the structure.

Continuing on with *Besotten Jenny* and its crew, with Basse and the four remaining 142nd infantrymen—Corporal William Sutton and Privates Alex Petrukovich, Arthur Pollock, and Alfred Worsham—riding on the back deck and Gangl and his men following in their vehicles, Lee continued along the east bank of the river. The road was hemmed in on the east side by a steep mountainside, forcing the column to continue almost due southward toward the market town of Hopfgarten until they came to a sharp left-hand curve onto the Ittererstrasse, the road leading uphill toward Itter village and the schloss. Lee could now see his objective, perched atop the hill barely a mile directly to his front, and he ordered his driver to move out carefully.

His caution was justified, for within minutes of turning onto the Ittererstrasse the column rounded an S-curve in the road and almost drove over a squad of Waffen-SS troops trying to set up a roadblock. The infantrymen riding on the tank's rear deck quickly opened fire, as did bow gunner McHaley and Gangl's troops in the truck, and the Waffen-SS men scurried into the surrounding woods without firing. Lee ordered Rushford to "open her up," and the tank slewed around another corner and up the twisting Ittererstrasse with the Wehrmacht vehicles close behind.

The mini convoy roared through the narrow streets of Itter village and then turned west onto the schlossweg, the narrow lane leading toward the castle. The schlossweg ended at the bridge leading to the castle's main gate, where Lee ordered Rushford to pull *Besotten Jenny* as far over to the side as possible and then motioned Gangl and the driver of the truck to move ahead and cross the bridge. As the Wehrmacht vehicles eased past the Sherman and on toward the gatehouse, Lee told the four infantryman atop the tank's rear deck to jump down and take up defensive positions. Turning to Rushford—who'd driven the several hundred yards from Itter village with his head and shoulders out of his hatch—Lee said to back the tank up slightly until it was in the center of the road and then turn it 180 degrees so the front of the vehicle would face toward the village. The turn was a delicate operation on the narrow roadway, but, by moving the steering levers in opposite directions and applying power, Rushford was able to rotate the tank in place.

Lee's rationale for the maneuver became clear moments later, when he told Rushford that they would be backing *Besotten Jenny* up the curving, sixty-foot-long access road toward the gatehouse. In response to quizzical looks from both Rushford and Basse, Lee quickly explained that during his brief earlier visit to the castle with Gangl, he'd realized that the access road was narrower than where the vehicle now sat and that the gatehouse's arched entryway was too low to allow the tank to move all the way into the schloss's lower courtyard. He wanted to get the tank as close as possible to the gatehouse, both to block the entry and to ensure that enemy troops couldn't get between the vehicle and the gate. While backing *Besotten Jenny* up the access road to the gatehouse would be challenging, Lee said, it would also ensure that enemy gunners couldn't get a shot at the tank's most vulnerable spot: the less heavily armored lower rear hull. With the plan agreed on, Lee ordered everyone but Rushford out of the tank and then climbed atop the turret and dropped into the commander's hatch.

Because the Sherman's rearview mirrors had been damaged several days earlier, Rushford had to rely on Lee's voice commands for guidance. As *Besotten Jenny* began creeping backward, so slowly that its movement was at first barely discernable to the anxious soldiers looking on, Lee relayed small course corrections via intercom. The initial half of the access road was relatively straight, but it also included the potentially most dangerous hurdle the tank had to surmount: the twenty-foot-long bridge spanning the ravine separating Schloss Itter from the rest of the ridgeline. The metal-reinforced concrete span was supported at either end by what appeared to be fairly robust, arched, dressed-stone piers, but the Sherman would undoubtedly be pushing the bridge well beyond its design limits. Should the span give way under the tank's immense weight, *Besotten Jenny* would drop some twenty-five feet to the bottom of the ravine—a distance that would disable the vehicle, rob the rescue force of its biggest gun, and almost certainly kill or severely injure Lee and Rushford.

When the Sherman backed onto the bridge, the span literally started to groan as the interior metal girders supporting the length of the structure began to bend. Chunks of the stone façade popped out and dropped into the ravine, and hairline cracks opened in the macadam road surface. Art Pollock, crouched nearby with his BAR[35] pointing back toward the village, turned at the sound, and was stunned to see that the bridge was actually swaying slightly from side to side.[36] Despite the obvious signs of distress, the span held, and after nearly a minute of high anxiety for Rushford, Lee, and the watching soldiers, *Besotten Jenny* rolled safely across—only to face another challenge. At the castle end of the span the roadway turned left toward the gatehouse at about a 15-degree angle, narrowing from twelve feet to just under eleven. The turn would be a tight one, with the nine-foot-wide tank having less than a foot of clearance on either side. If Rushford misjudged the angle of his turn or inadvertently applied too much power, the Sherman would smash through the low, cinder-block and wooden-plank guard rails lining the roadway and might well go tumbling down the slope on the other side. But again, Lee's precise instructions and Rushford's steady hand averted a possible disaster: *Besotten Jenny* made the turn with inches to spare and covered the remaining distance to the gatehouse without incident.

When Rushford had backed the Sherman to within a few feet of the arched gateway—through which the German vehicles had already passed—Lee told him to shut the engine down. Both men then climbed out of their respective hatches, jumped to the ground, and lit up celebratory smokes as Basse, Szymcyk, Seiner, McHaley, and the four infantrymen left their defensive positions on the village side of the bridge and trotted to join them. The Americans then moved through the open gates and into the snow-dusted lower courtyard, where Schrader and Gangl were waiting. With daylight fading, Lee was eager to organize the castle's defenses. But before he could begin issuing orders, the schlosshof's small arched gate swung open, and he and his men were engulfed by a wave of Gallic congratulations.

———

LEE'S RETURN WITH THE eagerly anticipated American rescue column drew all of Schloss Itter's French VIPs out of the safety of the Great Hall, across the walled terrace, and down the steps to the courtyard with smiles on their faces, cheers in their throats, and bottles of wine in their hands. That initial enthusiasm quickly dimmed, however, when they realized the limited extent of the relief force. Lee's assurances hours earlier that he would return with "the cavalry" had conjured in their minds images of a column of armor supported by masses of heavily armed soldiers; what they got instead was a single, somewhat shopworn tank, seven Americans, and, to the former prisoners' chagrin, more armed Germans. The French, to put it mildly, were decidedly unimpressed.

The former captives' mood darkened even more when they heard Lee telling Schrader—who'd returned to the castle in full uniform—about the Waffen-SS roadblock the relief force had encountered on the Ittererstrasse just north of Hopfgarten. The French knew there were hostile units in the area, of course—Blechschmidt had told them just that when he and his men had arrived earlier—but the fact that there were German troops still willing to confront American armor was a chilling reminder that the war was most certainly not yet over. Their peace of mind would have been further undermined had the French heard what Schrader reported to Lee: pulling the tanker to one side, the Waffen-SS man told him quietly that as Blechschmidt was deploying his handful of men along the castle's upper floors earlier in the afternoon, he'd seen hostile troops moving toward the schloss from the north, west, and south. Even more ominous, Schrader added, both he and the young Wehrmacht lieutenant had seen two Pak 40 antitank guns[37] being moved into positions from which they could fire toward the castle: one just inside the tree line on a parallel ridge directly east of the schloss and the other in a small clearing on the west bank of the Brixentaler Ache, southwest of the schloss.

Aware that the tactical situation had worsened significantly in just the past few hours and that an attack could come at any minute, Lee quickly began issuing orders. His first was directed at the expectant French, whom he told to take Schrader's wife and children and the female number prisoners and seek shelter in the basement storerooms. His order was greeted by an immediate outburst of Gallic outrage—Reynaud, Daladier, and the other men loudly protesting that they would rather die on the parapets than cower in the cellars. Lee cut off the dissent with a curt wave of his hand, reminding the Frenchmen that he was in sole command and adding that they wouldn't be any good to postwar France if they got themselves killed.

As the French former prisoners moved off, the men still grumbling, Lee motioned Basse, Gangl, Schrader, Dietrich, Höckel, and Blechschmidt together and quickly outlined his strategy. Since there weren't enough vehicles to move everyone in the castle back to Kufstein and given that the immediate area seemed to be crawling with enemy troops anyway, they would stay put, defend Schloss Itter, and wait to be relieved by the advancing 142nd Infantry. Lee would remain in overall command of the castle's ad hoc garrison—which now included ten Americans, one Waffen-SS man, and fourteen Wehrmacht soldiers—with Basse, Schrader, and Gangl acting as his lieutenants.

Though the defenders were likely to be hugely outnumbered, Lee said, they had several factors working in their favor. First, they were relatively well armed: In addition to Kar-98 and M1 Garand rifles, they had MP-40 and M3 submachine guns, Pollock's BAR, German and American pistols and hand grenades, and, most important, the .30-caliber and .50-caliber machine guns and 76mm cannon on *Besotten Jenny*. Second, Lee pointed out, attackers coming from the north, west, or south would have to surmount the encircling concertina-wire barriers and advance uphill while under intense fire from men atop the high walls on those sides. Third, enemy troops moving in from the east would be completely exposed as they negotiated the short schlossweg leading from the closest part of Itter village to the schloss, and in the final sixty feet of that distance the attackers would have to cross the narrow bridge over the ravine before even reaching the gatehouse. Fourth, Lee said, Schloss Itter's thick stone walls would offer protection from small-arms fire and, to a lesser extent, reduce the effectiveness of enemy artillery. Fifth, and possibly most important, Lee pointed out that should attackers actually breach the outer ramparts, the defenders could resort to a positively medieval tactic: they'd shepherd the VIPs into the schloss's tall central building—which Lee immediately dubbed the "keep"—and use the remaining ammunition, the grenades, and, if necessary, their fists to make the enemy fight for every stairwell, every hall, and every room.

Having laid out the battle plan, Lee set about deploying his troops. Gangl and Schrader would each be responsible for defending 180 degrees of the castle's perimeter, Lee said, the former on the south and the latter on the north. Each man would have junior officers as "squad leaders"—Dietrich and Blechschmidt with Gangl, and Höckel with Schrader—and three of the Wehrmacht enlisted soldiers. The three remaining German troops would be posted as lookouts on the top floor of the keep. All of the friendly

Germans would wear a strip of dark cloth tied around their left arms as a recognition symbol, Lee said. Until something happened, the troops could sleep and eat in shifts, but, when and if the shooting started, it would literally be every man to the battlements.

As the German officers moved off to take up their positions, Lee told Rushford, Szymczyk, Seiner, and McHaley to wait for him next to the tank, still parked a few feet in front of the gatehouse. Turning to Basse and the four GIs from the 142nd Infantry, Lee said they would be responsible for the area around the main gate, as well as for covering the approach road. Motioning them to follow, Lee trotted over to the gatehouse, where he and Basse did a quick recon as Pollock, Worsham, Petrukovich, and Sutton took up defensive positions just to the rear and on either side of *Besotten Jenny*.[38]

Exploring the thirty-foot-tall, forty-foot-wide gatehouse confirmed the two officers' initial impression: while it certainly wasn't impregnable, it would make a decent first line of defense against any direct enemy assault from the direction of the village or uphill from the south or east. Strongly built of stone, the structure had two sets of gates, one set at each end of the covered and arched central entryway. The outer gates had been installed as part of the schloss's conversion into a prison; built of thick, rough timber and pierced on one side by a small inset door, they opened outward and could be secured from the inside by several large padlocks. Set about fifteen feet further back, the inner gates were made of massive, metal-banded timbers, opened inward, and could be both locked and barred. Moreover, the central entryway was flanked by two tall stone towers pierced at the top by firing loops[39] that commanded the short access road. Two additional towers some forty feet to the rear of the gatehouse—on the west front corner of the schlosshof—overlooked the steep slopes leading up to the base of the castle's massive southern and western foundation walls. The front guard towers and the gatehouse's cramped upper floor were accessible via two small wooden doors, one to either side of the inner gates, while the schlosshof's tower had its own gate and internal circular staircase.

There were two possible weak spots in the defenses in and around the gatehouse, Lee and Basse agreed. The first was the area directly beneath the arched supports of the small bridge on the access road. Enemy troops who were able to work their way through the ravine and reach the base of the stone pier closest to the main gate would be able to cut through the concertina-wire barriers where they butted up against the pier while remaining almost impossible to engage: none of the firing loops in the gatehouse offered a clear line of sight, and the sloping shoulders of the small promontory on which the castle stood would block fire from the main walls. The second weak spot was the small arched doorway—the sally port[40]—at the base of the south foundation wall, right below the schlosshof's guard tower on the castle's south side. The door opened directly onto the sloping hillside leading down into the ravine. Built of thick, metal-reinforced timber, it was heavily barred from within and was overlooked by firing loops in the guard towers, but the placement of the openings in the curving walls of the towers would make it difficult to actually bring a weapon to bear on the slightly recessed door. Worse, small trees and underbrush on the hillside leading to the sally port meant that enemy troops who cut through the concertina wire might be able to make it from the ravine to the door unseen and blow it open before they could be stopped.

Standing before the front gate, Lee realized that the position of *Besotten Jenny* also presented a tactical problem. While his foresight in backing the vehicle up the access road spanning the ravine and parking it immediately in front of the gatehouse both protected its more vulnerable rear end and made any enemy assault up the approach road virtually suicidal, it also severely restricted the field of fire of the turret-mounted 76mm cannon and coaxial and hull-mounted .30-caliber machine guns. In order to ensure that the tank could cover the sally port and engage targets to the west and south of the schloss in addition to those immediately to the east, Lee ordered Rushford to move *Besotten Jenny* further from the gatehouse and park it just on the castle side of the bridge. Its engine roaring and with greasy smoke belching from its exhausts, the Sherman moved slowly forward. When it came to a stop, Rushford and the other crewmen jumped down and trotted back to the gatehouse, each man carrying his personal gear, a .45-caliber M3 submachine gun, and as much ammunition as he could carry.

Lee knew that repositioning the tank was a calculated risk: while the move would significantly increase the field of fire for the Sherman's main and secondary weapons, it would also make the vehicle more visible to antitank gunners and increase the likelihood of attack by infantrymen wielding the fearsome panzerfaust. To help prevent the latter, Lee told Basse to emplace one of the tank's machine guns in the gatehouse's small upper level. By kicking out some of the ceramic roof tiles, the defenders could create a firing position that would cover *Besotten Jenny* and also provide an elevated—if somewhat exposed—position from which to engage enemy troops attempting to move up the hillsides on either side of the bridge over the ravine. Though Lee would have preferred to use the tank's Browning .50-caliber for the overwatch task, its size and weight would make it too unwieldy to use in the gatehouse's cramped attic space. And of the tank's two lighter and smaller .30-caliber machine guns, Lee and Basse agreed that it made more sense to remove and resite the assistant driver's hull-mounted M1919A4 weapon: it had a more restricted arc of fire than the coaxial next to the main gun in the rotating turret and was easier to remove from its mount. Whistling to get McHaley's attention, Basse told him to go back to the tank, dismount the bow .30-caliber, retrieve its stowed tripod, and take the weapon and several cans of ammunition to the top of the gatehouse. Turning toward Worsham, Basse told him to help McHaley emplace the weapon and then act as the young tanker's assistant gunner.

Leaving Basse to deploy Pollock, Petrukovich, and Sutton as he saw fit, Lee moved over to where Rushford, Szymczyk, and Seiner were crouched just inside the first set of gates. Lee told them that while he realized that *Besotten Jenny* was in an exposed position, he wanted at least one of them in the buttoned-up vehicle at all times. Turning to Seiner, Lee said that, since there was virtually no chance they'd have to tangle with German armor, he wanted the Sherman's 76mm gun loaded with a high-explosive shell, which would be far more effective against troops than an armor-piercing round.[41] Finally, Lee said, at the first sign of a full-scale attack he wanted all three of them to get to *Besotten Jenny* as soon as possible; Basse would try to join them, but if the motor officer couldn't make it out to the Sherman, the three enlisted men should keep it in action as long as they could.

With the defense of the gatehouse organized, Lee headed across the small courtyard toward the schlosshof, noting as he did that the wire-topped parapet walls on either side were not tall enough to offer complete protection from incoming fire. Making a mental note to remind everyone that in the event of a firefight they'd have to crouch when traversing the lower courtyard and the equally exposed terrace between the schlosshof and the main building, Lee hurried toward the Great Hall. It was just after nine thirty, the sun was starting to set, and he wanted to ensure that all the "tame Krauts" were in position and alert before nightfall.

As he crossed the terrace, Lee was pleased to see that Gangl had placed two of his men behind a low wall that allowed them to cover both the castle's main entryway and the stairway leading up from the front courtyard. The soldiers saluted the American officer as he walked past them into the Great Hall, where Lee found Gangl and Schrader waiting for him. Together, the three men set off to inspect the defenses. Then it was down to the cellars to look in on the VIPs and Schrader's family, followed by a drawn-out strategy session among Lee, Gangl, and Schrader that evolved into a remarkably open discussion of the war and the uncertainties of the coming peace. It must have been a truly odd sight: the brash tanker from upstate New York and two highly decorated German officers, sitting around a table in the candlelit great hall of a medieval castle, speaking quietly of their experiences in a conflict that each man fervently hoped would end within hours.

Finally, talked out, the enemies-turned-allies went in search of places to catch a few hours' sleep. Lee ended up in what had until recently been the SS guards' dormitory on the first floor of the keep. Setting his helmet and M3 submachine gun on a bedside table, he picked one of the narrow beds at random and lay down on the bare mattress still wearing his boots and pistol belt. His foresight would soon be validated, for it would be a very short night.

CHAPTER 7

A CASTLE BESIEGED

JUST AFTER FOUR AM Jack Lee was jolted awake by the sudden banging of M1 Garands, the sharper crack of Kar-98s, and the mechanical chatter of a .30-caliber spitting out rounds in short, controlled bursts. Knowing instinctively that the rising crescendo of outgoing fire was coming from the gatehouse, Lee rolled off the bed, grabbed his helmet and M3, and ran from the room.

The young tanker raced down the hallway, across the Great Hall, and out the front door. As he reached the arched schlosshof gate leading from the terrace to the front courtyard, an MG-42 machine gun opened up from somewhere along the parallel ridgeline east of the castle, the weapon's characteristic ripping sound[1] clearly audible above the outgoing fire and its tracers looking like an unbroken red stream as they arced across the ravine and ricocheted off the castle's lower walls. Almost immediately the German weapon was answered by the slower, deeper thumping of *Besotten Jenny*'s .50-caliber Browning, and, as Lee ran the last few feet to the gatehouse, he could see the M2's own tracers stabbing into the trees near where the MG-42 must be. The German weapon quickly fell silent, its two-man crew no doubt seeking shelter from the .50-cal.'s deadly stream of thumb-sized rounds.

The big Browning continued to bang away as Lee reached the inner set of gates and yanked open the small wooden door leading to the guard tower on the west side of the gatehouse. Using his red-lensed flashlight[2] for illumination, he pounded up a flight of circular stone stairs until he reached the first firing loop, through which Sutton was methodically loosing rounds from his M1. To Lee's surprise the infantryman was firing not across the ravine but down into it, aiming into the darkness to the west of the tower. In response to Lee's shouted query, Sutton said that he'd spotted four troops who had apparently cut through the concertina wire—Waffen-SS he thought, though with only moonlight for illumination it was hard to be sure—dashing the thirty or forty feet upslope to the base of the foundation wall. They looked to be carrying grappling hooks and ropes but were spotted before they could put them to use. When he opened up on the enemy troops, Sutton said, they had scurried back downslope under covering fire from the woods and gone to ground.

Telling Sutton to save his ammo until he had a definite target, Lee continued up the circular stairway to the small door leading into the gatehouse's cramped upper level. Inside he found Worsham and McHaley lying prone behind the now-quiet .30-caliber, surrounded by spent brass and wreathed by floating dust kicked up by the machine gun's firing. As McHaley fed another belt of ammo into the weapon, he told Lee that when Sutton had started shooting at the interlopers, the west side of the gatehouse had almost immediately come under rifle and machine-pistol fire from troops hidden on the upper floor of the small inn on the schlossweg. He and Worsham had laid down suppressing fire, aiming at muzzle flashes and the occasional shadowy figure they could see silhouetted in the building's windows. Despite their somewhat exposed position, they themselves hadn't been directly targeted, and when the MG-42 had opened up, it seemed to be aimed at Sutton's position, not at them. When *Besotten Jenny's* .50-caliber had gotten into the act, McHaley said, the enemy fire had briefly shifted toward the tank but then died out completely.

Cautioning the two young soldiers to stay alert, Lee descended via the circular stairway in the guard tower on the eastern front corner of the gatehouse. Emerging back in the courtyard, Lee knocked gently on one of the inner gates and then eased it open enough to squeeze through into the covered entryway. As he moved inside, he found himself looking down the barrels of Petruchovich's M1 and Pollock's BAR; recognizing Lee, the infantrymen lowered their weapons and turned back toward Basse and Szymczyk, who were crouched on either side of the small door that pierced the right half of the outer gate. The door was open just enough to give a clear view of *Besotten Jenny*, and, as Lee moved up beside him, Basse whispered that Szymczyk and Rushford had just traded places when the shooting started. When the MG-42 opened up, Rushford had popped up in the commander's hatch, swiveled the big Browning around on its rotating ring mount, and started banging out .50-caliber rounds. Spent brass littered the top of the tank's turret, its rear deck, and the ground around it.

Conferring in whispers, Lee and Basse agreed that the enemy was obviously looking for a way into the schloss that didn't require a direct assault down the narrow, sloping approach road toward the sturdy and well-defended gatehouse. Since the Germans on the castle's upper levels hadn't fired when the GIs in the gatehouse did, the attackers might not yet have a clear idea of the defenders' numbers. Given that a full-scale attack wasn't likely until the besiegers had determined how many men and what type of weapons they were facing, Lee told Basse to rotate the GIs up to the main building in pairs so they could eat and clean up. In the meantime, Lee said, he was going to check on the "castle Krauts."

When he reached the schloss's Great Hall he was surprised to find most of the French VIPs gathered in front of the room's huge, ornate fireplace. Several large logs were burning fiercely, and, in reply to Lee's pointed query about why they all weren't in the cellars as he'd directed, Augusta Bruchlen responded simply that they'd been driven upstairs by the cold. They'd emerged—shivering, though all were wearing coats—just after Lee had raced down to the gatehouse, and despite the sounds of battle they'd decided that warmth was a more immediate concern than safety. On behalf of the others, Bruchlen asked Lee if they could remain in the Great Hall; he agreed, but only on the conditions that they stay away from the heavily curtained windows, that no one leave the building, and that they all immediately return to the cellars if the firing resumed. As he moved toward the stairway, Lee also cautioned them not to give in to the temptation to go back upstairs to the relative comfort of their rooms, pointing out that Sepp Gangl and his men were stationed on the keep's upper floors and that their defensive firing in the event of an attack would almost certainly attract a hail of enemy gunfire.

Heading up to the first floor, Lee found Blechschmidt sitting on a chair to one side of the French doors leading out onto the broad veranda that stretched the width of the building's south side. With crenellated, five-foot-high parapet walls, the structure offered a relatively safe perch from which to observe the ravine below. Using hand gestures and a few halting words of English, the young German officer explained that he'd stationed a man in the small, circular turret that projected a few feet over the wall at the veranda's eastern corner, from where the soldier could overlook both the front courtyard and the base of the south foundation wall. Blechschmidt then pointed to a man crouched in the shadows in the opposite corner, from where he could keep on eye on the large rear courtyard and the foundation wall to the west.

Lee clapped the German lieutenant on the shoulder and then moved down the hallway toward the heavy wooden door that led from the main building into the keep. Ascending the narrow stone stairs from floor to floor, he found two Germans on each, one peering out a window on the north side and the other on the south. Gangl and Schrader were on the fourth floor, standing just outside the door to Wimmer's former suite and looking out one of the two windows on the keep's east side. Joining them, Lee realized they were keeping an eye on two soldiers who had obviously climbed out the window and down onto the roof of the Great Hall. Gangl explained that he'd directed the men to take up observation positions behind the crenellations on the roof's far corners. Schrader added that two more men were similarly concealed on the roof of the keep.

Lee smiled his satisfaction with the officers' preparations. Noticing that sunlight was beginning to peek through the windows of Wimmer's former room, Lee checked his watch. Even as his mind registered the time—six AM—he heard the unmistakable rattle of an MP-40 coming from the floor directly below. Taking the stairs two at a time with the German officers close behind, Lee emerged on the third floor and immediately saw one of Gangl's troops—obviously the one who'd fired the MP-40—curled on the floor in one of the south-facing rooms. The man lay directly beneath a shattered window, and incoming bullets were making the curtains dance before thudding into the chamber's ornate wooden ceiling. Dropping to their knees, Lee and Gangl scrambled across the floor, grabbed the soldier by his ankles, and jerked him out into the relative safety of the hallway.

Propping the man against the wall, Gangl grilled him in rapid German, turning every few seconds to give Lee a rough translation. The soldier—a young Austrian-born private—had spotted a small group of Waffen-SS troopers approaching the castle from the direction of Hopfgarten. The intruders had already gotten past the concertina wire and were running upslope toward the base of the foundation wall when the young soldier—

who'd been drafted into the Wehrmacht just weeks before and had no combat experience—slammed the window open and in seconds emptied an entire thirty-two-round magazine at them. His rash action had had immediate consequences: in addition to rifle and machine-pistol fire aimed at the keep, an MG-42 had come briefly to life, raking the entire south side of the schloss before being suppressed by .50-caliber fire from Rushford in *Besotten Jenny*. And though Lee didn't know it at the time, the enemy machine-gun fire had come very close to eliminating one of the French VIPs: several rounds had slammed into a wall just inches from the head of Édouard Daladier, who was taking his customary early morning walk in the rear courtyard in defiance of Lee's order that all the French former prisoners remain inside the castle.[3]

Despite the heated response the young Wehrmacht trooper's act had elicited, his fire had also apparently succeeded in prompting the Waffen-SS men to pull back into the woods at the bottom of the ravine. Reports from Blechschmidt's two lookouts on the veranda and from the men on the keep's roof confirmed that no attackers had made it to the base of the foundation wall. Gangl and Schrader both concurred with Lee's assessment that the aborted assault was another attempt to probe the castle's defenses rather than to breach them, but all three officers also agreed that the coming of a new day—and with it, the increasing potential for the arrival of a significant Allied relief force—might well prompt the enemy to launch an all-out attack without waiting to find an exploitable chink in the castle's defenses.

Though the schloss's defenders had thus far managed to deal with the enemy's initial probes, Lee and the two German officers knew that a determined assault by what might well be several hundred battle-hardened Waffen-SS troops could have but one possible outcome. Only the timely arrival of a major relief force could guarantee the survival of Schloss Itter's French VIPs and their American and German guardians. And though Lee and his newfound allies didn't yet know it, the two forces dispatched to rescue them would both be significantly delayed—one by enemy action and the other by military bureaucracy.

––––––

BEFORE LEE AND his mixed armor-infantry, American-German rescue party left Kufstein the previous evening, the young tanker had been assured by

Colonel George E. Lynch that the 2nd Battalion of his 142nd Infantry Regiment would be "right behind them." As part of the 36th Infantry Division's advance from the Inn River valley eastward toward Kitzbühel, 2nd Battalion commander Lieutenant Colonel Marvin J. Coyle's four rifle companies—E, F, G, and H—and their supporting artillery and tank units were to strike southwest from Kufstein to Wörgl on the morning of May 5, and after securing the latter turn southeast and move down the Brixental Valley toward Hopfgarten.[4] The advance would take the 2nd Battalion right past the base of the ridge atop which Itter village sat, and Lynch was certain that Coyle and his men would be able to quickly relieve Lee and his troops. But, as so often happens in wartime, Lynch's plans were derailed and the 2nd Battalion's advance delayed by unforeseen circumstances.

The trouble started almost immediately after 2nd Battalion's jeeps, trucks, and half-tracks rolled out of Kufstein at seven AM, led by the attached M4 Shermans of Company B, 753rd Tank Battalion.[5] Coyle's orders from regimental commander Lynch directed him to follow Lieutenant Colonel Everett Simpson's 3rd Battalion as far as the junction leading to the Söll-Sankt Johann road, about three miles south of Kufstein, at which point Simpson's unit would turn directly east while 2nd Battalion moved on toward Wörgl. The only route toward the junction was a two-lane road that for about two miles of its length was sandwiched between the Inn River and a line of steep-sided hills, and near the hamlet of Kirchbichl the 3rd Battalion ran into a hastily emplaced timber-and-stone roadblock defended by Waffen-SS troops wielding small arms and panzerfausts. It took about thirty minutes to eliminate the resistance and another twenty for the GIs to clear the obstructions and reboard their vehicles, and 3rd Battalion had only moved about another half mile when it encountered a blown bridge. Though troops of the 111th Engineer Combat Battalion were immediately brought forward to deal with the situation, the two infantry units were halted for another ninety minutes.

Nor did the 2nd Battalion's luck improve. Almost as soon as Simpson's 3rd Battalion turned off at the road junction, Coyle's column encountered a massive crater—the result of demolition charges planted by withdrawing German units—spanning both of the road lanes in a built-up area with no available bypass. Fearing an ambush, Coyle deployed dismounted infantrymen to protect the leading tanks and the engineers who came forward to fill the crater. That effort took another hour, and it wasn't until eleven o'clock that the 2nd Battalion renewed its advance toward Wörgl. Though Austrian resistance fighters who greeted the arriving Americans insisted that all German troops had left the town, Coyle's soldiers undertook a thorough block-by-block clearance sweep, a process that occupied them for far longer than Coyle would have liked. Even as he prepared the battalion for the move east out of Wörgl, Coyle—having not heard from Lee since the previous night—was already wondering if his men would find anyone left to relieve at Schloss Itter.

Though Coyle didn't know it, the leader of the other American column trying to relieve Schloss Itter was also wondering whether he'd make it in time. Having gotten on the road just after sunup, Major John Kramers and his rescue force had initially made good time. As Meyer Levin later recalled:

> We romped along a fine road lined with cheering Polish, Czech, French and Russian ex-slaves and ex-prisoners, who here, as everywhere, seemed to have sprung up out of the ground the instant the liberation blew their way. It was a fine warm day[6] and the mountain scenery was first class and we had a fine tourist ride for some 20 miles on the road to Worgl.[7]

Their seemingly idyllic road trip through the Inn River valley soon turned sour, however. Just past Jenbach—about halfway between Innsbruck and Wörgl—Kramers's column was hailed by a group of Austrian anti-Nazi partisans who'd been fighting running battles with Waffen-SS units farther along the road. According to Levin:

> Our little party paused for reflection. There we were, alone in what was still Kraut land. Liberating a castle full of big names was important, but it was also important not to get killed in so doing, especially on the day when fighting was supposed to have stopped. To add point to the argument, there came a familiar whine, which we thought we had heard for the last time. Then the blast, and 100 yards away there was a black burst. The boys in the tanks promptly backed among some trees, for cover. The soldiers hopped off their truck, took positions in a ditch, and watched the shells come down.
>
> "They've seen us."
>
> "If they're shooting for us, that's lousy poor shooting."

"Yah, but it's eight-eights and they got observation on this road."

Major Kramers made a swift "reccy" up the road, did some radio talk with headquarters, and decided we couldn't clear the road to Itter without help.[8]

As Kramers was discussing the situation with Lutten, the French liaison officer, the radio in their jeep crackled. It was the division command post, and the news wasn't good. Not only would they not be getting reinforcements, the 103rd's chief of staff, Colonel Guy S. Meloy, was ordering the rescue force to turn around and head back toward Innsbruck. Thunderstruck, Kramers reminded the senior officer that the French VIPs were in mortal danger and, as respectfully as he could, asked why on earth he was being ordered to abort the mission when the rescuers were well over half the way to Itter. The answer left Kramers stunned: His column had crossed the map coordinates that marked the boundary between the 103rd and 36th divisions' respective areas of operation. He and his men were, in effect, "trespassing" in the 36th's territory.[9]

While Kramers well understood that moving unannounced through another division's area of operations could be dangerous—friendly forces unaware of his column's presence might well mistake it for an enemy unit and attack—he also believed at that point that his ad hoc detachment was the only force capable of saving Schloss Itter's French prisoners. Being careful not to sound insubordinate, Kramers pointed out to Meloy that the question of unit boundaries and areas of operational responsibility had not kept the initial rescue plan from being approved by the division commander, Major General McAuliffe, less than twelve hours earlier. Going further, he reminded the chief of staff that the murder of a gaggle of French VIPs by the Nazis would not reflect well on either American division. Struggling to keep his anger in check, Kramers all but pleaded to be allowed to keep going, but to no avail.

Directed in no uncertain terms to return to Innsbruck, the military-government officer made what under the circumstances was a very gutsy, and admittedly foolhardy, decision: he would send back the four tank destroyers and the infantrymen from the 409th as ordered, but he, Lutten, Sergeant Gris, and Čučković would continue to Schloss Itter in the jeep. How he planned to either liberate or defend the French VIPs is unclear, given that the only weaponry he now had at his command were the M3 submachine guns and .45-caliber pistols he, Lutten, and Gris were carrying. As Kramers was about to pull away, Levin and Schwab made their own bold decision: despite the obvious folly of driving deeper into what was still enemy-held territory—on roads quite possibly mined and almost certainly crawling with die-hard German troops—the two journalists immediately volunteered to follow along in their own jeep. As dangerous as the trip to Schloss Itter might turn out to be, neither man intended to miss what was shaping up to be one hell of a story.[10]

EVEN AS SCHLOSS ITTER'S two would-be relief forces were struggling to stay on the move, the castle's defenders were suffering a crisis of trust.

Just after eight AM, as Lee and Gangl were inspecting the defenses on the schloss's north side, firing erupted from the gatehouse. When the two officers got there, Basse explained that one of Gangl's men had apparently used a rope to lower himself from the veranda outside the VIPs' dining area to the base of the sloping foundation wall directly west of the gatehouse. One of the wall's supporting stone buttresses had hidden him from view until he took off running down into the ravine, heading in the direction of Hopfgarten. With a pointed glance at Gangl, Basse said that none of the "tame Krauts" had opened fire on their erstwhile comrade. By the time the Americans in the gatehouse realized what was happening, the escaping Wehrmacht trooper had run through the breach in the concertina made earlier by the Waffen-SS men and was well into the trees. Though the GIs had opened up with M1s and Pollock's BAR, they hadn't hit the fleeing soldier.[11]

A quick headcount by Gangl and Lieutenant Höckel showed the escapee to be a German-born soldier of no great political conviction who'd probably decided to go over to the Waffen-SS simply to avoid immediate execution should the castle be overrun. Whatever his motives, the man's escape was a dire development. He knew exactly how many troops were defending Schloss Itter, where they were positioned, the type and number of their weapons, and even how much ammunition they had—information he would almost certainly reveal to the SS men in order to demonstrate his loyalty. What must have been worse still, from Lee's point of view, was the fact that none of the other Germans had fired at the defector as he loped toward the trees. Did that mean that the man's comrades harbored the same idea—to find a way to give themselves up to the Waffen-SS and claim they'd been coerced into helping the Americans in hopes of avoiding a bullet in the back of the head?

While we don't know the exact course of the discussion Lee and Gangl must have had following the deserter's departure—were there recriminations, accusations, apologies?—we do know that Gangl was able to convince Lee of the remaining Wehrmacht troops' loyalty by the simple fact that the tanker allowed the Germans to keep their weapons. If Lee had harbored any doubts about the trustworthiness of the remaining German soldiers, he would have immediately disarmed them and locked them away in one of Schloss Itter's many cells. And though we can't say with certainty, it's also probable that having convinced Lee, Gangl then took the time to go about reminding his troops that the best chance they had of surviving the next few hours and going home to their families was to continue to throw in their lot with the Allies.

Having dealt with one setback, Lee was almost immediately faced with another. After their discussion about the German soldier's escape, the tanker and Gangl had gone up to the top floor of the keep to fill Schrader in on what had happened and to get a better view of any increased enemy activity that might have resulted from the German corporal's defection. They didn't have to wait long for an answer: just after eight thirty Lee, peering through binoculars, spotted two ominous weapons—a 20mm anti-aircraft cannon[12] and an 88mm gun—being emplaced in a tree line barely eight hundred yards to the northwest of the castle.[13] The sight likely made Lee cringe; the rapid-fire 20mm was lethal against soft-skinned vehicles and personnel, and the 88 had a fearsome and well-earned reputation as a killer of Allied tanks. But worse was yet to come. Gangl nudged Lee and pointed south down the Ittererstrasse toward Hopfgarten: a string of military trucks was emerging from the town and driving in the direction of the castle. After passing the junction with the Ittererstrasse, the vehicles stopped and began disgorging troops, who immediately ran into the woods at the base of the hill. Focusing the binoculars, Lee could easily see that the troops leaping from the tailgates of the trucks were wearing characteristic Waffen-SS camouflage.[14] The tanker estimated that the new arrivals numbered between 100 and 150, and Schrader pointed out that at least two of the vehicles bore the mailed-fist insignia of the 17th SS Panzer-Grenadier Division.

While the appearance of the 88 and the truckloads of troops was certainly not a positive development, Lee and the two German officers agreed that it could explain why the schloss had not yet been attacked in force. The enemy soldiers in the woods along the schlossweg and on the parallel ridgeline to the east were probably just a reconnaissance element tasked with probing the castle's defenses as they awaited the arrival of the main assault group. Though there was a slim chance that the 88 and the newly arrived Waffen-SS men were being deployed in order to engage the U.S. 36th Infantry Division rather than to assault Schloss Itter, the officers assumed— correctly, though they wouldn't know that for some time[15]—that the Waffen-SS troops had been specifically ordered to eliminate the French VIPs and their American and German protectors. And, that being the case, Lee, Gangl, and Schrader all understood that the enemy would waste little time before mounting an all-out attack on the castle.

Realizing that the 88 and the large contingent of Waffen-SS troops would pose as great a threat to the U.S. forces advancing from Kufstein as they did to those holed up in Schloss Itter, Lee knew he had to get the word out. But with *Besotten Jenny*'s radio inoperable—it had failed at some point between Wörgl and the castle—the question was, how? To Lee's surprise, Schrader had a simple answer: try the telephone. The officer pointed out that the handset in the ground-floor orderly room was connected directly to the telephone exchange in Wörgl, and as long as the lines hadn't been cut, they should be able to reach someone who could pass the word on to the Americans. Gangl suggested they call Alois Mayr and Rupert Hagleitner at the Neue Post Inn; who better to contact the U.S. forces than the local Austrian resistance leaders? Lee immediately agreed and told Gangl to make the call.

Within minutes the Wehrmacht officer was on the line with Mayr, who promised to pass the intelligence on to the first Americans he saw. Then, knowing that Schloss Itter would need all the defenders it could get, Gangl ordered Second Lieutenant Wegscheider and Corporal Linsen to get to the castle as quickly as they could. The two men immediately jumped in a kübelwagen and sped off toward Itter, accompanied by seventeen-year-old Hans Waltl, the only resistance member Mayr and Hagleitner felt they could spare. What would have been a twenty-minute drive in peacetime took the trio nearly forty-five, given that they were forced to take several sudden detours onto unpaved side roads to bypass Waffen-SS roadblocks on the main routes out of Wörgl. By looping to the north of the schloss and then approaching from the northeast end of the Ittererstrasse, the three men were able to avoid most of the troops moving into position between Hopfgarten and the castle, and Wegscheider—deciding that bravado was the only ploy that would get them past the gathering Waffen-SS troops—told Linsen to sound the kübelwagen's horn as they raced through Itter village and down the last few hundred yards of the schlossweg toward the gatehouse. The soldiers lining the road were apparently taken in by the ruse, because Wegscheider and his companions made it unscathed to the entrance to the schloss access road. Abandoning the kübelwagen, the three men ran the last yards to the gatehouse, where Gangl—who'd come down to warn Basse and the GIs of the men's arrival—welcomed them with a relieved smile.[16]

The hurried greetings over, Gangl told the new arrivals to follow him to the keep, where he wanted them to take up positions alongside their comrades. As the group traversed the Great Hall, Gangl realized that virtually all the French VIPs were in the rear courtyard in direct defiance of Lee's orders that they stay inside—Daladier and Jouhaux were strolling upright around the perimeter, looking like they hadn't a care in the world; Mabire, Reynaud, and the Cailliaus were taking souvenir photos of each other near the central fountain; Clemenceau, Gamelin, and Borotra were deep in discussion near the door leading down into the main building; and Augusta Bruchlen was just walking out of the Great Hall.[17] Even Schrader's wife and children were out enjoying the morning sunshine and bracing mountain air.

While we don't know how Gangl felt about the French VIPs' defiance of Lee's orders or their cavalier disregard for their own safety, we do know that any rebuke he might have been about to voice was rendered completely unnecessary by the 88mm round that at that moment slammed into the west side of the keep's third floor, destroying Gamelin's room and blasting loose a cascade of stone, shattered glass, and splintered furniture. Almost immediately the woods surrounding the castle erupted with automatic weapons and rifle fire; bullets hammered into the castle's walls and blew windows out of their frames. Then the 20mm cannon to the northwest added its voice to the chorus, coughing out fist-sized rounds that exploded on impact with the side of the keep, gouging holes in the stonework the size of dinner plates.

It was a few minutes after ten, and the battle for Schloss Itter had begun in earnest.

———

WHEN THE FIRING ERUPTED, Art Pollock and Al Worsham were crouched behind *Besotten Jenny*, smoking cigarettes and peering around opposite sides of the vehicle in the direction of the schlossweg and Itter village. The two infantrymen had gone out to provide security for Bill Rushford, who was inside, focusing his attention on trying to repair the Sherman's balky SCR-528 radio. They'd barely registered the sound of the 88 round detonating against the side of the keep when the tank was rocked violently backward on its suspension, the lurch accompanied by a harsh metallic clang so loud it almost deafened them. The two men knew instinctively that the Sherman had been hit by an antitank round, a perception immediately reinforced by flames that shot upward from the engine access grills atop *Besotten Jenny*'s rear deck. With the same thought in their heads—get away from it before it cooks off!—the two GIs took what seemed at the time to be the fastest escape route: they vaulted over the low guardrails lining the access road and slid down into the ravine, Pollock on the east side of the roadway and Worsham on the west.[18]

Struggling to stay upright on the treacherous slope and fearing that at any moment enemy troops would emerge from the nearby tree line, the six-foot-four-inch Pollock was frantically looking for some kind of cover when he heard Worsham yelling, "Pollock, Pollock, are you dead?"

"How the hell am I gonna answer you if I'm dead?" the BAR man responded. "Hell no, I'm not dead."

"Come underneath the bridge and up the other side. I'm over there," Worsham shouted.

Pollock hurried through the opening and found the rifleman waiting on the other side. Together the two GIs scrambled awkwardly uphill to the sally port, pounding on it and yelling until it was yanked inward far enough for them to squeeze through. To their amazement, the man opening the door for them was Rushford—they'd assumed he was dead.[19]

That the *Besotten Jenny*'s driver was still among the living was nothing short of a miracle. Rushford had been standing inside the vehicle, facing the radio set in its rack at the rear of the turret when the antitank round—most probably fired by the 75mm Pak 40 that Lee and the others had seen earlier on the parallel ridgeline east of the castle—slammed into the left side of the Sherman's upper hull halfway between the turret ring and the center set of road wheels. The armor-piercing projectile hit at an angle, punching a fist-sized hole in the tank's 38mm side armor and slicing through the left rear corner of the crew compartment just feet from Rushford's right leg. Barely missing the left-side fuel tank, the round tore into *Besotten Jenny*'s V-8 engine, completely destroying it and sparking an immediate fire. Momentarily stunned but miraculously unhurt, Rushford briefly hesitated before heaving open the loader's hatch and hauling himself onto the top of the turret. By the time he did so, both Pollock and Worsham had already gone over the walls and down into the ravine; Rushford chose a different escape route. Dropping from the turret top onto the narrow ledge atop the side hull, he jumped from the tank onto one of the narrow columns supporting the guardrail on one side of the access road and ran several feet along the wooden beam toward the gatehouse. Once clear of the fire, Rushford jumped down to the road surface, sprinted to the front gate—which Basse had opened for him—and lunged through just as the Sherman's fuel tanks blew, turning the vehicle into an inferno of flames and exploding machine-gun ammunition.[20]

Besotten Jenny's fiery demise galvanized the VIPs still sheltering in the rear courtyard. Reynaud shouted at Christiane Mabire and Augusta Bruchlen to collect the Cailliaus and Schrader's family and take them to the cellar; as she moved to comply, Mabire noticed that Schrader's wife was bleeding from several small cuts on her forehead and neck. As the group ran toward the main building—trailed by Daladier and Jouhaux—the young German woman explained that when the shooting started she'd thrown herself over her children and almost immediately been struck by a shower of stones blown out of the nearby parapet wall by the enemy fire.[21] Running into the Great Hall, Mabire and Bruchlen—who had herself been lightly struck by flying stones—gathered up the other VIPs crouching behind the furniture in front of the fireplace and hustled them all through the door leading to the cellars.[22]

Back in the rear courtyard, four of the six Frenchmen who moments before had been calmly enjoying the morning sun were huddled closely together beneath the surrounding parapet wall, having an unusually civil and remarkably calm discussion about what they should do next. That the men were not unduly perturbed by the enemy rounds smacking into the walls around them is not surprising: All had served in their nation's armed forces, and each had experienced combat to greater or lesser degrees. Nor is it surprising—given that each of the men was strong willed, to say the least—that they unanimously agreed to completely disregard Lee's orders to stay out of the fight. A second antitank round slamming into the already mortally wounded *Besotten Jenny* spurred the men to action; each hurried off to retrieve the weapons they'd liberated from the castle arms room the day before. Reynaud, decisive as ever, knew immediately what he would do:

> I soon saw that, as the tank was burning, the attackers could penetrate from the other side into the courtyard by the bridge which linked up with the flank of the mountain. I dodged into the castle. I got my tommy-gun[23] out of my trunk and went down to the [front] courtyard, where I found some soldiers. Clemenceau had already calmly posted himself at a loophole in case the attackers wished to take possession of the tank. I . . . took up a position near to him.[24]

Gamelin and Borotra soon reappeared, along with de La Rocque. The trio joined Reynaud and Clemenceau behind the parapet wall in the front courtyard, and all began firing enthusiastically—if somewhat randomly—toward the small inn on the schlossweg and into the trees on the south side of the ravine.[25]

When the Frenchmen had returned to the courtyard after retrieving their weapons, Gangl had ordered Wegscheider and Linsen to join their comrades on the upper floors of the keep and direct their fire down onto any Waffen-SS troopers attempting to reach the base of the foundation wall. As the two Germans moved off, Lee came running past them and slid into a crouch next to Gangl. After a quick pause to catch his breath, Lee motioned the German officer to follow him and then headed for the schlosshof gate and the steps leading to the front courtyard. Dashing down the stone steps, the two men emerged at the rear of the courtyard and took cover behind the parapet wall. Catching sight of the elderly Frenchmen a few yards farther along the wall, Lee caught Gangl's eye and, pointing at Reynaud and the others, smiled ruefully.

As the two men were pondering the sight of five of France's most fa-mous sons blasting away with obvious delight, the rear door of the gate-house swung open, and Basse, Seiner, and Pollock emerged in a low crouch. Motioning Seiner to stay by the door, Basse briefly conferred with Pollock, who nodded and moved to the eastern corner of the gatehouse. At a wave from Lee, Basse hurried over, being careful to stay crouched be-low the level of the parapet wall. Leaning in close to be heard above the din of the incoming rounds and the Frenchmen's MP-40s, the young motor officer explained that though the GIs in the gatehouse had begun laying down defensive fires almost as soon as *Besotten Jenny* was hit the first time, smoke from the furiously blazing tank was wafting back toward them, ob-scuring the schlossweg and the oncoming enemy. Basse's intent was to post Pollock on the upper floor of the schlosshof, from where he'd have a better, and hopefully smoke-free, line of sight up the access road.

While Lee and Basse were conferring, Reynaud moved closer to the gatehouse. Believing the elderly politician would be more exposed to en-emy fire in his new position, Lee was about to motion to Seiner to pull him back when Gangl, who obviously also recognized the danger, stood and dashed toward Reynaud. In his haste to stop the Frenchman the German officer ran almost fully erect, and he'd gone barely ten feet when he sud-denly dropped to the courtyard's cobblestones in an awkward heap, his visored hat rolling a few feet past him. Seiner, watching from his position by the rear door of the gatehouse, at first thought the officer had tripped. But when blood quickly began pooling around his head, it was obvious that Sepp Gangl, a man of valor who'd survived the hell of Stalingrad and the maelstrom of Normandy, had been cut down by a sniper's bullet.[26]

Though stunned by the sudden death of his unexpected ally, Lee had no time to mourn him. The volume of enemy small-arms fire from across the ravine was increasing, and several 88 rounds had crashed into the north wall. Shouting to be heard, Lee told Basse to hold the gatehouse as long as he could and then pull his men back up to the main building. Motioning that he was headed for the top of the keep to get a better idea of what was happening, Lee then headed for the stone steps.

Across the courtyard from Basse, Pollock was about to have his own problems. The young GI had moved into what he believed to be a relatively safe position behind the parapet wall on the east side of the gatehouse, prior to making a dash across the courtyard for the schlosshof. He'd momentarily

rested his BAR on the top of the wall and begun scanning for targets, looking away briefly when he saw Lee head up the steps. Just as he turned back,
a hail of enemy fire from the ridgeline east of the castle—off to his left—
forced him to drop to his belly.[27] As the rounds slapped into the side of the
stone wall next to him, Pollock low-crawled to the rear corner of the gatehouse and shouted to Basse that Waffen-SS troops were moving up the
steep slope on the north side. Certain that the main enemy effort would
be directed at the gatehouse and loath to spare any of the GIs protecting it,
Basse turned to Reynaud. Shouting to be heard above the raucous cacoph-
ony of hammering weapons, the young officer brusquely ordered the
Frenchman to take Clemenceau and hurry over to the other side of the castle to bolster its defenses.

The two Frenchmen scurried to the base of the same stone steps Lee had
just ascended and bolted upward. As Reynaud later recalled:

We ran to the other side of the castle in order to defend the surrounding
wall, although the ground fell away in a steep slope. A young Austrian
patriot [Hans Waltl] with a white and red brassard showed himself very
active. The Wehrmacht lieutenant [Wegscheider], glasses to his eyes,
pointed out targets against which to direct our fire. . . . I regret that I
cannot confirm that I killed one enemy.[28]

Fortunately, the defense of Schloss Itter did not solely depend on Reynaud's skill with an MP-40. Wegscheider, Waltl, and Clemenceau were also
blasting away, and the Wehrmacht troops in the keep—commanded by
Lee with the help of Schrader, Dietrich, Höckel, and Blechschmidt—were
pouring a far more accurate fire down on SS troops attacking from the north,
west, and east. Basse and the GIs in and around the gatehouse—aided by
Borotra, de La Rocque, and Gamelin—were holding their own as well,
though by this time Basse was becoming acutely aware that ammunition
was beginning to run low. McHaley, in the gatehouse's upper level, had
already gone through all but a few belts of the 1,300 .30-caliber rounds
they'd earlier removed from *Besotten Jenny*, and bullets were getting equally
short for the infantrymen's M1s, Pollock's BAR, and the three tankers' M3
submachine guns. De La Rocque and Gamelin were each down to only one
or two thirty-two-round magazines for their MP-40s, and Borotra's weapon
was empty. After cautioning all the gatehouse defenders to conserve their

ammo as much as possible, Basse motioned the French tennis star over and told him to inform Lee about the ammo situation.

Borotra, bent as low as his lanky frame would allow, nodded and bolted up the stone steps. Dodging and weaving as he ran across the terrace, he made it into the Great Hall unscathed and, not surprisingly, unwinded. He was about to start up the interior stairway in search of Lee when the tanker, followed by Schrader and several of the "tame" Wehrmacht soldiers, hurried in through the doors leading from the small patio on the castle's northwest corner, while rounds from the enemy 20mm anti-aircraft gun to the northwest gouged the exterior wall above the door. As Lee pointed out new ground-floor positions to the men, whom Borotra assumed had become too exposed on the patio, the tennis player quickly relayed Basse's message.

Lee grimly acknowledged that everybody was running short on ammo and was about to say something else when the shrill ringing of the orderly room telephone echoed through the cavernous room.

AFTER DECIDING TO CONTINUE on to Schloss Itter without infantry and armor support, Major John Kramers had pushed his under-armed, two-jeep relief force hard. The two vehicles had roared along the south bank of the Inn River, occasionally spotting groups of armed German troops in the trees bordering the road but—much to the Americans' surprise—encountering no roadblocks or resistance. As Meyer Levin recalled: "We whistled through the last 20 miles to Wörgl, which had still been unexplored on our side, and when we got to the place and saw a United States tank sitting there, we let out a joint gasp of relief."[29]

The tank, of course, was *Boche Buster*. Bill Elliot and his crew had been anxiously awaiting some kind of reinforcement since Lee had left them in Wörgl the evening before to guard the bridge; whether the tankers felt that two jeeps—one of which bore only reporters—constituted that reinforcement is unclear. Nonetheless, Kramers was an officer, and, when he asked for a situation report, Elliot told him it had been a tense but essentially uneventful night. The tank crew had parked their Sherman between two buildings about fifty feet from the span, thus screening themselves from view while still being able to maintain overwatch. They had heard a lot of enemy vehicle traffic moving through the town in the dark and, once dawn arrived, had seen trucks and dismounted troops heading south out of Wörgl on a road that snaked through the mountains toward the crossroads at Neiderau. No enemy units had attempted to cross the small bridge, Elliot said, and his men had not fired their weapons, nor had the ten or so Austrian partisans who'd stood vigil with them.

When Kramers asked about the situation at Schloss Itter, Elliot—pointing at the castle, just visible atop the ridgeline to the southeast—said he and his men had been hearing heavy small-arms fire and occasional artillery all morning and assumed from the heavy black smoke that Lee's tank had been destroyed. As Kramers, Levin, and the others trained their binoculars on the castle, noting the smoke pillar, several additional shells slammed into the schloss's northern foundation wall. When the military-government officer asked if they'd been able to speak with Lee, Elliot said they'd been out of radio contact even before *Besotten Jenny*'s apparent demise. Kramers then asked if there was any other way to communicate with the castle, and one of Rupert Hagleitner's partisans responded that the telephone connection from the town hall might still work. Leaving Elliot and his men with *Boche Buster*, Kramers, Lutten, Gris, Čučković, Levin, and Schwab jumped in their vehicles and, with one of the partisans sitting on the hood of the lead jeep giving directions, headed for the center of Wörgl.[30]

Roaring through deserted streets lined by buildings from which white flags fluttered, the jeeps made it to the town hall in minutes. Rushing inside, the men crowded around a small telephone booth tucked under a stairway and waited a few anxious moments while the young partisan dialed. To their surprise and relief, Lee picked up after only a few rings. Kramers took the phone, introduced himself, and then asked about the situation at the castle.

After telling Kramers that the castle's defenders were perilously short on ammo, Lee added, "They're shelling the bajabers out of us. Listen, better get some doughs [GIs] up here right away." Before Kramers could ask any more questions, he heard an explosion, and the line when dead.[31]

Though he knew Lee and his men needed immediate help, Kramers also knew that without significant backup he and his little group would likely not even survive the trip to the castle. As he was wondering aloud where he'd find the necessary help, Eric Schwab ran in from the street, yelling that there was an American column rolling toward them. Kramers and the others rushed outside just as six M4 Shermans from the 753rd Tank Battalion clattered into the plaza in front of the town hall, followed by half-tracks filled with men of the 142nd Infantry's Company E. Quickly locating the unit commander, Captain Joe W. Gill,[32] Kramers told him of the urgent need to get to Schloss Itter. Gill obviously had not gotten the word regarding his regimental commander's earlier sanctioning of Lee's rescue mission to the castle or of Lynch's promise to provide a relief force, as Meyer Levin recalled:

> "We're just supposed to travel down this road and make a link-up with the Hundred and Third. That's our mission. We haven't got any order to move out and attack a castle," [Gill said.]
>   "Who's got to give you the order?" [Kramers asked.]
>   "Colonel Lynch."
>   "Where's he?"
>   "He's just left us; he's gone back up the road someplace."[33]

Because Gill had more important things on his mind than chasing down his wayward regimental commander to ask about what most probably seemed to the young company commander a rather harebrained rescue effort, he tapped one of his platoon leaders, First Lieutenant Clifford J. Reinhard, to escort Kramers and his retinue. Then, Levin said, the group "chased off in search of Colonel Lynch. We burned up six miles of road in a style that would have gladdened the heart of Darryl Zanuck, and we caught up with a cloud of dust."[34]

While we don't know how Lynch reacted to the sudden appearance of one of his young lieutenants with Kramers's party in tow, or to Reinhard's news that Gill was unaware of the need to relieve Lee and his troops, we do know that the 142nd's regimental commander immediately sent Reinhard back to Wörgl with instructions for Gill. The Company E commander was to leave enough men to secure the town's eastern side and then assemble a relief force and move out for Schloss Itter following the Brixentalerstrasse through Söll-Leukental to Hopfgarten and then up the Ittererstrasse. Captain Carl P. Matney's Company G, Lynch said, would advance on the castle from the north, via the village of Mühltal.[35] Minutes later, Lynch added Company F to the mission, tasking Captain Glenn A. Goff to slot his men in behind Matney's unit.[36]

Racing back to Wörgl, Reinhard relayed Lynch's instructions to Gill, who tapped three Shermans of the 1st Section of the 753rd's Company D—the same tanks that had been unable to cross the bridge with Lee's party the day before—and Rushford's *Boche Buster* to spearhead the move to Schloss Itter. One platoon of GIs would remain in Wörgl; three others, including Reinhard's, would follow the Shermans in half-tracks; and Kramers's two jeeps would play tail-end Charlie.

The need to chase down Lynch and then put together the relief force meant that Gill and his column didn't leave Wörgl until almost one PM. Finally on the road, the convoy moved through streets now lined with white flags and growing numbers of welcoming Austrian civilians—many of them wonderfully attractive young women, as Levin later noted—who offered the GIs bottles of wine and bouquets of early spring flowers. Once out of Wörgl, however, the Americans began encountering a rather different sort of people. As Levin recalled: "German [soldiers] began to leak out of the woods. Some were just boys of sixteen who claimed they hadn't even fired their guns. Then there came older men, in twos, singly, in groups—all, of course, claiming they'd been forced into the fight against their will."[37] Consisting mainly of volksturm (elderly civilian militiamen) Hitler Youth and second- or third-line Wehrmacht reserve troops, most of those attempting to surrender to Gill's infantrymen were simply disarmed and told to make their way toward the POW cage being set up just south of Kufstein.

But not all German troops in Tyrol were ready to call it quits. As Gill's men moved out into the farmland between Wörgl and Söll-Leukental—barely a mile from where they'd started—they began encountering Waffen-SS men who were vastly more motivated and obviously willing to fight. Sporadic sniper fire erupted, and, Levin wrote, "the old tense expressions settled in. [The U.S. troops] moved cautiously behind the tanks, taking cover in the field. Nobody wanted to get hurt on this day-after-the-last-day of fighting."[38] The GIs' caution was more than justified, for as they dispersed on either side of the Brixentalerstrasse, they came under fire from two MG-42s hidden in log-and-sandbag bunkers on a hillside to their south. Though the American tanks quickly silenced the machine guns with HE rounds, Waffen-SS troops engaged the infantrymen with increasingly heavy small-arms fire.[39]

On the far left flank of the advancing column Reinhard's platoon had crossed to the opposite side of the Brixentaler Ache via a small footbridge they'd found intact. This put the men a few hundred yards ahead of the lead elements of Company G, which was advancing southeast along the two-lane road that paralleled the river. Matney's unit had encountered only sporadic resistance since leaving the outskirts of Wörgl; indeed, it seemed that most of the Waffen-SS men in the area immediately east of the town were concentrating their efforts against the American troops and vehicles that were obviously intent on moving toward Hopfgarten. That force, which now consisted of the bulk of Gill's Company E bolstered by Goff's Company F, was deployed across the southwest side of the valley between the bordering hills and the river.[40]

As Reinhard and his men moved forward in single file beside the trees lining the riverbank, the young lieutenant was probably beginning to think that crossing the Brixentaler Ache had not been the smartest idea he'd had that day. While doing so had allowed the platoon to largely avoid enemy contact and thus advance fairly quickly, the bank's meandering curve to the southeast meant that the GIs were being steadily separated even more from the bulk of Company E, which was beginning to turn almost directly south along the road leading to Hopfgarten. Moreover, the character of the Ache—which flows northwest toward its rendezvous with the Inn—would also have given the infantry officer pause: though only about four feet deep, the river is fast flowing and constantly roiled by a rocky bed and dozens of small cataracts.[41] Loaded down with weapons, ammunition, and personal gear, Reinhard and his men likely wouldn't have been able to safely wade across.

As the young platoon leader was pondering his next move, several jeeps bearing soldiers of Company G's small reconnaissance detachment rumbled across the field behind him and slewed to a stop. As Reinhard walked over to speak to the new arrivals, he noted that one of the men wasn't carrying a weapon, nor was he wearing a regulation uniform. Glancing at a small insignia sewn to the man's British-style field jacket, Reinhard realized that he was a civilian reporter. Though the young infantry officer didn't know it at the time, the man was French-Canadian war correspondent (and future premier of Quebec)[42] René Lévesque. The then twenty-three-year-old journalist had spent the previous months attached to various U.S. Army units and had witnessed the liberation of Dachau. He'd been accompanying the 142nd Infantry for several days and had chosen to ride along with Company G on the rescue mission to Itter.

As Lévesque later recalled in his memoirs,[43] he was about to introduce himself to the men from Company E when a shout from the GI acting as point man for Reinhard's platoon focused everyone's immediate attention on a strange apparition: a tall, thin, and athletic-looking man—apparently an Austrian peasant from the look of his clothes—was approaching, "running at an unhurried pace, jogging before the invention of the word. Being a tennis buff I recognized him almost immediately," Lévesque later recalled. "It was Borotra, an all-time champion. He was hardly winded and told us that he'd just walked out of the chateau-prison of Itter a few kilometers up the road."[44] Borotra, the famed Bounding Basque, had escaped from Schloss Itter yet again. But this time his goal was more than just his own freedom, he said; this time, he'd made it over the walls bearing both a message and a plan.

———

WHILE KRAMERS'S CALL to Schloss Itter from the Wörgl town hall had let the castle's defenders know that help was actually on the way, it hadn't improved their immediate situation. Their ammunition was perilously low, Gangl was dead and two of his Wehrmacht troops were seriously wounded, and though the Waffen-SS attackers hadn't yet managed to breach the fortress's walls, they were pressing their attack with what Jack Lee would later call "extreme vigor."

At about the same time that Cliff Reinhard was relaying Lynch's instructions for a rescue force to Company E commander Gill, Lee realized that he was running out of options. The telephone line had been Schloss Itter's last communications link with the outside world, and it had been severed before Lee was able to give Kramers any intel about the location, strength, or weaponry of the attacking Waffen-SS troops. Without that information the relief force could well end up wasting precious time fighting enemies it might otherwise be able to avoid, and anything that delayed the advancing Americans only made it more likely that Schloss Itter's VIPs and their defenders wouldn't survive the afternoon.

At this critical juncture Jean Borotra stepped forward with an audacious— and quite possibly suicidal—proposal. He would go over the wall and make his way to the nearest Americans to both hurry them up and show them the quickest way to get to the castle. When Lee rightly pointed out that the tennis star's chances of making it through the enemy cordon were slim, at best, Borotra replied that his previous escape attempts had given him a unique knowledge of the surrounding terrain and of several ways to leave the castle unobserved. He confidently predicted that he'd reach the advancing Americans "in no time," and Lee, with no other options, reluctantly agreed to let the tall Frenchman try.

After disguising himself as an Austrian refugee—complete with ragged bedroll and gnarled walking stick—Borotra waited for a brief lull in the firing and then clambered over one of the low parapet walls on the castle's north side. He dropped some fifteen feet to the ground, rolled easily, and in seconds was back on his feet. His daily training runs stood him in good stead, for he dashed quickly across forty yards of open ground, made it into the woods that bordered the castle's northwest side, and started down the steep slope toward the river. After carefully eluding several groups of SS men, some of whom were firing upslope at the castle, Borotra burst from the trees at the bottom of the hill and came face to face with two soldiers manning an MG-42 machine gun sited so it could fire at both the castle and at any Americans approaching from the direction of Söll-Leukental.[45]

No doubt equally as startled by Borotra's sudden appearance as the Frenchman was by theirs, the Waffen-SS men nonetheless held their fire, apparently taken in by the tennis star's "harmless refugee" disguise. He reinforced their first impression by calmly bending down to gather some herbs and then relieving himself against a nearby tree. When it was clear that the soldiers had dismissed him as a possible threat, he sauntered to the bank of a large stream and, holding his bedroll and walking stick over his head, waded into the swift-flowing, waist-deep water. Though he slipped once or twice, he kept his footing and made it to the other side. Climbing to the top of the bank he looked back at the soldiers, tossed them a friendly wave, and started toward Söll-Leukental. As soon as he thought it safe, he began the slow and steady jog that ultimately led him to Reinhard and Lévesque.[46]

Within minutes of that meeting Borotra was talking to Lynch, who had set up his regimental command post in a farmhouse only a half mile away, from where he could see the castle silhouetted atop the towering ridgeline to his south. After delivering his message—that the situation at Schloss Itter was dire and help was needed immediately—the Frenchman presented his plan: he would lead the American infantrymen back to the castle via the quick route up the north slope and along the way point out to them all the German positions he'd observed. His only request was that he be given an American uniform and a weapon.

Suitably attired and armed, Borotra led Reinhard's platoon and most of Matney's Company G back across the open farmland toward Schloss Itter. After eliminating the MG-42 and its two-man crew, the Americans crossed the stream—aided by ropes—and started up the steep hillside, killing two more Waffen-SS men and capturing twelve without a single U.S. casualty.[47] Borotra led the way, determined to be the first to reach his beleaguered comrades in the castle. Unfortunately, that honor would not be his.

When the bulk of Company E and all of Company G had turned south onto the road to Hopfgarten, the resistance that had bedeviled them on the way out of Wörgl slackened considerably. Though occasionally fired on by snipers and the odd machine gun, the column had been able to quicken its pace down the Brixentalerstrasse. Upon reaching the northern outskirts of Hopfgarten, Company G had dropped out to secure the town, allowing Gill and his company to start north up the steep and narrow Ittererstrasse toward the castle. It wasn't a cakewalk; the GIs encountered several well-defended roadblocks, and at one point an antitank gun mounted on a half-track fired at the lead Sherman. It missed, and one of the other M4s quickly knocked out the German vehicle with an AP round and then killed its fleeing crew with .30-caliber machine-gun fire.[48] But Gill—now with his battalion commander, Marvin Coyle, riding along with him—was a man on a mission, and he pushed his men up the road as fast as he could. As Meyer Levin recalled: "There were short bursts of fire—machine guns, burp guns, ours, theirs. [But] the tanks reached [Itter] village. They let out a long roll of machine-gun fire, and presently a few dozen jerries came piling out of the houses, hands up. In a few minutes, the Joes were through the town."[49]

As SOON AS BOROTRA had gone over the wall, Lee—always the pragmatist—had begun planning what he and his shrinking command would do if the relief force didn't show up in time. Securing the agreement of Weygand and Gamelin—both of whom had deferred to the young American throughout the battle despite their own exalted ranks—Lee began pulling defenders off the walls and shepherding them and the French VIPs toward the keep. The American tanker, aided by Schrader and the other German officers, deployed the troops and the armed Frenchmen at windows and the top of each staircase.

Daladier, for his part, sequestered himself in one of the second-floor bedrooms, where:

> two of the German soldiers who had come with [Gangl] had taken up positions, with their rifles resting on the window sills. They pointed out [SS troops] firing at the "castle" from a few hundred yards away, near the little electric plant, on the edge of the forest. The two soldiers returned the fire. I took advantage of a moment of calm to exchange a few words with our defenders. They told me in German that they were Polish. When I told them I was French, one of them started shaking my hand while the other pulled a bottle out of his coat and offered it to me. It was a bottle of Fernet Branca; where the devil did he get that? I drank a bit; it was really bad. Then he laughed and told me Hitler was kaput.[50]

Down on the schlossweg, a squad of Waffen-SS troops was at that moment pressing the attack. Just as one of them settled into position to fire a panzerfaust at the front gate, the sound of automatic weapons and tank guns behind them in the village signaled a radical change in the tactical situation. Seconds later the SS men evaporated into the woods, just as *Boche Buster* rolled to a stop at the village end of the schlossweg, its appearance prompting Daladier's newfound friend to stop laughing, point out the window, and yell "panzer!"[51] It was just after four PM.

Within minutes the castle's jubilant defenders—American, French, and German—poured down into the front courtyard, out the gate, and past *Besotten Jenny*'s still-smoldering hulk toward the men and vehicles of the rescue force. As a small truck bearing Rupert Hagleitner, several of his resistance fighters, and Andreas Krobot rolled down the schlossweg, Lee thanked Gill for arriving in true Wild West fashion: just in the nick of time. Lee and Basse then walked over to where Elliot was nonchalantly leaning against *Boche Buster*. Feigning irritation, Lee looked the young tanker in the eye and said simply, "What kept you?"

CHAPTER 8

AFTERMATH

As Captain Joe Gill's infantrymen quickly set about establishing a security perimeter around Schloss Itter, 142nd Infantry Regiment commander George Lynch ordered John Kramers to maneuver the chattering, gesticulating French VIPs and liberated number prisoners back into the castle's front courtyard. The jubilant crowd squeezed through the gatehouse portals, Meyer Levin and René Lévesque dashing from person to person gathering quotes and Eric Schwab photographing civilians and soldiers alike.

A very tired Jack Lee walked up to Lynch, saluted, and, gesturing at the French VIPs loudly thanking Zvonko Čučković and Andreas Krobot for their courageous rides, said, "Take them colonel, they're all yours."[1] Lynch smiled and was about to respond when Čučković, spotting Kurt-Siegfried Schrader in his Waffen-SS uniform, let out a yell and rushed toward the startled officer as if to attack him. Krobot jumped between the two men, restraining the Croat handyman and explaining that the German had helped protect the French VIPs "with his life."[2] As an only slightly less angry Čučković moved away, Schrader approached Lynch. Saluting far more smartly than had the exhausted Lee, the German said he had the pleasure to formally hand over the French former prisoners, who had been "under his protection."

Protecting the liberated VIPs was also high on Lynch's task list, of course—there were still armed enemy units in the area, after all, and no cease-fire had yet been officially declared—and he had received orders from Major General McAuliffe to move the former prisoners as soon as possible to the 103rd Infantry Division's command post in Innsbruck. Through Kramers, Lynch directed the French to return to their rooms, pack only what they could carry in hand luggage, and then assemble in the castle's Great Hall while he set about organizing the first leg of their journey back to France.

While thrilled to have been rescued, the VIPs were obviously not willing to let go of the enmity, rivalries, and petty backbiting that had characterized their time at Schloss Itter. As they drifted into the Great Hall with their bags, several of them took the opportunity to voice their complaints to Kramers. As Meyer Levin later wrote, "Some of them whispered about others who had been quite friendly with the German commandant of Itter, and Major Kramers shrewdly observed that perhaps some of these people were as happy to be liberated from each other's company as they were to be liberated from imprisonment."[3]

René Lévesque was equally struck by the fact that liberation had obviously done nothing to ease the personal animosities of the French VIPs. When he entered the Great Hall to continue his interviews, the young Canadian war correspondent found them "sitting around in little groups seeming very disinclined to talk to one another."[4] Lévesque noted that Daladier and Reynaud were seated in opposite corners of the room and studiously avoiding each other.

Despite the obvious tension, the young reporter could not pass up the chance to interview two such august personages. Initially unsure which gentleman to approach first, Lévesque took a decidedly pragmatic approach: respecting the chronology of their public service, he began with Daladier.

The "old bull of the Vaucluse"[5] had thinned down a little, but he was still a rugged customer, though he had a hesitant look as if he might be worried about awkward questions. As far as that went, he'd had plenty of time to prepare himself. "Monsieur le Premier Ministré," I asked him after we'd been formally introduced, "would you mind sharing with us some of the reflections that time and distance have certainly given you a chance to elaborate?" "Cher Monsieur," he replied, "I have indeed many things to reveal, and above all a great many things to set straight. I intend to publish a full account as soon as I return to France. But here, you understand," he said, lowering his voice, "there are indiscreet ears belonging to certain individuals who will be unmasked in my memoirs as they deserve to be. I can hardly say more."[6]

The "old bull" obviously intended Lévesque to realize that the "indiscreet ears" belonged to his arch political enemy, for as he finished speaking, he shot what the young reporter called "a murderous look" at Reynaud, who was sitting across the room "affecting the most complete indifference." When Lévesque approached Reynaud, whom he described as a "dry, pointed little fellow," he was treated to a virtual repeat of his conversation with Daladier:

> He too, Reynaud said, had plenty to expose, and certain people—same murderous look—had better watch themselves! Not only were [Daladier and Reynaud] not on speaking terms, they could hardly wait to carve each other up. None the wiser, I had to settle for a simple statement of our discovery without further adornment.[7]

Once all the VIPs were ready, Kramers shepherded them down to the courtyard, out the front gate, and onto the schlossweg, where Krobot and the female former number prisoners were waiting with bags in hand. Soldiers loaded their luggage into the back of a two-and-a-half-ton truck waiting in front of the church. Schloss Itter's former prisoners boarded a line of waiting jeeps—the French being careful, of course, to segregate themselves into the same little groups they'd formed during their imprisonment. Just before seven PM the convoy of vehicles set off for Innsbruck, with Kramers's jeep leading the way and a truckload of 142nd infantrymen following to provide security.[8]

The French VIPs stayed in Innsbruck overnight and were suitably feted by, and photographed with, the 103rd's MacAuliffe. On May 6 they were driven across the German border to Augsburg, and that evening they dined with Seventh Army commander Alexander Patch. The American general had originally intended to fly the French notables home from Augsburg aboard a U.S. Army Air Forces C-47, but French 1st Army commander Jean de Lattre de Tassigny asked permission to undertake the VIPs' return to France. Patch agreed, and on May 7 the former prisoners were driven to de Lattre's headquarters in Lindau, on the German shore of Lake Constance.

Upon the group's arrival, Weygand, Borotra, and de La Rocque were led away; the 1st Army commander announced that the trio would be put on trial in France for their "collaborationist" activities. The other former prisoners were treated to yet another sumptuous banquet, and the following morning all but Daladier were driven to Strasbourg, where they boarded General de Gaulle's personal aircraft for the flight to Paris. The Bull of the Vaucluse, for his part, drove to Paris with his son Jean, an officer on de Lattre's staff.[9]

For Krobot and the female former number prisoners, the way home led east, not west. After ensuring that they'd all received a thorough medical examination and enjoyed several days of good food and clean beds courtesy of the U.S. Army, Kramers deposited them at a displaced-persons camp operated by the United Nations Relief and Rehabilitation Administration.

That Zvonko Čučković did not accompany his fellow former prisoners was the result of some quick thinking on his part. Within hours of the liberation of Schloss Itter the Croat convinced French liaison officer Eric Lutten that someone should gather up all the personal items the VIPs had not been able to take with them and then ensure that the articles were safely reunited with their owners—in France. Zvonko volunteered for the mission, of course, and was given a travel document authorizing him to accompany the items to Paris and stipulating that he report back to French authorities in Austria by May 23. He made the trip, returned on schedule, and within weeks was repatriated to Yugoslavia.[10]

The aftermath of the Schloss Itter battle was rather anticlimactic for Jack Lee and his men. The four infantrymen who'd taken part in the fight—Pollock, Worsham, Petruckovich, and Sutton—rejoined their unit, then assembling in Itter village. After turning Gangl's body over to the priest at St. Joseph's Church, Lee sent Basse and *Boche Buster* back to rejoin the 23rd TB. Once the burnt-out *Besotten Jenny* had been unceremoniously towed away by a tank-recovery vehicle, Lee and his four crewmen, accompanied by the surviving "tame" Germans, boarded a truck for the ride back to Kufstein. There the Wehrmacht men who'd risked their lives to help the GIs defend the French notables were marched off to a POW cage for processing.

The end of the battle for Schloss Itter did not mark the end of the castle's role in World War II history, however. Even before the French VIPs had departed for Innsbruck, the 142nd Infantry's George Lynch made the fortress his regimental command post, and over the following twenty-four hours he helped broker—through meetings with Georg von Hengl—a local cease-fire and the ultimate surrender of all German forces in Tyrol. Following Germany's unconditional capitulation in the early morning hours of May 7, Schloss Itter became (though for less than twenty-four hours) the provisional headquarters of Allied occupation forces in Austria.[11]

Several weeks after Germany's surrender Basse and Lee were recognized for their leadership during the battle for Schloss Itter, the former with the Silver Star and the latter with the Distinguished Service Cross.[12] Lee's citation noted his

> extraordinary heroism in action, as Commanding Officer of Company B, 23rd Tank Battalion, in the vicinity of Wörgl, Austria, and the Itter Castle on 4–5 May 1945. Captain Lee with a small group of soldiers infiltrated into hostile territory, demoralized enemy forces, prevented the destruction of two key bridges, and caused 200 German soldiers to surrender. He found many prominent French prisoners at Itter Castle, and immediately organized a defense with both American and German troops. Despite a fanatical SS attack and heavy artillery barrage, Captain Lee's men held until friendly troops arrived. Captain Lee's initiative, boldness, courage, resourcefulness and outstanding qualities of leadership exemplify the highest traditions of the Army and the United States.[13]

———

WHILE THE BATTLE OF SCHLOSS Itter may have been a defining moment in the lives of many of its participants, it was not—except for Sepp Gangl and those unnamed attackers who may have died in the assault—the final moment. The various key players in the last full-fledged ground combat action of World War II in Europe—the French, Germans, Americans, and others— went back to their normal lives, and it is only right that we briefly examine how some of those lives played out.

THE FRENCH

ÉDOUARD DALADIER

The Bull of the Vaucluse returned to politics after the war, serving as a deputy in France's Constituent Assembly and from 1953 to 1958 as mayor of Avignon. His son Jean later compiled and edited Daladier's wartime diaries. Published as *Journal de Captivité, 1940–1945* (*Prison Journal, 1940–1945*) several years after Daladier's death in October 1970 at age eighty-six, the book did exactly what the former Schloss Itter captive had told René Levesque it would do: excoriate his political rivals, especially Paul Reynaud.

MAURICE GAMELIN

Following his postwar return to France, Gamelin devoted himself to completing his memoirs, titled *Servir*. The three-volume work—much of which was written during the general's time in Schloss Itter—was published in 1946 and 1947 to relatively lukewarm reviews. In 1954 Gamelin published a further volume covering his World War I service. He died in April 1958 at the age of eighty-six.

LÉON JOUHAUX AND AUGUSTA BRUCHLEN

His years of imprisonment may have further damaged Léon Jouhaux's health, but they didn't dim his dedication to the workers of France or to the international labor movement. After his liberation he resumed his leadership of the CGT, but in 1947 the organization's Communist members forced his resignation. In reaction to what he saw as increasing Communist domination of the French labor movement he helped found the left-centrist Workers' Force, which he led for the remainder of his life. In 1947 Jouhaux was also elected president of the French National Economic Council and in 1951 helped establish the International Labor Organization as an agency of the United Nations. Jouhaux was awarded the Nobel Peace Prize in 1951 and died on April 28, 1954.

Augusta Bruchlen aided Jouhaux in all his postwar efforts on behalf of workers, and she adopted the name Augusta Léon-Jouhaux following their marriage in 1948. She was an important labor leader in her own right, serving as director of the International Labor Organization's Paris office from 1950 to 1971. *Prison pour hommes d'Etat*, her account of the Schloss Itter years, was published in 1973. This remarkable woman was named a commander of the Légion d'honneur in May 1992 and a Grand Officier of the same in July 2001. She died at the age of 104 on April 28, 2003, forty-nine years to the day after Léon Jouhaux.

PAUL REYNAUD AND CHRISTIANE MABIRE

Like his archrival Daladier, Paul Reynaud returned to politics soon after his liberation from Schloss Itter. He won election to the Chamber of

Deputies in 1946 and over the following decade held several cabinet posts, including minister of finance and economic affairs. Published in 1951, *Au Coeur de la Mêlée* (titled *In the Thick of the Fight* in English) the larger of Reynaud's two wartime memoirs,[14] devoted only 4 of more than 680 pages to events at Schloss Itter; the majority of the book was dedicated to explaining his own actions and generally belittling those of his many political rivals—including Daladier, of course. Reynaud was initially a strong supporter of Charles de Gaulle, though in 1962 he broke with the former general over what he saw as de Gaulle's drive to consolidate his power through manipulation of the constitution. After losing his seat in the Chamber of Deputies, Reynaud dedicated himself to writing on various topics. He died at age eighty-seven on September 21, 1966.

Christiane Mabire married Reynaud in December 1949 and ultimately bore three children: sons Serge and Alexandre and daughter Evelyne. After her husband's death Madame Reynaud led a very private life. She wrote a short, unpublished memoir dealing with her experiences in Ravensbrück and Schloss Itter before passing away in 2002 at the age of eighty-nine.[15]

Marcel Granger

After his liberation from Schloss Itter, Granger personally carried two suitcases full of documents back to Paris: one contained Maxime Weygand's voluminous notes for his intended postwar memoirs, and the other Paul Reynaud's notes for his book. While some sources indicate that Granger then returned to North Africa, it has proven impossible to discover any solid details about the final years of the man whom Édouard Daladier described in his memoir of the Schloss Itter years as "a true gentleman" and "a fine man, highly patriotic and brave, and a wonderful example of the average Frenchman."[16]

Jean Borotra

Though in the immediate postwar years the French government considered trying the Bounding Basque as a collaborator for his service in the Vichy government, nothing came of the charges, and Borotra's popularity was undiminished. He resumed his commercial career, working until 1975. Nor did he give up tennis; he served as vice president of the French Lawn Tennis Association and continued to play in international senior competitions well into his nineties. Borotra died in June 1994 at age ninety-five.

MAXIME AND MARIE-RENÉE-JOSÉPHINE WEYGAND

The general and his wife were apprehensive about how they would be received upon their return to France, and rightly so. Maxime Weygand was arrested by the French government on May 10, 1945, and charged with "attempts against the internal security of the state." The following July the High Court of Justice ordered the seizure of all his property and put the aged and ill former general under guard at a Paris hospital. Called as a witness in the trial of Marshal Philippe Pétain, Weygand did verbal battle with Paul Reynaud, who was acting for the prosecution. Weygand's own trial sputtered on for three years, and he was finally acquitted in 1948. He returned to writing, turning out books and articles on a host of subjects. Marie-Renée-Joséphine died in 1961, and Weygand himself passed away on January 28, 1965, at age ninety-eight.

MICHEL CLEMENCEAU

The son of the Tiger entered the rough and tumble of post–World War II French politics, serving in the first and second National Constituent Assemblies from 1946 to 1951. After withdrawing from politics, he returned to private industry and died on March 4, 1964, at ninety-one.

FRANÇOIS DE LA ROCQUE

During his time at Schloss Itter the former leader of the Croix de feu wrote what would ultimately prove to be his final political tract. Titled *Au service de l'avenir* (*Serving the Future*), the book was published in 1946, repeated his fundamental political and moral beliefs, and was obviously meant as a first attempt at rehabilitating his reputation. De La Rocque did not live to see that effort succeed, however. Placed under police supervision and then house arrest following his return to France, he died in April 1946 during surgery meant to alleviate lingering pain from one of his World War I injuries.

MARIE-AGNÈS AND ALFRED CAILLIAU

Though the Cailliaus' imprisonment at Schloss Itter lasted barely a month, the harsh conditions they'd experienced before arriving at the Austrian fortress left lasting scars—both physical and mental. Alfred returned to work as an engineer but was plagued by poor health until his death in December 1956 at the age of seventy-nine. Marie-Agnès was awarded the Légion d'honneur in June 1975 in recognition of her wartime activities on behalf of the French resistance. Her personal reminiscence of her eventful life, *Souvenirs personnels*, was published following her death in March 1982 at the age of ninety-three.

THE NUMBER PRISONERS

Sadly, it has proven impossible to track Andres Krobot or any of the female number prisoners following their handover to the UNRRA.

ZVONIMIR ČUČKOVIĆ

Following his return to Yugoslavia at the conclusion of his brief postliberation trip to Paris, Zvonko Čučković set up a small electrical contracting business in Belgrade. He consolidated the incredibly detailed notes he'd kept during his time at Schloss Itter into the manuscript "Zwei Jahren auf Schloss Itter," and provided copies to both the West German and the French governments. Čučković corresponded with several of the French notables after the war, and he provided Augusta Léon-Jouhaux with many of the details she used in her book *Prison pour hommes d'Etat*. Čučković died in Belgrade in 1984.

THE GERMANS

JOSEF GANGL

Following the liberation of Schloss Itter the Wehrmacht officer's body was first taken to St. Joseph's Church in Itter village but was eventually interred in Wörgl's main municipal cemetery. Gangl is considered an Austrian national hero because of his alliance with the anti-Nazi resistance movement, his efforts to protect the civilian population of Wörgl, and his participation in the defense of the French VIPs at Schloss Itter. A major street in Wörgl is named after him.

SEBASTIAN WIMMER

Despite his efforts to disappear, Schloss Itter's former commandant was arrested within weeks after Allied forces occupied Tyrol. He was held at the fortress of Kufstein, the medieval castle overlooking the city, which was run as a POW camp by the French (who were the primary occupation force in that part of Austria). Thérèse Wimmer contacted the Jouhauxs and other former Itter prisoners, asking them to intervene on her husband's behalf.

Several of the former VIP prisoners did so, via the French government's occupation headquarters, the Mission de Contrôle en Autriche.[17]

As an SS-TV officer, Wimmer was automatically considered a war criminal and logically should have been tried for his role in the 1939 Polish massacres and his administrative duties at Dachau and Madjanek. Inexplicably, he was released by the French in 1949, after which he went to work as a common laborer on a farm near Wörgl. His continued heavy drinking apparently drove his wife away, for in May 1951 he returned alone to his hometown of Dingolfing, Bavaria, and lived with his father at Bruckstrasse 101. He killed himself there on December 10, 1952, at the age of fifty.

STEFAN OTTO

Though his name appears on several postwar lists of suspected war criminals, the former SD officer was apparently never apprehended, tried, or imprisoned. As of this writing no information has come to light about his whereabouts or status.

KURT-SIEGFRIED SCHRADER

Following their liberation the French VIPs at Schloss Itter gave Schrader a note, in French, which read "On May 4 [sic], 1945, Captain S. Schrader ensured the safety of the French detainees at Itter castle and stayed with them during the German attacks."[18] While not exactly a ringing endorsement, the letter—which was signed by all of the VIPs—helped ensure that the decorated Waffen-SS officer spent only a relatively short period of time as a POW. After his release in 1947 he rejoined his family and worked for several years as a bricklayer. In the early 1950s the family moved to Münster, in northwestern Germany, and in 1953 Schrader was appointed to a position in the Interior Ministry of the state of North Rhein-Westphalia. He retired from that post in 1980 and reportedly died in the mid-1990s.

THE AMERICANS

JOHN T. KRAMERS

As interesting an experience as the Schloss Itter rescue operation might have been for the 103rd Infantry Division military-government officer, it was only one of many in John Kramers's long career. He remained in the army after World War II, serving as a military attaché in the U.S. embassies in Finland, Egypt, Algeria, and Ethiopia, among others. His last assignment was as the garrison commander at Fort Indiantown Gap, Pennsylvania, and he retired from the army in 1967 as a colonel. After obtaining a degree in business from the University of Pennsylvania, he worked as a financial advisor, retiring in 2004. I am pleased to say that he was alive and well at age ninety-five at the time of this writing.

THE 142ND INFANTRY REGIMENT SOLDIERS

After rejoining their unit following the relief of Schloss Itter, the four GIs were told that they would be put in for decorations stemming from their actions in the battle, but none ever received an award. The four men eventually returned to the United States and, like millions of other former service members, got on with life. Unfortunately, for three of the four all I have been able to discover about their postwar lives are the dates and places of their deaths: Alex Petrukovich, Illinois, November 1973; William Sutton, Wisconsin, June 1979; and Alfred Worsham, Kentucky, June 1993. Arthur Pollock, on the other hand, is alive and remarkably well at the time of this writing: eighty-eight-years-old and in good health, and working five days a week in the family business.

THE 23RD TANK BATTALION SOLDIERS

As with the GIs from the 142nd Infantry Regiment, for three of *Besotten Jenny*'s four crew members I could locate only the dates and places of their deaths: Herbert G. McHaley, Indiana, November 1988; William T. Rushford, Michigan, March 1988; and Edward J. Szymczyk, December 1998. And, as in the case of Art Pollock, I was pleased to find Edward J. Seiner doing well at eighty-eight years of age; he is not, however, still working five-day weeks.

HARRY J. BASSE

Jack Lee's second in command returned to California after the war, and he and his wife went into farming near Anaheim. They grew oranges until Harry retired in the early 1960s, and one of the groves they sold was razed to help make way for Disneyland. Harry spent his retirement doing the things he enjoyed: hunting, fishing, and spending time with his extended family. He was in good health until his last two years, according to his son. Harry Basse died in Bishop, California, on October 4, 1991, at the age of eighty-one.

JOHN C. LEE JR.

The man who engineered the rescue of the French VIPs and the defense of Schloss Itter attempted to jump-start his postwar life even before leaving the service. On the advice of his father, who in addition to being a Norwich physician was also an important player in Democratic Party politics in Chenango County, New York, while still in Germany with the 23rd Tank Battalion, Jack Lee filed the paperwork necessary to make himself a candidate for the Democratic nomination for county sheriff. It was apparently the first time a U.S. military officer serving overseas sought a stateside political office.

Not coincidentally, Lee's candidacy was announced in his home county the same week that Meyer Levin's account of the fight for Schloss Itter, "We Liberated Who's Who," appeared in the *Saturday Evening Post*. While the magazine piece and several laudatory articles about Lee's actions in the battle—coupled with news of the young tank officer's Distinguished Service Cross—undoubtedly helped garner him some votes, Lee was ultimately unable to parlay his war record into public office; he lost the election by a substantial margin.

Lee finally returned to the United States in late January 1946 and was released from active duty at Fort Dix, New Jersey, on February 2, and transferred to the inactive reserve with the rank of captain.[19] And from that point on his life seems to have gone into a slow but seemingly inexorable downward spiral. Though he played several seasons of minor league football with the New Jersey Giants of the short-lived American Association, he was unable to win a berth on a pro team and turned to coaching local semipro and farm-club teams. He found work as a bartender, and, not surprisingly, his own drinking increased. At some point—the exact date is unclear—he and his wife, Virginia, split up, and she took their young son[20] to California and eventually obtained a divorce. In the early 1950s Lee decided to go into the hospitality business and made a deal to buy the historic Eagle Hotel in New Berlin, New York. He took possession of the structure but was ultimately unable to make the final payments, and when the former owner took him to court, Lee lost the hotel. In a separate legal difficulty, Lee was charged with assaulting his sister's estranged husband and was ultimately fined $50 and put on probation.

Details of Jack Lee's subsequent life are few, though we do know some things. He married a second time, to a woman named Stella Evans, a waitress whom he'd met while working as a bartender. She eventually divorced him—also because of his drinking. After the failure of his second marriage Lee lived for a few years in Texas City, Texas, but by the time of his father's death in 1961 he was living in Long Beach, California; during his time in the Golden State (perhaps searching for Virginia and his son?) he apparently spent many hours with his old friend Harry Basse. How Lee made his living is unclear, as is the date when he returned to Norwich. At some point he married for a third time, to the former Nellie Porter, though he never had additional children. As to the last important date in Jack Lee's life there is no doubt: he died at Chenango Memorial Hospital in Norwich on January 15, 1973, at the relatively young age of fifty-four. The cause of death was listed as "asphyxiation," likely as the result of acute alcohol poisoning.[21]

While Lee's obituary in the local newspaper mentioned his role in the battle for Schloss Itter—which the piece's author located in France rather than Austria—the man who'd led the rescue mission and the castle's defense had perhaps the most succinct summation of that improbable fight: A few months before his death, Lee was asked by a reporter in Norwich how he felt about the long-ago incident. The hero of "the Last Battle" thought for a minute and then replied, "Well, it was just the damnedest thing."

ACKNOWLEDGMENTS

WRITING HISTORY IS ALWAYS CHALLENGING, in that the passage of time often obscures the truth rather than revealing it. Eyewitnesses pass away, memories fade, and records—if they were kept at all—are destroyed as being no longer relevant or simply disappear into bureaucratic oblivion. And there is an added difficulty when we try to write accurate accounts of military actions: the exhaustion, fear, exhilaration, panic, and sheer volume of war ensure that participants in the same battle will forever remember it in profoundly different ways.

That being said, it is the historian's duty to diligently search out whatever documents remain and, if writing about relatively recent events, any participants who may still be alive. Much as a detective evaluates evidence through knowledge of the subject and the application of both logic and common sense, the historian assesses the available information and then weaves all the various strands into an account that is as accurate and complete as possible. For many who choose to write history, myself included, the hunt for the information on which the final story is based is the most enjoyable part of the process, even though it is often the most frustrating.

Fortunately, in researching *The Last Battle* I have been ably and generously assisted by a number of people in the United States and abroad. Their help has been immensely important, and I greatly appreciate it. Any errors or omissions in this volume are, of course, mine alone.

Above all, I wish to thank my wife, Margaret Spragins Harding. This book would literally not have been possible without her love, support, counsel, limitless patience, and extraordinary skills as a French linguist. She is the most remarkable human being I have ever encountered, and I am truly blessed to have her in my life.

I would also particularly like to thank Dr. Alfred Beck, an eminent historian and true gentleman, who many years ago—when we both worked at the U.S. Army Center of Military History—first told me of an odd little battle in Austria in May 1945 that involved Germans, Americans, and a gaggle of French VIPs. Thanks also to my agent, Scott Mendel, for his excellent advice and guidance; Robert Pigeon, my editor at Da Capo, for his friendship and assistance in shaping and improving the manuscript; and Bryce Zabel, friend and screenwriter, for suggesting that the Schloss Itter story would make just as good a book as it will a screenplay.

I am also indebted to:

IN THE UNITED STATES:

My colleagues Michael W. Robbins, David Lauterborn, Dan Smith, and Jennifer Berry at Weider History Group's *Military History* magazine for putting up with my frequent absences and almost continuous preoccupation while writing this book.

Karen Jensen and Wendy Palitz, both of Weider's *World War II* magazine; editor Karen for commissioning me to write the article from which this book evolved, and art director Wendy for both her friendship and the article's wonderful design.

Thomas Culbert and Mike Constandy for their dogged research work at the National Archives.

Joe Basse for providing information on, and photos of, his father, Harry Basse.

Robert D. Lee for providing information on, and photos of, his uncle John C. Lee.

John Kramers, Arthur Pollock, and Edward Seiner for their personal recollections of the battle for Schloss Itter.

Victoria Haglan for her excellent German translations.

Patricia E. Evans, Chenango County, New York, historian, for locating and providing background material on John Lee and his family.

Gail Wiese, Jennifer Payne, and Kelly Gonzalez of Norwich University's Archives and Special Collections for their help in researching John Lee's time at the university.

Veterans of the 12th Armored Division F. George Hatt and Steve Czecha and 23rd Tank Battalion veterans James Francis and John McBride, all for their help in researching their units and the men who served in them.

Lisa Sharik and the staff of the Texas Military Forces Museum and Kyle Wiskow and the staff of the 12th Armored Division Museum for their research assistance.

John P. Moore for providing vital background information on Kurt-Siegfried Schrader.

John Browning for information on his brother William Browning, squad leader in Company E, 142nd Infantry Regiment.

Ron Thomassin for providing photos of Harry Basse.

Megan Lewis at the U.S. Holocaust Memorial Museum for her research efforts on Sebastian Wimmer and Stefan Otto.

IN AUSTRIA:

The staff of Gemiende Itter, who were tremendously helpful both via e-mail and during my visit to Schloss Itter; Robert Kaller of Vienna's Institut für Zeitgeschichte; Hedi Wechner, current mayor of Wörgl; Otto Hagleitner, for information on his father, Rupert; and Dr. Wilfred Beimroh and the staff of the Tiroler Landesarchiv.

IN FRANCE:

Evelyne Demey Paul-Reynaud, for sharing family history and photographs of her parents taken while they were imprisoned in Schloss Itter.

Lise Pommois, for sharing photos of 23rd Tank Battalion operations in Alsace.

IN GERMANY:

The research and reference staffs of the Stadtarchive Ludwigsburg, KZ-Gedenkstätte Dachau, and the Bundesarchiv's Militärarchiv.

IN POLAND:

Marta Grudzińska at the Majdanek Museum and Archive for information on Sebastian Wimmer's activities at the infamous concentration camp.

IN SWITZERLAND:

Remo Becci, archivist of the United Nations International Labor Organization office in Geneva, for providing background information on and photographs of Augusta Léon-Jouhaux.

BIBLIOGRAPHY

PRIMARY SOURCES

OFFICIAL DOCUMENTS

Many of the sources below are part of the National Archives and Record Administration's Modern Military Records Center in College Park, MD; these are indicated with the abbreviation NARA MMRC.

Armored Force Field Manual, Tactics and Technique. U.S. War Department. March 1942. Archives II, NARA MMRC.

Battalion Diary for Month of May 1945. 753rd Tank Battalion. Oct. 31, 1945. NARA MMRC.

Battlegroup Buddenbrock, 16 March–4 May 1945, by Generalmajor Jobst Freiherr von Buddenbrock. Foreign Military Studies, 1945–1954. Department of the Army, Washington, DC, 1956.

Company History, 1–8 May 1945. Company D, 753rd Tank Battalion. May 10, 1945. NARA MMRC.

Final Strike Assessment, Wörgl M/Y, Austria. Photo Interpretation Officer, 301st Bombardment Group (Heavy), Feb. 23, 1945. NARA MMRC.

General Order 212. HQs., U.S. Forces, European Theater, Aug. 29, 1945.

The German Replacement Army (Ersatzheer). Military Intelligence Division, War Department, Washington, DC, April 1944. NARA MMRC.

Himmler's Files from Hallein. Office of the Military Governor for Germany (U.S.), Office of the Director of Intelligence, Nov. 8, 1945. NARA MMRC.

Historical Narrative for May 1945. HQs., 753rd Tank Battalion, n.d. NARA MMRC.

History of the 142nd Infantry Regiment, 36th Division, Sept. 3, 1943–May 8, 1945 (Volume II, France, Germany, Austria). HQs., 142nd Infantry Regiment, n.d. NARA MMRC.

Journal of Operations, 1944–1945. HQs., 17th Armored Infantry Battalion, n.d. NARA MMRC.

Kampf um die Alpenfestung Nord, by General der Gebirgstruppen Georg Ritter von Hengl. Foreign Military Studies, 1945–1954. Department of the Army, Washington, DC, 1956.

Operations in Germany, 1–10 May 1945. 23rd Tank Battalion, 12th Armored Division, Feb. 15, 1946. NARA MMRC.

Operations in Germany and Austria, May 1945. HQs., 103rd Infantry Division, July 1945. NARA MMRC.

Operations in Germany and Austria, 1–10 May 1945. HQs., 142nd Infantry Regiment, 36th Infantry Division, May 25, 1945. NARA MMRC.

Operations in Germany, Austria and Italy, May 1945. HQs., 103rd Infantry Division, n.d. NARA MMRC.

Personalakten für Gangl, Josef, Heeres-Personalamt, Oberkommando der Wehrmacht. Berlin, n.d. NARA MMRC.

Regimental History, 409th Infantry Regiment, 1–10 May 1945. NARA MMRC.

Resistance and Persecution in Austria, 1938–1945. Austrian Federal Press Service, Vienna, 1988.

Rocket Projectors in the Eastern Theater. Foreign Military Studies, 1945–1954. Department of the Army, Washington, DC, 1956.

7th Werfer Brigade, 24 March–30 April 1945, by Generalmajor Dr. Kurt Paape. Foreign Military Studies, 1945–1954. Department of the Army, Washington, DC, 1956.

Special Narrative Report, Mission to Wörgl M/Y, Austria. Office of the Intelligence Officer, 301st Bombardment Group (Heavy), Feb. 23, 1945. NARA MMRC.

SS Personalakten für Wimmer, Sebastian, SS-Hauptamt. Berlin, n.d. NARA MMRC.

Tank, Medium, M4A3. Technical Manual 9–759. War Department, Washington, DC, September 1944. NARA MMRC.

Unit Journal, 1–10 May 1945. HQs., 142nd Infantry Regiment, 36th Infantry Division, NARA MMRC.

Widerstand und Verfolgung in Tirol, 1934–1945: Eine Dokumentation, Dokumentationsarchiv des Österreichischen Widerstandes. Vienna, 1984.

INTERVIEWS

Duvall, Calbert. Company B, 23rd Tank Battalion. Conducted via e-mail, June 20, 2012.

Kramers, John T. Military Government Section, 103rd Infantry Division. Audio-recorded June 8, 2012.

Pollock, Arthur P. Company E, 142nd Infantry Regiment. Audio-recorded Nov. 3, 2011.

Seiner, Edward J. Company B, 23rd Tank Battalion. Audio-recorded Oct. 28, 2011.

Unpublished Manuscripts

Čučković, Zvonimir. "Zwei Jahren auf Schloss Itter." Handwritten, n.d. Archiv KZ-Gedenkstätte Dachau.

"Die Wahrheit Über Schloss Itter." Privatarchiv Otto Molden: Zur Geschichte der Österreichschen Widerstandsbewegung Gegen Hitler, 1938–1945. Institut für Zeitgeschichte, Universität Wien, Vienna, n.d.

Flanagan, Drew. "Resistance from the Right: François de La Rocque and the Réseau Klan." Department of History, Wesleyan University, Middletown, CT, 2010.

Schrader, Kurt-Siegfried. "Erinnerungen, Gedanken, Erkenntnisse." 1993.

SECONDARY SOURCES

Books

Alexander, Martin S. *The Republic in Danger: General Maurice Gamelin and the Politics of French Defence, 1933–1940*. Cambridge: Cambridge University Press, 1992.

Bischof, Günter, Fritz Plasser, and Barbara Stelzl-Marx, eds. *New Perspectives on Austrians and World War II*. New Brunswick: Transaction Publishers, 2009.

Cailliau de Gaulle, Marie-Agnès. *Souvenirs personnels*. Paris: Parole et Silence, 2006.

Craven, W. F., and J. L. Cate. *Europe: ARGUMENT to VE-Day, January 1944 to May 1945*. The Army Air Forces in World War II. Washington, DC: U.S. Government Printing Office, 1951.

Daladier, Édouard. *Prison Journal, 1940–1945*. Boulder: Westview Press, 1995.

de La Rocque, François. *Disciplines d'Action*. Paris: Parti social français, 1941.

Demey, Evelyne. *Paul Reynaud, mon père*. Paris: Plon-Opera Mundi, 1980.

Dulles, Allen. *The Secret Surrender*. New York: Harper & Row, 1966.

East, William, and William F. Gleason. *The 409th Infantry in World War II*. Ed. Julius J. Urban. Washington, DC: Infantry Journal Press, 1947.

Ferguson, John C. *Hellcats: The 12th Armored Division in World War II*. Abilene, TX: State House Press, 2004.

Francis, Jim. *A History of the 23rd Tank Battalion, 1943–1945*. Privately published, 2004.

François-Poncet, André. *Carnets d'un captif*. Paris: Librairie Artheme Fayard, 1952.

Gates, Eleanor M. *The End of the Affair: The Collapse of the Anglo-French Alliance, 1930–40*. Berkeley: University of California Press, 1981.

Haupt, Werner. *Deutsche Spezialdivisionen, 1935–1945: Gebirgsjäger, Fallschirmjäger, Waffen-SS.* Wölfersheim-Berstadt: Podzun-Pallas, 1995.

Koop, Volker. *In Hitler's Hand: Die Sonder-und Ehrenhäftlinge der SS.* Köln: Böhlau, 2011.

Lanckoronska, Karolina. *Michelangelo in Ravensbrück: One Woman's War Against the Nazis.* Translated by Noel Clark. Cambridge, MA: Da Capo, 2006.

Lasik, Aleksander. *Struktura Organizacyjna Oraz Obsada Osobowa Stanowisk Kierowniczych W Obozie Koncentracyjnym Na Majdanku W Latach 1941–1944.* Majdanek: State Museum at Majdanek, 2003.

Léon-Jouhaux, Augusta. *Prison pour hommes d'Etat.* Paris: Denöel/Gontheir, 1973.

Lévesque, René. *Memoires.* Montréal: Editions Québec/Amérique, 1986.

Liszt, Franz, La Mara, and Constance Bache. *From Rome to the End: Letters of Franz Liszt, Vol. 2.* San Diego: Icon Group International, 2008.

Long, Robert P. *Castle Hotels of Europe.* East Meadow, NY: Hastings House, 1962.

Lucas, James. *Alpine Elite: German Mountain Troops of World War II.* London: Jane's Publishing, 1980.

Luza, Radomír V. *The Resistance in Austria, 1938–1945.* Minneapolis: University of Minnesota Press, 1984.

MacDonald, Charles B. *European Theater of Operations: The Last Offensive.* United States Army in World War II. Washington, DC: U.S. Government Printing Office, 1993.

Mackenzie, W. J. M. *The Secret History of SOE: Special Operations Executive, 1940–1945.* London: St. Ermin's, 2002.

Mitcham, Samuel W., Jr. *The Rise of the Wehrmacht: The German Armed Forces and World War II.* Vol. 1. Westport, CT: Praeger Security International, 2008.

Molden, Fritz. *Fires in the Night: The Sacrifices and Significance of the Austrian Resistance, 1938–1945.* Translated by Harry Zohn. Boulder: Westview Press, 1989.

Monroe-Jones, Edward. *Crossing the Zorn: The January 1945 Battle at Herrlisheim as Told by the American and German Soldiers Who Fought It.* Jefferson, NC: McFarland, 2010.

Moore, John P. *Signal Officers of the Waffen-SS (Nachrichtenoffiziere der Waffen-SS).* Portland, OR: John P. Moore Publishing, 1995.

Mueller, Ralph, and Jerry Turk. *Report After Action: The Story of the 103d Infantry Division.* Nashville: Battery Press, 1987.

Munoz, Antonio J., editor and translator. *The Last Levy: Waffen-SS Officer Roster, March 1, 1945.* Bayside, NY: Axis Europa Books, 2001.

Nobécourt, Jacques. *Le colonel de La Rocque (1885–1946), ou, Les pièges de nationalisme chrétien.* Paris: Librairie Artheme Fayard, 1996.

O'Donnell, Patrick K. *The Brenner Assignment: The Untold Story of the Most Daring Spy Mission of World War II*. Cambridge, MA: Da Capo, 2008.

Pogue, Forrest C. *European Theater of Operations: The Supreme Command*. United States Army in World War II. Washington, DC: U.S. Government Printing Office, 1954.

Reynaud, Paul. *Carnets de captivité, 1941–1945*. Paris: Fayard, 1997.

———. *In the Thick of the Fight, 1930–1945*. Translated by James D. Lambert. New York: Simon and Schuster, 1955.

Ross, Alex. *The Rest Is Noise: Listening to the 20th Century*. New York: Picador, 2008.

Schwab, Gerald. *OSS Agents in Hitler's Heartland: Destination Innsbruck*. Westport, CT: Praeger, 1996.

Singer, Barnett. *Maxime Weygand: A Biography of the French General in Two World Wars*. Jefferson, NC: McFarland, 2008.

Smyth, Sir John. *Jean Borotra, the Bounding Basque: His Life of Work and Play*. London: Stanley Paul, 1974.

Steinböck, Erwin. *Österreichs Militärisches Potential im März, 1938*. Wien: Verlag für Geschichte und Politik, 1988.

Sydnor, Charles W. *Soldiers of Destruction: The SS Death's Head Division, 1939–1945*. Princeton, NJ: Princeton University Press, 1990.

Turner, Barry. *Countdown to Victory: The Final European Campaigns of World War II*. New York: William Morrow, 2004.

Van Goethem, Geert. *The Amsterdam International: The World of the International Federation of Trade Unions (IFTU), 1913–1945*. Burlington, VT: Ashgate, 2006.

von Steiner, Kurt. *Resistance Fighter: Anti-Nazi Terror Tactics of the Austrian Underground*. Boulder: Paladin Press, 1986.

Weygand, Maxime. *Recalled to Service: The Memoirs of General Maxime Weygand*. Garden City, NY: Doubleday, 1952.

Williamson, Gordon. *Gebirgsjäger: German Mountain Trooper 1939–45*. Oxford: Osprey, 2003.

NEWSPAPER ARTICLES

Note: The articles in this section are listed in chronological order.

Binghamton Press (Binghamton, NY):

"Norwich Lieutenant Proves Hero in Reich War-End Rescue Fight." June 7, 1945.

"Captain Lee in Chenago Sheriff Race." July 23, 1945.

"17 Tier Men Are on Latest Returnee List." Jan. 25, 1946.

"John C. Lee, Jr., Ordered Held for Jury." Feb. 25, 1953.

"Lee Fined $50 in Assault, Sister Freed." Mar. 10, 1953.

"Lee Indicted by Chenango Grand Jury." Apr. 10, 1953.
"Lee Vacates New Berlin Hotel." July 3, 1953.

Evening Sun (Norwich, NY):

"John C. Lee Dies, Freed de Gaulle Kin." Jan. 15, 1973.

New York Times:

"Mme. Menter's Good Fortune." Nov. 25, 1885.
"Freed: Daladier, Blum, Reynaud, Niemoller, Schuschnigg, Gamelin." May 6, 1945.
"Reynaud Relates Reich Prison Life." Aug. 15, 1945.
"Borotra Relates War Experiences." March 18, 1947.
"Paul Reynaud Married." May 14, 1950.
"Gen. Gamelin Dead." Apr. 19, 1958.
"Gen. Maxime Weygand Dead." Jan. 29, 1965.
"Paul Reynaud Dies; Led France in 1940." Sept. 22, 1966.
"Daladier, Signer of Munich Pact, Dies at 86." Oct. 12, 1970.

Norwich Record (Northfield, VT):

"Capt. Jack Lee, '42, Rescues Daladier in Castle Battle." June 22, 1945.

Norwich Sun (Norwich, NY):

"Lee Receives Award." Mar. 17, 1945.
"Lee Receives Promotion." May 28, 1945.
"Capt. John C. Lee Jr., Led Rescuers of Daladier, Ex-French Premier." June 4 and 7, 1945.
"Thrilling Story About Captain John C. Lee Appears in 'Post.'" July 18, 1945.
"Capt. Lee Seeks Democratic Nomination for Sheriff." July 21, 1945.

MAGAZINE/JOURNAL ARTICLES

Bachinger, Eleonore, Martin McKee, and Anna Gilmore. "Tobacco Policies in Nazi Germany: Not as Simple as It Seems." *Public Health* 122, no. 5 (May 2008): 497–505.
Distel, Barbara. "KZ-Kommandos an Idyllischen Orten: Dachauer Aussen- lager in Österreich." *KZ Aussenlager—Geschichte und Erinnerung* (1999).
"France: Trials, Tribulations." *Time*, Sept. 30, 1940.
"Gamelin Speaks." *Time*, Nov. 13, 1939.
Harding, Stephen. "The Battle for Castle Itter." *World War II* (Aug.–Sept. 2008).
"Kampf um Schloss Itter." *Neue Illustrierte*, Mar. 26, 1961.

Kennedy, Sean. "Accompanying the Marshal: La Rocque and the *Progrès Social Français* Under Vichy." *French History* 15, no. 2 (2001).

Levin, Meyer. "We Liberated Who's Who." *Saturday Evening Post,* July 21, 1945.

"Maurice Gamelin: Good Grey General." *Time*, Aug. 14, 1939.

"Reynaud Marriage Revealed." *Time*, May 22, 1950.

"Where Is Gamelin?" *Time*, June 10, 1940.

NOTES

CHAPTER ONE

1. Some sources date the earliest parts of the castle to 902. Most of the information regarding Schloss Itter's early history is drawn from "Die Geschichte von Itter," a pamphlet produced by Austria's Hohe-Salve Regional Tourist Board, and *Castle Hotels of Europe*, by Robert P. Long.

2. Reigned 893–930.

3. A palatinate was a territory administered on behalf of a king or emperor by a count. In the Holy Roman Empire, a count palatinate was known in German as a *pfalzgraf*.

4. Initially a collection of small huts and workshops used by the craftsmen who built the castle, the village of Itter evolved into a community built around the staffing and maintenance of the fortress. In return for their labor, the villagers were offered protection within the schloss in times of civil strife.

5. Led by social and political reformer Michael Gaismayr, the revolt sought to replace the church-dominated feudal system with a republic. While successful in several military engagements against reactionary forces, Gaismayr and his followers were defeated at Radstadt in July 1526. Gaismayr fled to Venice and ultimately Padua, where on April 15, 1532, he was assassinated by Austrian agents.

6. See Augusta Léon-Jouhaux, *Prison pour hommes d'Etat*, 23. As noted later in this volume, she was labor leader León Jouhaux's secretary, companion, and future wife and was imprisoned with him at Itter from 1943 to 1945.

7. Until his coronation in 1806 the king had been styled Maximilian IV Josef, prince-elector of Bavaria.

8. Menter apparently purchased the castle using funds she'd earned on the concert circuit, though a brief article in the Nov. 25, 1885, edition of the *New York Times* ("Mme. Menter's Good Fortune") indicated that the purchase was largely financed by 400,000 rubles left to her in the will of an elderly Russian admirer.

9. Ibid.

10. Liszt, La Mara, and Bache, *From Rome to the End*, 377.

11. Menter returned to Germany after the castle's sale and lived near Munich for the remainder of her life. She died on Feb. 23, 1918.

12. Widely referred to as the Wörgl Experiment, the effort was the brainchild of the town's mayor, Michael Unterguggenberger. He sought to economically empower his town and the surrounding region by replacing standard currency with what's known as "stamp scrip," a local currency that would remain in use and in circulation rather than being hoarded by bankers. While the idea managed to revive the local Wörgl economy, it was terminated by the Austrian National Bank in 1933.

13. This translates literally as "Eastern March," a reference to Austria's tenth-century status as a "march," or buffer, between Bavaria and the Slavs.

14. For clarity's sake, all French, Wehrmacht, and SS ranks in this book are expressed in their U.S. Army equivalents. Von Bock went on to play leading roles in the invasions of Poland, France, and Russia, and was killed on May 4, 1945, when a British fighter-bomber strafed his car.

15. An acronym for the full name of the dreaded Nazi secret police, the Geheime Staatspolizei.

16. See Richard Germann's excellent essay "Austrian Soldiers and Generals in World War II," in *New Perspectives on Austrians and World War II*, ed. Bischof, Plasser, and Stelzl-Marx, for a fascinating discussion of why Austrian soldiers so willingly donned Wehrmacht uniforms.

17. Ibid., 29.

18. Among the willing were Otto Skorzeny, the Waffen-SS commando leader who rescued Benito Mussolini from captivity in September 1943, and Ernst Kaltenbrunner, chief of the Reich Main Security Office.

19. Those considered unreliable included between 30 and 50 percent of all officers in the Bundesheer, who were dismissed. All were closely watched by the Gestapo through the end of the war.

20. Luza, *The Resistance in Austria*, 14.

21. Ultimately, many Austrians arrested by the Nazis would be imprisoned—and many would perish—in concentration and labor camps established within Austria itself, including the infamous Mauthausen-Gusen camp complex near Linz, some 120 miles northeast of Schloss Itter.

22. The German name is Deutscher Bund zur Bekämpfung der Tabakgefahren. For a fascinating discussion of the Nazis' antismoking activities, see Bachinger, McKee, and Gilmore, "Tobacco Policies in Nazi Germany."

23. For his part in the horrors of the Nazis' Final Solution, Pohl was charged by the Allies with crimes against humanity and a staggering array of war crimes. Found guilty, he was hanged on June 7, 1951.

24. Known as Konzentrationslager-Hauptlager, shortened in German to KZ-Hauptlager, Dachau was located about ten miles northwest of Munich

and established in March 1933 as the first regular Nazi concentration camp. It was the administrative and operational model for all subsequent camps, both within and outside Germany.

25. Koop, *In Hitler's Hand*, 32.

26. Sources vary on whether this officer's name was Petz or Peez, and in his handwritten postwar memoir, "Zwei Jahren auf Schloss Itter" (in the archive collection of the KZ-Gedenkstätte Dachau), Zvonimir Čučković refers to him as the latter. While the names would sound very similar to a nonnative German speaker like Čučković, the spelling "Petz" would be the more common German usage, and I have chosen to favor it.

27. Sited about 112 miles northeast of Dachau, hard on the Czech border, Flossenbürg was opened in 1938. It initially held common criminals and Jews but ultimately housed political prisoners and Soviet POWs. Its inmates were used as slave laborers in nearby granite quarries.

28. Details on the conversion are drawn from "Zwei Jahren auf Schloss Itter" and Léon-Jouhaux, *Prison pour hommes d'Etat*, 8–10.

29. The SS-Totenkopfverbände (SS-TV), or "Death's Head Units," administered the concentration-camp system.

30. Thanks to Čučković's memoirs, we know that twenty-two of the twenty-seven members of the work detail were political prisoners, four were classed as "common criminals," and one was an "asocial," a term the Nazis used to refer to such groups as homosexuals and the mentally ill. We also know that the prisoner work detail included five Germans, eight Austrians, a Yugoslav, a Czech, seven Russians, and five Poles.

31. In European usage, "first floor" is the floor above the ground floor—thus in fact "second floor" in American usage.

32. The Heeresunteroffiziersschule für Gebirgsjäger, as it was known in German, was one of two similar institutions within the Third Reich tasked with training NCOs bound for military units especially trained for mountain warfare. The other was at Mittenwald, Germany.

33. As far as can be determined, none of the prisoners who served on the Schloss Itter work detail and were returned to Dachau and Flossenbürg in April 1943 survived the war. Nor, apparently, did Petz.

34. Details on Čučković's life both before and during the war are drawn from "Zwei Jahren auf Schloss Itter."

35. Ema Čučković, neé Freyberg, was born in 1910 in Nordhausen, Germany. Čučković's son was born in Yugoslavia in 1933.

36. In his handwritten memoir, Čučković identifies thirteen of these men by name: SS-Sergeant First Class Oschbald; SS-Staff Sergeants Maschalek, Gilde, and Kunz; and SS-Corporals Euba, Jackl, Nowotny, Delus, Resner, Fischer, Bliesmer, Schulz, and Greiner.

37. Čučković identifies this woman as Rosel Harmske, "SS-Aufseherin [female auxiliary] aus Ravensbrück." A second female SS member who

occasionally worked at Schloss Itter and whom Čučković identifies only as "Kühn, SS-Aufseherin aus Ravensbrück," may have been Anna Kühn. When she joined the SS at Ravensbrück in 1942, she was fifty-seven years old, making her the oldest known woman to have served in the SS concentration-camp system.

38. In German, SS-Sonderkommando. The word "commando," in this sense, refers to the original South African Boer concept of a special-purpose unit, rather than an individual covert-operations soldier.

39. Upon joining the SS, Wimmer received the member number (*mitgliedsnummer*) 264374. Details of Wimmer's service are drawn from his personnel file, *SS Personalakten für Wimmer, Sebastian, SS-Hauptamt.*

40. While he was not the brightest of recruits, Wimmer's background as a police officer ensured (as it did for many of his former law-enforcement colleagues) an officer's commission, rather than being relegated to the enlisted ranks.

41. When the SS took control of all of Germany's concentration camps in 1934 and established the SS-TV, it organized that group into six named wachtruppen, or guard units. Wachtruppe Oberbayern (Upper Bavaria) was stationed at Dachau, and just before Wimmer joined it in 1935 the unit was enlarged and redesignated Wachsturmbann Oberbayern.

42. The other two were SS-Totenkopfstandarte 2 Brandenburg at Oranienburg concentration camp and SS-Totenkopfstandarte 3 Thüringen at Buchenwald. A fourth, SS-Totenkopfstandarte 4 Ostmark, was formed in Vienna following the 1938 Anschluss. More than ten additional SS-Totenkopfstandarten were formed during the course of World War II.

43. The other two Totenkopfstandarten, Brandenburg and Thüringen, were involved in identical activities.

44. The four thousand Jews who survived the initial shootings were later confined in a ghetto; in 1942 all were sent to Treblinka concentration camp and subsequently killed.

45. See Sydnor, *Soldiers of Destruction*, 40–42.

46. By the time Germany invaded the Soviet Union in 1941, the einsatzgruppen had so perfected their murderous technique that they were able to kill more than thirty-three thousand people in two days at Babi Yar, a ravine near Kiev, Ukraine.

47. The 3rd SS Panzer Division is also often, and incorrectly, referred to as SS Division Totenkopf.

CHAPTER TWO

1. Čučković, "Zwei Jahren auf Schloss Itter," 25.

2. Initially mobilized into the local Avignon regiment, Daladier was quickly posted to the 2e Régiment de la Légion Étrangère, the Foreign Legion's 2nd Regiment. The unit was in need of French noncommissioned of-

ficers to lead the many foreign volunteers flocking to France's aid. When his battalion was essentially destroyed, Sergeant Daladier was transferred to the 209th Infantry Regiment, which saw continuous combat near Verdun. Commissioned in 1916, Daladier proved to be a brave and effective combat leader, and he finished the war as a lieutenant with both the Croix de guerre and the Légion d'honneur. See Daladier, *In Defense of France*, 12–21.

3. Daladier's aggressive response was at least partly the result of his belief—one widely held among France's left-leaning political parties—that the riots actually constituted an attempted fascist coup.

4. He also became the first socialist, and the first Jew, to hold the office.

5. See the introduction to Daladier's *Prison Journal*.

6. Their political differences were exacerbated by the fact that their mistresses were social rivals, despite having known each other since childhood. Daladier's mistress was Jeanne de Crussol; Reynaud's was Hélène de Portes. Each woman took every opportunity to publicly and privately malign the other's man and, of course, to report to her own lover every word spoken against him by his political rival. Daladier's relationship had originated after the 1932 death of his wife, Madeline. Reynaud, on the other hand, remained legally married to his first wife, the former Jeanne Henri-Robert, until 1948. His relationship with Hélène de Portes was an open secret, one not contested by his wife.

7. In addition to some twenty-seven politicians, *Massilia*'s passenger list included thirty-three other passengers, among them Mendès-France's wife and two sons and Mandel's mistress.

8. Le Verdon-sur-Mer was a harbor at the mouth of the Gironde River, some fifty-four miles northwest of Bordeaux. The French government had relocated to Bordeaux on June 10.

9. Daladier, *Prison Journal*, 2. Recognizing the irony in the general's cables, Daladier said on the same page of his journal, "Strange fellow, this General Noguès, who felt he had to ask the government for permission to rebel."

10. In the military usage, a rank roughly equivalent to a U.S. general of the armies.

11. Daladier, *Prison Journal*, 193.

12. Buchenwald was built in 1937. Though it was not a designated extermination camp, an estimated fifty-six thousand people died or were executed there before the camp's April 1945 liberation by elements of the U.S. 6th Armored Division.

13. For additional details on Daladier's time in Buchenwald, see both Daladier, *Prison Journal*, and Léon-Jouhaux, *Prison pour hommes d'Etat*.

14. Daladier, *Prison Journal*, 199. The two men were to have very different fates. Blum spent the remainder of the war in Buchenwald and, briefly, Dachau, and was liberated by Allied troops in May 1945. He returned to politics and was briefly prime minister in 1946–1947. He died in 1950.

Mandel, sadly, did not survive the war. He was executed in Paris in July 1944 by the French fascist paramilitary force known as the Milice.

15. Known in German as Feldgendarmerie, these troops were widely hated within the Wehrmacht because of their habit of summarily executing any soldier they believed to be a deserter or malingerer. They were scornfully referred to as *kettenhunde,* or chained dogs, because of the gorgets (a flat metal crescent suspended around their necks on a light chain) that were the emblems of their authority.

16. For an in-depth discussion of Gamelin's family background and military connections, see Martin S. Alexander's excellent *The Republic in Danger.*

17. Gamelin also ruthlessly put down a revolt by restive Druze tribes in the Syrian hill country. According to a *Time* magazine account (Aug. 14, 1939), Gamelin was present when French aircraft and artillery killed more than 1,400 civilians in Damascus.

18. Singer, *Maxime Weygand,* 65. This book is an excellent in-depth look at Weygand's life and career.

19. Alexander, *The Republic in Danger,* 30.

20. Conseil Supérieur de la Guerre, France's highest military council, headed by the country's prime minister.

21. Italian in origin, "generalissimo" refers to a military commander who has operational control of all of a nation's armed forces—land, sea, and air—and is subordinate only to the head of state, or is himself the head of state. In addition to Weygand and Gamelin, in the 1930s and 1940s the term was applied to such disparate individuals as Chiang Kai-shek, Joseph Stalin, Francisco Franco, and Hitler.

22. "France: Trials, Tribulations," *Time,* Sept. 30, 1940.

23. This was the French national police, formed in 1812. Following the capitulation, the Sûreté—like all of France's other law-enforcement agencies—became subordinate to the Germans in occupied France and to the Vichy government elsewhere. Following the German occupation of Vichy in November 1942, all Sûreté personnel and resources came under direct German control.

24. Daladier, *Prison Journal,* 9.

25. Both Čučković and Augusta Léon-Jouhaux mention Jouhaux's health issues, with emphasis on his heart condition.

26. Details of Jouhaux's early life are largely drawn from his 1951 Nobel Peace Prize acceptance speech.

27. Ibid.

28. Ibid.

29. Van Goethem, *The Amsterdam International,* 100.

30. Ibid., 260.

31. Various writers have rendered her last name in different forms—including Brücklin, Broukhlin, and Brucklen—usually depending on the

language in which they were writing. Since she and Jouhaux most often used Bruchlen, I have chosen to use that spelling in this volume.

32. The agency charged with conducting intelligence-gathering operations outside the United Kingdom, often referred to as MI6.

33. Mackenzie, *The Secret History of SOE*, 269.

34. There is some confusion in the historical record about the exact date of Jouhaux's arrest, with some sources mentioning Nov. 12. However, since Jouhaux's secretary and eventual wife, Augusta, believes it was Nov. 26, I have chosen to use that date.

35. Léon-Jouhaux, *Prison pour hommes d'Etat*, 11.

36. Though he'd decided to be as "correct" as conditions allowed, it apparently didn't occur to Wimmer to have the chilling quotation from Dante's *Inferno* removed from the wall in the castle's entrance hall. Virtually every VIP prisoner confined at Schloss Itter mentioned seeing the grim greeting upon first arrival.

37. Room assignments would change several times as new "guests" arrived. See Čučković, "Zwei Jahren auf Schloss Itter," 57–59.

38. Léon-Jouhaux, *Prison pour hommes d'Etat*, 14.

CHAPTER THREE

1. As mentioned in the notes to chapter 2, de Portes had been Reynaud's openly acknowledged mistress for several years, despite his continuing marriage to Jeanne Henri-Robert Reynaud. Often portrayed as the evil genius who controlled Reynaud—and thus, his government—from behind the scenes, de Portes's actual influence over events during the months of Reynaud's premiership is both open to debate and outside the scope of this volume. For a fascinating discussion of the countess's relationship with Reynaud and influence on French politics, see Gates, *The End of the Affair*.

2. The first concentration camp in Oranienburg was established in 1933 and bore the name of the town but was subsequently closed and replaced by the nearby—and vastly larger—Sachsenhausen complex. In his memoirs, Reynaud refers to the camp by its earlier name.

3. Reynaud, *In the Thick of the Fight*, 652. Though nearly seven hundred pages long, Reynaud's memoir devotes just four pages to his time at Schloss Itter. He covers that period in exhaustive detail, however, in his *Carnets de captivité, 1941–1945*.

4. Details on Borotra's life are drawn from Smyth, *Jean Borotra, the Bounding Basque*.

5. Ibid., 103–104.

6. Ibid., 113–115.

7. Ibid., 124.

8. Ibid., 144.

9. Reynaud, *Carnets de captivité*, 272–273. See also Reynaud, *In the Thick of the Fight*, 651.

10. Léon-Jouhaux, *Prison pour hommes d'Etat*, 27.

11. Lanckoronska, *Michelangelo in Ravensbrück*, 219. Christiane Mabire is described by the volume's author, the Polish countess Karolina Lanckoronska, following their first meeting in the German concentration camp.

12. In "Zwei Jahren auf Schloss Itter" Zvonimir Čučković lists Mabire's arrival date as June 17, but other sources—including both Reynaud and Bruchlen—cite July 2. Given that Mabire did not arrive at Itter until after Bruchlen, who reached the castle on June 19, I believe the July date to be correct.

13. Léon-Jouhaux, *Prison pour hommes d'Etat*, 15.

14. Daladier, *Prison Journal*, 211–212.

15. As Barnett Singer points out in *Maxime Weygand*, most historians agree that Weygand was the unintended product of an affair between Belgian Lt. Col. Alfred van der Smissen and Melanie Zichy Ferraris, daughter of Austrian foreign minister and chancellor Klemens von Metternich. Singer also believes that Weygand was actually born in 1865, though I have chosen to use the more widely accepted 1867 date.

16. Daladier, *Prison Journal*, 252.

17. Čučković, "Zwei Jahren auf Schloss Itter," 30.

18. Literally the Second Bureau, the organization tracked the strength, capability, and disposition of potential enemies, while the Premier (First) Bureau compiled the same information for French and allied forces.

19. Reynaud, *Carnets de captivité*, 269.

20. Jacques Nobécourt, author of *Le colonel de La Rocque*, published by Librairie Artheme Fayard in 1996.

21. Ibid., 193.

22. He used the term in his 1941 volume *Disciplines d'Action*, 12.

23. Nobécourt, *Le colonel de La Rocque*, 777.

24. Notably Jacques Nobécourt.

25. This description was offered by her son, Pierre Cailliau, in his introduction to her 1970 memoir, *Souvenirs personnels*, 12.

26. Ibid., 41–42.

27. Denys was plagued by ill-health throughout his life and, sadly, died of meningitis at the age of twenty-two.

28. Koop, *In Hitler's Hand*, 44–45. Most of the VIPs held at the hotel were high-ranking French military officers.

29. Cailliau de Gaulle, *Souvenirs personnels*, 94–95.

30. Belgian-born Alfred Cailliau had become a French citizen after he and Marie-Agnès moved to the Le Havre area after World War I.

31. Reynaud, *Carnets de captivité*, 312.

32. The former prime minister's penchant for taking off his clothes whenever the weather was warm enough is mentioned in the memoirs of both

Reynaud and Augusta Léon-Jouhaux. Daladier himself, however, makes no mention of his nudism in his own memoir.

33. Some sources render the cook's last name as "Korbart" or "Krobet," but Zvonimir Čučković—who shared a room with him for almost two years and presumably knew best—gives the man's name as Krobot, so I have chosen to use that spelling. Čučković also says Krobot was transferred to Itter from Dachau in August 1943.

34. Sadly, we know the full names of only two of these unfortunates: Gertrud Seibold and Gisela Sinneck-Barta. For the others, we have only first names: Sofia, Ommi, Luci, Maria, Josefa, and Olma. While Krobot and Čučković shared a room in the castle's main building, the female inmate-servants slept on straw scattered over the floor of the schlosshof's cramped upper level.

35. Čučković, "Zwei Jahren auf Schloss Itter," 10.

36. Ibid. Daladier mentions the radio several times in *Prison Journal*, as does Augusta Léon-Jouhaux in *Prison pour hommes d'Etat*. Both indicate that it was capable of picking up stations as far afield as North Africa, the Soviet Union, and, when atmospheric conditions were right, even North America.

37. Smyth, *The Bounding Basque*, 154–155.

38. Daladier, *Prison Journal*, 335.

CHAPTER FOUR

1. World War II Soviet "fronts" were roughly equivalent to army groups in the U.S. Army. Made up of multiple field armies, each of which comprised several corps, the 3rd Ukrainian Front by April 1945 totaled some one million men.

2. In U.S. usage, numbered armies are identified by words, not numerals.

3. Seventh Army was under the command of Lieutenant General George S. Patton, who relinquished command to Patch following the island's seizure.

4. For more details on Eisenhower's overall plan for Austria and southern Germany, see MacDonald, *European Theater of Operations*, 436–438.

5. Patton was promoted to full general on April 14, 1945. Devers gained four-star rank on March 8, 1945.

6. The individual units assigned to each of Seventh Army's three corps— the other two being VI and XV—changed fairly frequently, with divisions being moved between corps as the tactical situation demanded.

7. Panzer-grenadier units combined tanks, truck-borne infantry, and artillery, antitank, and engineer elements.

8. Details on von Hengl's mission, force, and activities are drawn from his 1946 monograph *Kampf um die Alpenfestung Nord*, prepared as part of the U.S.-government-produced Foreign Military Studies, 1945–1954.

9. Grossdeutschland was the German army's premier combat division (and not, as widely believed, a Waffen-SS organization). Von Hengl's belief

that elements of the division were present in Tyrol at this point in the war may not be accurate, in that most official histories (both German and American) indicate that Grossdeutschland ended the war in northern Germany. Of course, it is entirely possible that some members of the division had been sent to Austria under circumstances that are no longer clear.

10. *Kampf um die Alpenfestung Nord*, 2–3.

11. OKW is usually translated as High Command of the Armed Forces, and Führungsstab B was one of two operational headquarters under OKW.

12. In the event, those few units of the two larger organizations that did manage to make it into Tyrol didn't get far enough east to be of any real help to von Hengl.

13. Born in 1901, Hans Buchner was a highly regarded German-born gebirgsjäger officer. After World War II he joined the West German Bundeswehr, eventually rising to the rank of general. From 1956 to 1959 he commanded the Bundeswehr's 1st Gebirgsjäger Division.

14. Giehl was the commandant of the Heeresunteroffiziersschule für Gebirgsjäger in Wörgl.

15. Also referred to in some records as "Reserve Division Innsbruck."

16. The source of the Inn River is in Switzerland, and it flows northeastward through Tyrol and into Germany.

17. See note 9 above. If these troops were not from Grossdeutschland, it is likely they were drawn from various Wehrmacht units that had retreated into Austria from Bavaria.

18. *Kampf um die Alpenfestung Nord*, 2–3.

19. Details on the formation, organization, and operations of the Austrian resistance are drawn primarily from Luza, *The Resistance in Austria*, and the Austrian Federal Press Service's *Resistance and Persecution in Austria, 1938–1945*.

20. In German, Provisorisches Österreichisches Nationalkomitee.

21. Established by presidential military order on June 13, 1942, the OSS was both an intelligence-collection and analysis agency and a covert-operations organization. Headed by World War I hero William J. Donovan, the OSS saw service in both the European and the Pacific theater.

22. "O5" was a clever rendering of the first letter of the German word for Austria, Österreich, which when typed without the umlaut is printed as "Oe." Thus, the capital letter *O* followed by the number 5 (indicating the fifth letter of the alphabet, *e*) equals Ö for Austria. The symbol was created by a young Austrian medical student, Jörg Unterreiner. Resistance members would daub the symbol in paint on the sides of buildings, on streetcars, and, if they were particularly brave (or foolhardy), on the sides of German military vehicles.

23. For two especially engrossing accounts of OSS operations in Austria, see Schwab, *OSS Agents in Hitler's Heartland*, and O'Donnell, *The Brenner Assignment*.

24. Luza, *The Resistance in Austria*, 245–246.

25. Between 1935 and 1937, for example, the German-born socialist Waldemar von Knoeringen (1906–1971) established small anti-Nazi cells in Wörgl and several nearby towns.

26. The Feb. 22 attack and one the following day were part of the 15th Air Force's contribution to Operation Clarion, a joint U.S.-British effort to completely paralyze the Third Reich's already much-degraded rail and communications networks by specifically targeting smaller cities and towns that might not have been heavily attacked thus far. Several thousand aircraft participated, flying from bases in France, England, and Italy. For details, see Craven and Cate, *Europe*, 731–732.

27. *Personalakten für Gangl, Josef.*

28. Biographical information for Gangl is drawn primarily from his personalakten and from data provided by the Stadtarchiv Ludwigsburg in Germany and the Tiroler Landesarchiv in Innsbruck, Austria.

29. While details about Sepp Gangl's siblings are sketchy, it appears that he had at least two brothers and one sister.

30. I have been unable to determine the name or gender of their second child.

31. A play on the German term *blitzkrieg* or "lightning war," *sitzkrieg* literally means "sitting war."

32. Taus, now Domažlice, is in the Plzeň Region of the Czech Republic.

33. "Combined-arms," in this context, means a coordinated and integrated operation by mutually supportive armor, infantry, and artillery units backed by tactical aircraft.

34. Werfer means "thrower," and nebelwerfer is literally translated as "fog thrower." The term originally was used to describe single-barrel, cannon-like weapons used to fire smoke or gas shells.

35. And the numbers were even more impressive with larger werfer units. According to *Rocket Projectors in the Eastern Theater*, a postwar history written as part of the U.S. government's Foreign Military Studies series, in ten seconds a werfer regiment could fire 324 rockets, and a brigade 648.

36. Formally designated 15cm Panzerwerfer 42 auf Selbstfahrlafette Sd.Kfz.4/1, the Opel-built Maultier weighed just over nine tons, carried between twenty and forty werfer rounds, and had a top speed on paved roads of about twenty-five miles per hour.

37. Organizational and equipment details drawn from *Die Nebel-und Werfertruppe (Regimentsbögen)*, vol. 1, 322, as listed on the excellent German research site Lexikon der Wehrmacht.

38. The award—an eight-pointed star with a swastika in the center—was given in recognition of the recipient's bravery and outstanding achievement in combat. Awardees had to have already received both the Iron Cross Second Class and First Class.

39. Paape had taken command of the brigade in late March. He wrote a fascinating postwar account of the unit's final days, *7th Werfer Brigade, 24 March–30 April 1945*, as part of the U.S. Army's Foreign Military Studies series.

40. On March 10, 1945, Hitler had issued a "Führer Order" directing the creation of mobile courts-martial units whose task was to find and punish any member of the Wehrmacht or SS, regardless of rank, who was neglecting his duty. Negotiating with Allied forces or collaborating with local resistance organizations was grounds for immediate execution.

41. Named after Fritz Todt, the engineer and high-ranking Nazi who founded it, the Organization Todt (OT) was the Third Reich's primary civil- and military-construction agency. In the prewar years OT constructed Germany's autobahns and frontier fortifications, and after September 1939 it expanded into military construction throughout the Reich and the occupied territories. The organization used "compulsory" workers almost exclusively; initially these were German citizens unfit for military service, but, as the war progressed, the workforce was predominantly made up of slave laborers: prisoners of war, political prisoners, and concentration-camp inmates.

42. Details on the meeting are drawn from *Resistance and Persecution in Austria, 1938–1945*, 594–595.

43. Though Battle Group Forster was in reserve at Wörgl, the actual defense of the city and its environs had been made part of Giehl's responsibility.

44. According to von Hengl's postwar account, the initial American attack was followed by an intense artillery barrage aimed at the next town to the south, Oberaudorf, which was packed with refugees and from which all German military units had already withdrawn. Von Hengl called a brief truce, crossed the front lines under a white flag, and convinced the Americans not to shell any town in which German forces were not actually visible. His mission accomplished, the general crossed the front lines once again and resumed the fight.

45. The full text of the message, translated in *Headquarters, 103d Infantry Division, Operations in Germany, Austria and Italy, May 1945*, 4, read: "At the present juncture of the war, everything depends on a stubborn and inflexible determination to hold on at all costs. The display of white flags, the removal of an antitank barrier, desertion from the *Volksturm* or similar manifestations are offenses which must be ruthlessly punished. All male persons inhabiting a house showing a white flag will be shot. No hesitation in executing these orders can be permitted any longer. 'Male persons' who are to be considered responsible in this respect are those aged 14 years or over."

CHAPTER FIVE

1. *Prison Journal*, 292.
2. Ibid., 294.

3. Ibid., 296.

4. Ibid., 283.

5. A fiery, 80-proof German brandy.

6. For example, in the summer of 1944 Čučković was able to repair a small electric motor that Wimmer intended to use in the farmhouse he and his wife were renovating (possibly as a postwar hideout) about 1.5 miles northeast of Schloss Itter. The SS-TV officer gave the Croat 30 Reichsmarks and allowed him to spend time with his wife, Ema, and son, Zvonimir, who had traveled down from the outskirts of Munich and were staying with a family in Itter village. For five nights Čučković was allowed to leave the castle by himself after dark but had to be back in each morning by six. See Čučković, "Zwei Jahren auf Schloss Itter," 40.

7. All three incidents are described in Čučković, "Zwei Jahren auf Schloss Itter," 39–41.

8. Daladier, *Prison Journal*, 317–318.

9. Reynaud, *In the Thick of the Fight*, 653.

10. Even after the war the area around Schloss Itter continued to be a way station for former Nazis seeking to escape Allied justice. Among the most infamous was Adolf Eichmann, one of the primary organizers of the Holocaust. As part of his escape to Argentina in 1950, the former SS-TV officer crossed into Austria at Kufstein and, with the help of local sympathizers, made his way to Innsbruck. From there he crossed into Italy and then traveled on to South America. Abducted by Israeli agents in 1960, he was taken to Israel, tried for war crimes and crimes against humanity, and executed in 1962.

11. Daladier, *Prison Journal*, 336. Among those accompanying Weiter was his adjutant, whom Daladier described as "tall and fat, a real thug."

12. Reynaud's postwar account says May 1, but Weiter killed himself sometime between one AM and six AM on May 2. Nor was Weiter the only senior SS man to commit suicide in the vicinity of Schloss Itter. Just days after the Dachau commandant killed himself, SS-Major Hermann Müller-John, commander and bandmaster of the ninety-six-man orchestra of the Leibstandarte Adolf Hitler—the führer's bodyguard regiment—killed his wife, his nineteen-year-old daughter, and himself in a farmhouse within a few miles of Itter. He apparently wished to avoid postwar prosecution for his involvement—and that of the band members he led—in the murder of some fifty Jews on the night of Sept. 18–19, 1939, in Blonie, Poland.

13. Reynaud, *In the Thick of the Fight*, 653.

14. Ibid.

15. Ibid.

16. The bulk of the information used in this volume concerning Schrader's early life and wartime career is drawn from his ultimately unpublished postwar memoir, "Erinnerungen, Gedanken, Erkenntnisse"

("Memories, Thoughts, Insights"), and from Schrader's entry in John P. Moore's excellent *Signal Officers of the Waffen-SS*.

17. Schrader, "Erinnerungen, Gedanken, Erkenntnisse," 5.

18. Known in German as the Reichsarbeitdienst, or R.A.D., the organization had been created in 1931 as the Freiwilliger Arbeitsdienst (Voluntary Labor Service) as a way to provide work for Germany's many unemployed people. Structured along military lines, it undertook civic construction projects. Following the Nazis' assumption of power, service in the renamed R.A.D. was made compulsory for all German males between eighteen and twenty-five. Upon completion of that service young men entered the military for two years.

19. Schrader's SS-number was 353 103.

20. Schrader, "Erinnerungen, Gedanken, Erkenntnisse," 16.

21. Ibid., 20.

22. The date usually observed for the official formation of the Waffen-SS as a distinctly military organization is August 1940.

23. Ibid., 28–29.

24. Ibid., 30.

25. Essentially the German equivalent of the U.S. jeep, the kübelwagen was an inexpensive, four-door convertible-top military utility vehicle designed by Ferdinand Porsche.

26. Ibid., 31.

27. Schrader takes pains to point out that it was a regular passenger train, not a military troop train.

28. Schrader, "Erinnerungen, Gedanken, Erkenntnisse," 36.

29. Čučković's reference to "Mühltal" can be confusing, as there are several small villages by that name within twenty miles of Schloss Itter. The Wimmers' farmhouse was actually in an area now known as Itter-Mühltal, just east of Niederau.

30. This exchange and the account of Čučković's ride to Innsbruck are drawn from Čučković, "Zwei Jahren auf Schloss Itter," 51–53.

31. As commander of the 101st Airborne Division when it was encircled by the Germans at Bastogne, Belgium, in December 1944, McAuliffe famously responded to a demand for surrender with a one-word reply: "Nuts!"

32. This man was apparently part of the 103rd Infantry Division's military-government section; unfortunately, his name is lost to history.

33. Reynaud, *In the Thick of the Fight*, 654.

34. Schrader, "Erinnerungen, Gedanken, Erkenntnisse," 36.

35. This incident is recounted in Reynaud, *In the Thick of the Fight*, 654.

36. Unfortunately, we have no first names for most of the soldiers who chose to join Sepp Gangl in protecting the people of Wörgl.

37. While the vast majority of German military personnel who surrendered to U.S. forces in Europe survived the process, it was certainly not

unheard of for GIs to summarily execute prisoners—most notably in the days after the June 1944 Normandy landings and in the wake of the December 1944 Waffen-SS murder of eighty-four American POWs in Malmedy, Belgium, during the Battle of the Bulge. However, the Allied liberation of the Nazis' concentration, extermination, and slave-labor camps led to a spike in the number of German prisoners—especially Waffen-SS and SS-TV members—killed while attempting to surrender or following surrender. On April 29, 1945, the day Dachau was liberated by elements of the U.S. 42nd and 45th Infantry divisions, between sixteen and approximately fifty of the camp's SS-TV guards were killed by American troops, many after surrendering.

38. *Operations in Germany, 1–10 May 1945,* 68–70.

CHAPTER SIX

1. An 1806 graduate of West Point—and its superintendent from 1814 to 1818—Partridge came to believe that the national military academy system exemplified by his alma mater had created and was perpetuating a closed military elite. He strenuously advocated the establishment of state militias led by officers trained in private, regional military colleges. He established seven such institutions himself, with Norwich being the first and ultimately most successful.

2. Indeed, because its founder established the principles of what evolved into the Reserve Officer Training Corps program, Norwich University bills itself as the birthplace of ROTC, though there is some disagreement as to where the first ROTC unit was constituted.

3. Though most Norwich graduates were commissioned into the cavalry branch, such an assignment was not a foregone conclusion. Graduates could request assignment to another branch, or their first branch choice might be turned down by the army if officers were needed in other fields. Of the seventy-nine graduates in Lee's class of 1942, sixty—including Lee—were assigned to the cavalry, thirteen to the army air forces, and two each to the engineer corps, signal corps, and chemical warfare service.

4. The U.S. War Department's 1930 establishment of the mechanized force ensured that the horse's days in army service were numbered. Mounted cavalry units were converted to mechanized organizations as quickly as funding and vehicles could be provided. While military horsemanship was taught in all four years of Lee's time at Norwich, he and his fellow students also received instruction in the operation and use of armored cars and other military vehicles during their junior and senior years. As it happened, Lee and the other members of his Class of 1942 were the last Norwich cadets to receive horse-cavalry training. In March 1943 the school's entire corps of cadets was taken directly into military service, and from then until the end of the war Norwich did not accept students, instead

acting as an auxiliary training school for army aviation cadets. By the time regular instruction resumed in 1946, the university had disposed of all its horses and officially discontinued cavalry training. From then on Lee and his classmates were referred to as the Horsemen of '42.

5. The woman's maiden name remains unclear.

6. Construction had begun in January 1942. The post was renamed Fort Campbell in 1950, and as of this writing remains the home installation of the 101st Airborne Division, the 5th Special Forces Group, and the 160th Special Operations Aviation Regiment.

7. Organizational details for both the 12th AD and 23rd TB are drawn from Ferguson, *Hellcats*, and Francis, *A History of the 23rd Tank Battalion*.

8. A coaxial machine gun is mounted inside the tank's turret, alongside and parallel to the main gun. The machine gun fires in the same direction as the main gun and is used against such "soft" targets as unarmored vehicles and troops in the open.

9. *Armored Force Field Manual*, 10.

10. "Capt. Jack Lee, '42, Rescues Daladier in Castle Battle," *Norwich Record* (Northfield, VT), June 22, 1945, 5.

11. Basse by all accounts was a very nice man. In a 2012 interview with the author, Calbert Duvall, a driver in Company B's 2nd Platoon, related an example of Basse's kindness: while the 23rd was still at Camp Barkley, Duvall's young wife and infant daughter arrived from upstate New York for a very brief visit. Duvall was supposed to have guard duty, but Basse pulled the eight-hour detail in the young soldier's place so Duvall could spend the time with his family.

12. Built between 1913 and 1919 by Germany's Vulcan AG shipyard and originally intended for service with the Hamburg-Amerika Line, the twenty-two-thousand-ton vessel was transferred in 1920 to Britain as part of the war reparations the Allies awarded themselves at the Paris Peace Conference. The ship passed to Canadian Pacific in 1921 and was initially named *Empress of China* but became *Empress of Australia* the following year. It reentered transatlantic passenger service after World War II and was scrapped in 1952.

13. Francis, *History of the 23rd Tank Battalion*, 10–12.

14. Some sources give the name as *Besotten Jinny*, but the version used in this volume is the one most commonly cited. The actual origin of the name is lost to history, but it may be a reference to the nickname of Lee's first wife, Virginia.

15. LST stands for "Landing Ship, Tank." The large, flat-bottomed vessels carried their cargo of armored vehicles right up onto the beach and off-loaded them through large bow doors. The modern U.S. Army uses an even larger variant known as an LSV (Logistics Support Vessel) to move armored vehicles and other cargo.

16. See Francis, *History of the 23rd Tank Battalion*, 18, and Ferguson, *Hellcats*, 57–60.

17. Montgomery Cunningham Meigs, a 1940 graduate of West Point, was twenty-four when he was killed. The scion of a family with a long military history, Meigs was the son of a naval officer. His own son, the future General Montgomery C. Meigs, was born one month after Lt. Col. Meigs's death.

18. *Operations in Germany, 1–10 May 1945*. For a full account of the Herrlisheim battle, see Edward Monroe-Jones's excellent *Crossing the Zorn*.

19. The "Easy 8" moniker came from the fact that the M4A3(76)W was also referred to as the M4A3E8. Second-generation examples of the Easy 8 were built with the Horizontal Volute Spring Suspension (HVSS) system and had wider tracks and other detail changes.

20. Earlier Sherman models had carried the projectiles in the side sponsons above the tracks; the rounds would almost always detonate if the hull was breached by antitank fire, so in later-model M4s the main-gun ammunition was stored in bins under the turret floor. The bins were surrounded by a water-antifreeze mixture that greatly reduced the risk of the ammunition cooking off and catastrophically destroying the tank.

21. General Orders 33, HQs., 12th Armored Division, April 19, 1945. Lee was also awarded the Purple Heart for wounds received sometime in March 1945, but the nature of the wounds and exactly how and where they were inflicted remain unclear.

22. As World War II ground on in Europe, the army needed immediate reinforcements in its infantry units. When the numbers of white soldiers pulled from other tasks failed to fill the gap, the still-segregated army allowed black soldiers in Europe-based service and support units to volunteer. Some two thousand men did, and after truncated infantry training in France they were allocated to white-officered units in the 12th and 14th Armored divisions. While the black soldiers in the 17th AIB's Company D proved themselves to be both brave and highly competent infantrymen, they did not—as some sources (including the author's own 2005 magazine article) have erroneously indicated—participate in the Schloss Itter operation.

23. *Operations in Germany, 1–10 May 1945*, 84.

24. A few days earlier, as the 103rd had moved into Garmisch-Partenkirchen in southern Germany, Kramers had led his group of jeep-borne civil-military government soldiers up the driveway of a particularly imposing villa. Intending to use the home as a command post, Kramers informed the residents that they had fifteen minutes to pack a single bag and leave. An elderly man walked slowly out of the house and up to Kramers, who was bent over the hood of his jeep studying a map. "I am Richard Strauss, the composer," the man said, proffering part of the manuscript of

his *Der Rosenkavalier* and a certificate proclaiming him to be an honorary citizen of Morgantown, West Virginia. Kramers, a fan of classical music in general and Strauss's work in particular, decided he could find a suitable command post elsewhere. After posting an "Off Limits" sign in front of Strauss's villa, Kramers and his men moved on. This incident is recounted in Alex Ross's excellent *The Rest Is Noise*, 373–374. Kramers also related this event to the author in a June 8, 2012, telephone interview. And, according to a postwar history of the 103rd Infantry Division, Strauss's son, Franz, his Jewish wife, and their two teenaged sons had spent the entire war in the composer's home. The elder Strauss told Kramers and his men that Franz's wife "was the only free Jewess in Germany during Hitler's reign." Her safety, it seems, stemmed from the fact that Strauss's popularity with the German people was so great that even the Nazis couldn't touch them. See Mueller and Turk, *Report After Action*, 140.

25. The actual term used in the Free French forces was Enseigne de vaisseau de première classe, but since Lutten was attached to an American unit, he went by "lieutenant."

26. Levin, "We Liberated Who's Who," 98.

27. Pronounced "Simzik."

28. The basic account of Lee's initial recon to Wörgl and Schloss Itter is drawn from *Operations in Germany, 1–10 May 1945*, 68–70, and from *Resistance and Persecution in Austria*, 594–598.

29. Schrader, "Erinnerungen, Gedanken, Erkenntnisse," 36.

30. It remains unclear which two men they were.

31. Demey, *Paul Reynaud*, 144.

32. Daladier, *Prison Journal*, 337.

33. Unfortunately I have been unable to determine the names of the other two members of *Boche Buster*'s crew.

34. The account of the 753rd's actions in support of the Schloss Itter operation is drawn from *Battalion Diary for Month of May 1945*, 1–3, and *Company History, 1–8 May 1945*, 1–2.

35. Designed during World War I by John Browning, the Browning Automatic Rifle was chambered for a .30–06 round. In World War II the Model 1918A2 was normally the sole automatic weapon in each eight-man infantry squad.

36. Interview with Arthur P. Pollock.

37. While not perhaps as lethal as the famed German 88mm anti-aircraft/antitank gun, the more mobile 75mm Panzerabwehrkanone (Pak) 40 was more than capable of knocking out a Sherman under most circumstances.

38. Interview with Pollock.

39. Tall, narrow openings in a castle's defensive walls originally intended to allow defenders to fire arrows at attackers while remaining protected. The embrasures were wider on the inside than on the outside, allowing the defender a wide field of fire despite the narrowness of the exterior opening.

40. A common feature in medieval castles, a sally port allowed the troops of the castle's garrison to mount quick raids outside the walls without having to open the main gate.

41. Interview with Edward J. Seiner.

CHAPTER SEVEN

1. Introduced in 1942, the Maschinengewehr-42's readily identifiable sound resulted from a rate of fire of more than one thousand rounds per minute.

2. The red lens provides illumination in low light without revealing the user's position as a white light would.

3. Daladier, *Prison Journal*, 337.

4. The 142nd's actions in support of the Schloss Itter rescue operation are drawn from *Operations in Germany and Austria, 1–10 May 1945*, 4–6.

5. *Battalion Diary for Month of May 1945*.

6. Levin was speaking in comparative terms: the high temperature in the area that day, according to the weather forecast included in the 103rd Infantry Division's daily operations report for May 5, was 38 degrees F.

7. Levin, "We Liberated Who's Who," 96.

8. Ibid.

9. As it happened, Kramers's small force was not the only 103rd ID unit operating in the 36th ID's area. A small element of the division's 103rd Reconnaissance Troop under the command of Lieutenant Herbert had reached the outskirts of Wörgl on the afternoon of May 4, spent the night, and was making its way back toward Innsbruck even as Kramers was arguing with the division's chief of staff. The recon troops did not know about the French VIPs at Itter; the GIs' only mission was to establish contact with the lead elements of the 36th ID and then return to Innsbruck to report that contact. How the two groups failed to encounter each other on the road along the Inn River remains a mystery. See *Regimental History, 409th Infantry Regiment, 1–10 May 1945*, 68–71.

10. Levin, "We Liberated Who'ss Who," 96.

11. *Operations in Germany, 1–10 May 1945*, 70.

12. According to the account of the action in *Resistance and Persecution in Austria, 1938–1945* (597), the weapon was a 2cm Flak 30.

13. *Operations in Germany, 1–10 May 1945*, 70.

14. Ibid.

15. Paul Reynaud, in his *In the Thick of the Fight* (655), says that after the event he was informed by General Émile Antoine Béthouart, then commander of the French 1st Army Corps and postwar French high commissioner in Austria, that the Waffen-SS soldiers were there specifically to kill the French VIPs.

16. *Resistance and Persecution in Austria, 1938–1945*, 598.

17. Cailliau de Gaulle, *Souvenirs personnels*, 101.

18. Interview with Arthur P. Pollock.

19. Ibid.

20. Fortunately for all concerned, *Besotten Jenny*'s "wet" storage kept its 76mm main-gun ammunition from detonating.

21. Schrader, "Erinnerungen, Gedanken, Erkenntnisse."

22. Ibid., and Léon-Jouhaux, *Prison pour hommes d'Etat*, 154.

23. Reynaud is using "tommy-gun" in the generic sense, to mean any type of submachine gun. The weapon he wielded during the fight for the castle was actually a German MP-40 machine pistol.

24. Reynaud, *In the Thick of the Fight*, 655.

25. Cailliau de Gaulle, *Souvenirs personnels*, 101.

26. Interview with Edward J. Seiner.

27. Interview with Pollock.

28. Reynaud, *In the Thick of the Fight*, 655.

29. Levin, "We Liberated Who's Who," 98.

30. Ibid.

31. Ibid.

32. Gill was himself a bona fide hero; just over two weeks earlier he'd personally led an attack on an enemy position that ultimately resulted in his being decorated with the Distinguished Service Cross, the nation's second-highest military award for valor.

33. Levin, "We Liberated Who's Who," 98.

34. Ibid.

35. *Operations in Germany and Austria, 1–10 May 1945*, 2. Mühltal, as mentioned earlier in this volume, is about a mile northeast of Schloss Itter, on the road from Wörgl east to Söll.

36. *Unit Journal, 1–10 May 1945*, 53.

37. Levin, "We Liberated Who's Who," 98.

38. Ibid.

39. Ibid.

40. Ibid.

41. Indeed, the Brixentaler Ache is still a popular destination for whitewater kayakers.

42. He was also the postwar founder of the separatist Parti Québécois and a prime mover in his province's attempts to gain political independence from the Canadian Confederation.

43. Lévesque, *Memoires*, 96–99.

44. Ibid., 98.

45. Léon-Jouhaux, *Prison pour hommes d'Etat*, 156. See also Smyth, *Jean Borotra, the Bounding Basque*, 157–158.

46. Léon-Jouhaux, *Prison pour hommes d'Etat*, 157.

47. *Operations in Germany and Austria, 1–10 May 1945*.

48. Ibid.

49. Levin, "We Liberated Who's Who," 98.

50. Daladier, *Prison Journal*, 338.

51. Ibid.

CHAPTER EIGHT

1. Levin, "We Liberated Who's Who," 98.

2. Schrader, "Erinnerungen, Gedanken, Erkenntnisse," 36. The reason for Čučković's outburst is unclear; he almost certainly would have encountered Schrader—both in civilian clothes and in uniform—during the latter's earlier visits to Schloss Itter. We can only assume that the now-free Čučković felt that he could display his true feelings about the man wearing the death's-head collar insignia that was the symbol of so much horror and tragedy throughout Europe.

3. Levin, "We Liberated Who's Who," 98.

4. Lévesque, *Memoires*, 98–99.

5. A nickname given to the solidly built Daladier years earlier by the Parisian press.

6. Lévesque, *Memoires*, 98–99.

7. Ibid.

8. *Operations in Germany and Austria, 1–10 May 1945*, 3.

9. Cailliau de Gaulle, *Souvenirs personnels*, 102–105, and Daladier, *Prison Journal*, 340–341.

10. Čučković, "Zwei Jahren auf Schloss Itter," 68–69.

11. Late in 1945 Schloss Itter was purchased by Wilhelm Woldrich, an Innsbruck hotelier who completely refurbished the castle and added an outdoor swimming pool and a larger garage. In 1964 the Hotel Schloss Itter was sold to a Frau Bettina McDuff, who in 1972 sold it to a Lichtenstein-based company, which, according to some sources, was owned at least in part by one-time Austrian Formula 1 race driver Niki Lauda. In the late 1980s the castle was purchased by Dr. Ernst Bosin, an Austrian attorney with offices in Kufstein, Wörgl, and Orlando, Florida. The hotel ceased operation about that time and has been closed to the public since then.

12. The DSC is awarded for extreme gallantry and risk of life in combat; it is second in order of precedence only to the Medal of Honor. The Silver Star is the third-highest U.S. military decoration for valor in combat.

13. General Order 212. I am indebted to Robert Lee for providing the original document.

14. The other being *Carnets de captivité*.

15. I am indebted to Mr. Reynaud's daughter, Evelyne Demey Paul-Reynaud, for information on her mother's later life.

16. Daladier, *Prison Journal*, 244.

17. Léon-Jouhaux, *Prison pour hommes d'Etat*, 149.

18. The letter is quoted in Schrader, "Erinnerungen, Gedanken, Erkenntnisse," 40.

19. Lee remained in the inactive reserve until his honorable discharge on December 20, 1952.

20. It has proven impossible to determine the child's name or birth date, or to discover what ultimately happened to him and his mother. Jack Lee apparently never saw either of them again.

21. I am indebted to James Dunne, Norwich sports writer and local historian, for details on Jack Lee's later life.

INDEX